Educational Psychology

D1374793

Educational Psychology

Topics in Applied Psychology

Norah Frederickson

Andy Miller

Tony Cline

PART OF HACHETTE LIVRE UK

First published in Great Britain in 2008 by
Hodder Education, part of Hachette Livre UK,
338 Euston Road, London NW1 3BH

www.hoddereducation.com

The advice and information in this book are believed to be true and
accurate at the date of going to press, but neither the authors nor the publisher
can accept any legal responsibility or liability for any errors or omissions.

Every effort has been made to trace and acknowledge the owners of copyright.
The publishers will be glad to make suitable arrangements with any
copyright holders whom it has not been possible to contact.

British Library Cataloguing in Publication Data
A catalogue record for this book is available from the British Library

Library of Congress Cataloging-in-Publication Data
A catalog record for this book is available from the Library of Congress

10 05466 75X

ISBN 978 0 340 92893 6

1 2 3 4 5 6 7 8 9 10

Cover & section opener © Kent Weakley/iStockphoto.com

Typeset in 10pt Berling Roman by Servis Filmsetting Ltd., Manchester
Printed and bound in Malta

What do you think about this book? Or any other Hodder
Education title? Please send your comments to the
feedback section on www.hoddereducation.com.

Contents

Series preface

Psychology is still one of the most popular subjects for study at undergraduate degree level. As well as providing the student with a range of academic and applied skills that are valued by a broad range of employers, a psychology degree also serves as the basis for subsequent training and a career in professional psychology. A substantial proportion of students entering a degree programme in Psychology do so with a subsequent career in applied psychology firmly in mind, and as a result the number of applied psychology courses available at undergraduate level has significantly increased over recent years. In some cases these courses supplement core academic areas and in others they provide the student with a flavour of what they might experience as a professional psychologist.

Topics in Applied Psychology represents a series of six textbooks designed to provide a comprehensive academic and professional insight into specific areas of professional psychology. The texts cover the areas of **Clinical Psychology, Criminal Psychology, Educational Psychology, Health Psychology, Sports and Exercise Psychology**, and **Organizational and Work Psychology**, and each text is written and edited by the foremost professional and academic figures in each of these areas.

Each textbook is based on a similar academic formula which combines a comprehensive review of cutting-edge research and professional knowledge with accessible teaching and learning features. The books are also structured so they can be used as an integrated teaching support for a one-term or one-semester course in each of their relevant areas of applied psychology. Given the increasing importance of applying psychological knowledge across a growing range of areas of practice, we feel this series is timely and comprehensive. We hope you find each book in the series readable, enlightening, accessible and instructive.

Graham Davey
University of Sussex, Brighton, UK
September 2007

Preface

How can this book be used?

In this preface we outline for students and tutors the range of ways in which this book can be used to support teaching and learning about educational psychology. We first consider *purpose* – *why* you may have decided to open the book. We then discuss *approach* – *how* the chapters are structured and may be used to achieve each of a number of purposes. In the third section we focus on *content* – *what* areas of knowledge and understanding are addressed and sequencing options available. We finish this introduction with some thoughts about what is involved in applying psychology to education.

Purpose

We first consider a number of different purposes for which this textbook might be used, focusing in particular on the needs and priorities of different target readerships.

Advanced level undergraduate psychology degree option

The primary audience we have had in mind in writing this book are advanced level undergraduate psychology students and tutors. Tutors will find material suitable for a one-term or one-semester Level 2 or Level 3 undergraduate course. Subject benchmarking statements for psychology suggest that a virtuous circle often exists 'between theory and empirical data, the results of which may find their expression in applications to educational, health, industrial/commercial and other situations' and specifies that a degree programme should feature 'the ability to extrapolate and comprehend the applications of knowledge within the areas of psychology' (QAA, 2002: 4). The book will support the achievement of this purpose in the area of educational psychology.

For students, educational psychology has a number of advantages in supporting this purpose. The main context of application in educational psychology is the school context. While there are other areas of educational psychology practice, in families and in the community, we will only touch on them occasionally in this book, which will focus mainly on the school. All students have had experience of school, which in most cases is recent. We hope this broad familiarity will enable a ready grasp of the applications of psychology that are described. In addition students are encouraged, specifically in Chapter 1, to think about other possible applications to schools from the courses studied in the first and second year of the degree programme.

Application to educational psychology training

For anyone who might be interested in applying for professional training as an educational psychologist, Chapter 1 *What do educational psychologists do?* is an obvious starting point for finding out about the professional role and training. For the serious applicant each chapter offers insights about aspects of professional practice and ways in which psychology can be applied in educational contexts. The criteria used by selection panels for educational psychology training programmes commonly include: *knowledge of ways in which psychology can be applied in educational, childcare and community contexts* and/or *experience of applying psychology theory and research in work with children*. This book will contribute to the knowledge required by the first of these criteria and will assist both in planning and reflecting on relevant experience for addressing the second criterion.

Professional training in educational psychology

In the initial stages of doctoral professional training programmes in educational psychology there is often a need for trainees to update their knowledge of psychological theory and research relevant to professional practice. While many trainees will have completed their undergraduate psychology degree within the previous couple of years, for some it will have been completed a number of years prior to that, and for some there may have been less emphasis on the actual application of psychology in educational contexts. We hope that this book will serve these purposes well and be of value on the initial set reading list for these programmes.

Approach

This book is designed to be used to support a range of different course formats:

- A one term/semester lecture course.

- A seminar group meeting weekly alongside a lecture course.

- A problem-based learning (PBL) course, structured as a series of tutor-facilitated or self-directed learning group meetings (for example, see Hmelo-Silver, 2004).

Across each of these formats the text is designed to encourage and support a problem-orientated approach to learning. This orientation has been selected to engage interest and develop critical analysis. It also aids the presentation of issues in practice contexts in ways that facilitate the representation of different perspectives and the development of a realistic appreciation of both the contributions and current limitations in the application of psychology.

The problem-orientated approach is reflected in a number of different ways. The titles of the chapters pose questions highlighting controversies and dilemmas in research and practice. For example: *'Be still, be quiet, be docile.' How ethical are behavioural approaches to classroom management?* and *Do modern methods of teaching reading cause dyslexia?* Each chapter contains at least one focus box which features a suitable stimulus or 'trigger' for use by a PBL or seminar group as starting point on the topic in question. This will often be a vignette or case study from the professional practice of educational psychologists, but newspaper reports and other relevant material are also included. Information on current theories and research is presented in relation to issues arising from the case study material. Using a variety of activities in the text, students are encouraged to critically evaluate potential implications of the different areas of research reviewed for practice and policy in education and to identify limitations of current methods and knowledge in the pursuit of 'evidence-based' practice.

New topics are frequently introduced in a way that encourages students to access (and, where working in groups, to share) existing knowledge of relevance to the scenarios presented. This is intended to assist them in building upon, extending to a more advanced level and, crucially, seeking to integrate information from topics covered in the core domains during the first two years of their degree: biological, cognitive, developmental, personality and individual differences, and social psychology.

Each of the chapters follows a similar overall structure:

- An introductory paragraph orientates the reader to the topic.

- A set of intended learning outcomes is then presented.

- The text is organized in a number of sections addressing different facets of the topic and focused round 'focus boxes' containing stimulus material, activities, examples of applications and more detailed discussion of methodological or ethical issues.

- A summary of the main issues addressed in the chapter is presented.

- Key concepts and terms are listed.

- Sample essay titles are suggested.

- Recommendations for further reading are provided.

The problem-orientated approach is represented throughout. For example, the sample essay titles suggested include two representative of this approach, e.g.:

- Design an evidence-based intervention programme for Alex (Activity box 8.1), justifying the approaches you decide to include with reference to relevant literature.

- You have been asked to give a talk to sixth form volunteers on 'Supporting children with ASD in school: Key insights from psychology'. Explain what you will include in your talk and why.

Alongside these are two more conventional essay titles, such as:

- To what extent can a 'theory of mind' deficit account for the triad of impairments in autism?

- Evaluate the strengths and weaknesses of research evidence on the use of social stories with children who have ASD.

It is our objective throughout to maximize the flexibility with which the book can be used to meet the purposes of different tutors and groups of learners.

Content

An introductory chapter (Chapter 1) focuses on the role and training of educational psychologists. This chapter both provides a basis for those that follow and seeks to draw together some overarching themes and to encourage learners to make connections with information from topics covered in the core domains – biological, cognitive, developmental, personality and individual differences and social psychology – covered during the first two years of the undergraduate psychology degree.

The remaining chapters are organized into two sections. Section 1: *Cognition, learning and instruction* contains chapters which reflect educational psychologists' work in relation to the core purposes of schools in promoting learning and raising achievement. They draw primarily on cognitive development, cognitive psychology and individual differences. Section 2: *Social, emotional and behavioural issues in school* contains chapters which reflect educational psychologists' work in relation to the social context and ethos of the school and school's responsibilities in providing for the behaviour and well-being of the pupils. They draw primarily on social development and social psychology.

It is recommended that Chapter 1 be used as both the starting and finishing point of the course. Initially it will provide an orientation to the work of educational psychologists. At the end of the course an educational psychologist from a neighbouring educational psychology service might be invited to give a talk on their work. This may be particularly useful where there is no chartered educational psychologist on the staff. The suggested essay questions for Chapter 1 will also be most appropriately addressed at the end of the course as they seek to integrate topic areas, allow more scope for individual interests to be followed and challenge the highest achieving students.

Otherwise, with the aim of allowing maximum flexibility, the chapters have been written so that they can be studied in any order. The associated disadvantage is that while there are a small number of themes that re-occur across chapters, this re-occurrence is not flagged up in the text. Rather, sufficient background is provided in each chapter for it to stand alone. This also means that chapters can readily be used to support contributions to other third level courses, for example contributing four lectures on educational psychology to a course on applied psychology.

Applying psychology to education

In Chapter 1 the work of educational psychologists will be described in detail and the way in which they operate as scientist-practitioners highlighted in particular. However, it has long been recognized that the application of psychology to education is not a matter of direct translation – 'You make a great, a very great mistake if you think that psychology, being the science of minds' laws, is something from which you can deduce definite programmes and schemes and methods of instruction for immediate classroom use. Psychology is a science and teaching is an art: and sciences never generate arts directly out of themselves. An intermediary, inventive mind must make the application, by using its originality' (James, 1899: 23–24).

In this book we hope to illustrate both elements in William James' formula for the successful application of psychology to education: first, the basis in psychological science which allows clear principles and guidelines to be developed in particular areas of practice; second, the creativity, inventiveness and 'professional artistry' that is also involved in undertaking the process of translation into practice with different people in different contexts. It is this combination, we believe, that makes educational psychology such a fascinating field of study and practice.

Norah Frederickson
Andy Miller
Tony Cline

1 What do educational psychologists do?

Norah Frederickson and Andy Miller

Educational psychology seems to be rather a mysterious profession. An education officer who claimed to have read over 1000 reports written by educational psychologists (EPs) wrote an article (Wood, 1998) entitled *Okay then, so what do educational psychologists do?* UK governments have appeared similarly baffled in that three reviews of the role and function of educational psychologists have been carried out since the turn of the century, one in Scotland (Scottish Executive, 2002) one in England and Wales (DfEE, 2000a) and a further one in England (Farrell et al, 2006). Our main objective is that by the end of this chapter you will be able to answer the question in the title, and will have gained an appreciation of some of the issues in the professional practice of educational psychology that lead to the question being asked.

We begin this chapter by identifying the different levels at which educational psychologists work (from individual child to local authority) and the core activities that they undertake. We consider similarities and differences between the work of educational psychologists in different places and at different times in the history of the profession. A case study of an educational psychologist's work in response to a teacher's concern about a child is presented to illustrate the way in which different activities are typically integrated and informed both by psychological theory and research and professional ethics and practice guidelines. The resulting central conceptualization of the role of the educational psychologist as 'scientist-practitioner' is then examined, highlighting a number of current issues and possible future developments. The chapter concludes with information on training as an educational psychologist.

Learning outcomes

When you have completed this chapter you should be able to:

1. Describe what educational psychologists do and identify some of the key issues in their practice.
2. Evaluate the extent to which educational psychologists can be described as scientist-practitioners.
3. Outline the requirements for training as an educational psychologist and locate more detailed information if required.

How much do different accounts of educational psychology practice agree?

In this section we examine different descriptions of educational psychologists' work – from individual educational psychologists, from government reports and from information provided to the public from local authority educational psychology services. In Activity box 1.1 we start by looking at what educational psychologists say they do.

Activity 1.1

What do educational psychologists say they do?

Read the following four descriptions by educational psychologists (EPs) of their work. Apart from their obvious enthusiasm, what do they have in common? How many different aspects of educational psychologists' work are mentioned?

Use just the information in these four extracts to write a one paragraph description of what educational psychologists do. If possible, compare your paragraph with that produced by someone else. As you read the rest of the chapter annotate your paragraph to reflect the further information you obtain.

Callum started nursery and was a handful for staff. He was running around, barging into other children and not settling to any kind of activity without a lot of adult prompting. I worked with his teachers through the nursery and reception years, slowly working out his strengths and difficulties and the best ways to teach him. I had to observe him in his class, talk to his parents, carry out assessment work with him and discuss ways forward with his teachers. Approaches were developed which took advantage of Callum's desire to actively explore the world around him. By the end of the process Callum was clearly enjoying school and was no longer a cause for concern. This is an example of the rewards of educational psychology. Sometimes you're not as successful as you'd like, but if you are, you see progress, and that's fulfilling. I also find it an intellectually stimulating job because it combines practice and theory. (Nick Bozic*)

I enjoy meeting with children and young people, getting to know them and exploring with them their issues. Helping them to see things differently gives me a real buzz. My work with groups of people, like parents and teachers, is enjoyable on a different level. Sharing with them some of the things that the research has shown, which might make a difference and help them to work more effectively, can be very satisfying. I also relish research aspects that I get to do, and find that my curiosity for why something happens still excites me. (Phil Jones*)

The job is about testing hypotheses. It's not saying: "I know this is correct," it's about problem-solving and trying out possible solutions. I bring *psychology to teachers and we share perspectives. We devise interventions together (such as introducing a paired reading programme) and evaluate them. I work with individual children and with groups, as well as with staff. Recently, I've been working for half an hour a week with a group of 10 children; it's been about them developing more positive interactions with each other. The best part is being involved in a situation – whether it's a school or a child – over the long term and seeing the changes. (Anne-Marie Baverstock**)*

A 13-year-old girl was having real difficulties with school attendance, manifested by anxious behaviour and a huge fear of going out. I used an approach based on personal construct psychology – where I got to understand what was linked to this child's fears and then put a scheme in place within the school to support her social relationships. I did the same with her parents. Her attendance picked up radically once she'd made better connections with her peer group and she was back in full-time learning within weeks. It was enormously rewarding. (Kairen Cullen*)

*   From *Vital Support for Children in Need* by Kate Hilpern, *The Independent*, 8th January 2004, Special Supplement on Educational Psychology, p. II.
** From *Emergency in Class* by Caitlin Davis, *The Independent*, 3rd February 2005, Careers, p. 10.

On the website of the Department for Children, Schools and Families the role of Educational Psychology Services in England is described as 'the promotion of learning, attainment and the healthy emotional development of children and young people aged 0 to 19, through the application of psychology, by working with early years settings, schools (and other education providers), children and their families, other local authority officers, practitioners and other agencies'. In the last 10 years reviews of educational psychology services in England and Wales (DfEE, 2000a) and in Scotland (Scottish Executive, 2002) have identified very similar levels of work and core activities. The examples of work across levels and core activities shown in Table 1.1 are taken from the Scottish report. More information about educational psychologists' practice in different parts of the UK, and in many countries internationally can be found in Jimerson, Oakland and Farrell (2007). See Squires and Farrell (2007) for an account of educational psychology practice in England and Topping et al (2007) for a description of educational psychology practice in Scotland.

One issue that emerges from the international literature is a potentially confusing difference in terminology. In North America psychologists undertaking the range of core activities undertaken by educational psychologists in the UK are called 'school psychologists'. As can be seen from Table 1.2, the American Psychological Association has a separate division for educational psychologists who are academic psychologists, like cognitive or social psychologists, whose field of study is the processes of teaching and learning. In the UK both academic

Level	Core functions				
	Consultation	**Assessment**	**Intervention**	**Training**	**Research**
Child and family	Individual discussions Contribution to IEPs Home visits Parents meetings Review meetings, as appropriate	Overall assessment in context Standardized assessment instruments Identifying special needs	Behaviour management programmes Individual and family therapy Working with small groups (e.g. self-harm, social skills, anger management)	Talks to groups of children (e.g. anti-bullying groups) Parenting skills	Single case studies Interactive video research with families
School or establishment	Joint working with staff Advice on programmes for children and young people Contribution to strategic planning Policy advice for schools, children's homes Review meetings, as appropriate	Contribution to school assessment policy and procedure	Contribution to whole-establishment interventions (e.g. anti-bullying programmes, playground behaviour, discipline, raising achievement) Contribution to special exam arrangements Contribution to curricular innovation/ initiatives Joint working with class/ subject teacher/LST Supporting inclusion Supporting special college placements	Staff training Disseminating evidence-based practice	Design, implementation and evaluation of action research in single establishments and groups of schools

Table 1.1 Examples of the levels of work and core activities of educational psychologists.

Source: Scottish Executive, 2002.

Level	Core functions				
	Consultation	**Assessment**	**Intervention**	**Training**	**Research**
Education authority/ Council	Contribution to strategic planning	Contribution to authority assessment policy and procedure Contribution to Best Value reviews	Contribution to establishing authority-wide interventions (e.g. anti-bullying initiatives, alternatives to exclusion, promoting social inclusion, resource allocation)	Authority-wide training in all areas relevant to psychology Input to multi-disciplinary conferences	Design, implementation and evaluation of authority-wide action research (e.g. early intervention, raising achievement) Informing evidence-based policy and practice
IEPs, individual education plan; LST, learning support teacher.					

Table 1.1 *(continued)*

Division 15: *Educational psychology*	Is concerned with theory, methodology, and applications to a broad spectrum of teaching, training, and learning issues
Division 16: *School psychology*	Is composed of scientific-practitioner psychologists … engaged in the delivery of comprehensive psychological services to children, adolescents, and families in schools and other applied settings

Table 1.2. American Psychological Association Divisions of Educational and **School Psychology**

psychologists with research interests in education and those working in professional practice with children may be called educational psychologists, although as we shall see in the last part of this chapter, only those qualified to work in professional practice are eligible to become Chartered Educational Psychologists with the **British Psychological Society (BPS)**. In this book 'educational psychologist/psychology' will be used to refer to applied practitioners and their work. As can be seen from the contents of this book, the psychology on which they draw in practice is not limited to research on teaching, training and learning, but draws widely on behavioural, cognitive, social and developmental psychology and may also be informed by research in occupational psychology, clinical psychology and neuropsychology.

Despite the broad similarities in educational psychology practice, apparent internationally as well as nationally, there are some variations between different local authorities in the UK. For example, Buckinghamshire Educational Psychology Service list the following core activities on their website:

- Consultation.

- Psychological assessment and intervention.

- Problem-solving and solution finding.

- Therapeutic work with individual and groups.

- Training and development of other professionals.

- Multi-agency working.

- Research and evaluation.

Leicestershire Educational Psychology Service list the following levels of practice in their 2006/7 Service Guide:

- Multi-agency work.

- Work with the Local Education Authority and County Council.

- Work within the Community.

- Work with schools and other organizations.

- Work with the adults who care for and educate children and young people.

- Work with groups of children.

- Work with individual children and young people.

It is of interest that 'work within the community' is a new level of work, not listed in the previous year's service guide. However this addition is not surprising in the light of the recommendations of the most recent review of the functions of educational psychologists (Farrell et al, 2006). The recommendations of this report are discussed in the next section of this chapter which considers the ongoing development of the profession of educational psychology. But first, Activity box 1.2 provides an opportunity to source information from the websites of educational psychology services.

Educational psychology: A historical perspective

The first local authority educational psychologist in the UK was appointed by the London County Council in 1913 and held the half time post for almost 20

Activity 1.2

What do educational psychology services say they do?

Most educational psychologists are employed by local authorities (although a small percentage are self-employed and undertake work for parents, social services departments and voluntary agencies). Visit the websites of at least six local authorities, including the one in which you are living. How do the accounts of what the educational psychology services do fit into the grid shown in Table 1.1? Update the paragraph you produced in Activity box 1.1 describing what educational psychologists do (you may need to add another paragraph, but do keep the description as succinct as possible).

years. The individual appointed to the post was Cyril Burt, who was later to become head of the psychology department at University College, London (UCL), and, later still, the subject of one of the most widely publicized controversies in modern psychology, concerning research ethics and data falsification (Macintosh, 1995). Burt was given the following brief:

- To report on problematic cases referred by teachers, doctors or magistrates for individual investigation.

- To construct and standardize tests.

- To organize and carry out surveys of large and representative samples of the entire school inhabitants.

- To be ready to report on any specific problem raised by the Education Officer or Committee.

There are clear parallels with the range of practice apparent today. In addition Burt's description of his work with individual children indicates an interactionist perspective which appears strikingly contemporary almost 90 years later.

> *Whatever the problem might be, instead of calling each child up to the office . . . I always found it far more effective to study him, as it were, in situ, and that of course meant visiting him in the school, calling at his home, and watching him with his play fellows larking in the streets. (Burt, 1964 address to the Association of Educational Psychologist's Conference, transcribed and reported in Rushton, 2002: 565.)*

Of particular interest also, given our later discussion in this chapter of the conceptualization of the role of the educational psychologist as that of scientist-practitioner, is the place Burt saw for research in all aspects of professional practice, including individual case work.

> *All my work in the Council's schools was of the nature of research. Even the individual cases . . . had each to form the subject of a small intensive investigation. (Burt, 1964, in Rushton, 2002: 565.)*

While Burt's model of practice was highly regarded by his employers in London (Maliphant, 1998), it did not immediately become established nationwide. Initially the number of educational psychologists increased slowly and many were based in child guidance clinics run by health, rather than education departments of the local authorities. The child guidance clinic teams comprised child psychiatrists, psychiatric social workers and educational psychologists, offering the potential advantage of enabling a multidisciplinary approach. However there were many tensions. The psychiatrists were usually designated as team leaders and often adopted a narrow medical model which the psychologists did not consider appropriate to educational and social problems. The psychologists generally had a much more limited role than the one Burt had created which, in some cases, became confined primarily to **psychometric testing**.

The report of the first committee of enquiry into the work of educational psychologists, the Summerfield Report (DES, 1968), recommended that educational psychologists should be administratively responsible to local authority education departments but did not challenge the narrow focus on individual case work. Indeed in 1975 a DES circular identified the desirability of obtaining an assessment report from an educational psychologist in the special education ascertainment procedures run by the school doctors. This created something of a dilemma for educational psychologists: 'On the one hand they would like to spend more time on advisory and treatment activities, but on the other hand their "coming of age" relies on their having achieved official recognition for their contribution to assessment procedures as required in Circular 2/75' (Quicke, 1982: 39). Many argued for change, for a reconstruction of the educational psychologist's role. In an influential edited volume (Gillham, 1978) three main directions for change were advocated:

- Decreasing emphasis on individual work with children individually referred.

- Increasing emphasis on indirect methods aimed at the organization, policy and structure of schools and the attitudes and behaviour of adults towards children.

- Increasing emphasis on preventative work, especially through courses for parents and teachers.

This period has been described 'as a time when the profession was beginning to gird its loins and drag itself out of . . . the sterile treadmill of individual casework, psychometrics, and the professional suffocation of child guidance' (Dessent, 1992: 34). However the 1981 Education Act enshrined in legislation and extended the role for educational psychologists in advising on the special educational needs of individual children which had been introduced in the 1975 guidance circular. The new legal requirement to produce psychological advice to inform the **Statement of Special Educational Needs** issued by the local authority led to pessimism about reconstructing a broader professional role.

Under the 1981 Education Act procedures, educational psychologists are firmly nailed and fastened as assessors of needs and definers of resources. They are likely to find themselves seeing and assessing an ever increasing number of individual pupils . . . (Dessent, 1988: 74).

The majority of educational psychologists continue to work in services dominated by open referral systems, are forced into a primarily reactive role and are frequently overwhelmed by administration and paperwork (Knapman et al, 1987: 29).

From the accounts of contemporary practice contained in the first part of the chapter it is clear that educational psychology has found ways of re-establishing a broader role to some extent, but that balancing demands for statutory and other assessments with prevention and intervention remains very much a live issue. The role of educational psychologists in the statutory assessment of special educational needs (SEN) has been reaffirmed in subsequent revisions of the legislation, most recently in the Special Educational Needs and Disability Act (DfEE, 2001). In fact, it was the stimulus for the next governmental review of the work of educational psychologists following the 1997 Green Paper which set out the Government's vision for raising the achievement of children with SEN.

The Green Paper recognised the wide ranging responsibilities of educational psychologists. In doing so it observed that the growing pressure for statements has led to educational psychologists spending more of their time carrying out statutory assessments, at the expense of providing early intervention and support when the child's needs are first identified. The Green Paper made a commitment to explore ways of changing the balance of educational psychologists' work to ensure their expertise is used more effectively. (DfEE, 2000a:1).

Rather than coming up with radical solutions, this report focused on publicizing descriptions of strategies some services had found to be successful in balancing conflicting demands and shifting practice.

Given the 32 year gap between the publication of the previous two governmental reports on the work of educational psychologists, it is perhaps surprising that the next one was to appear only six years later. This report (Farrell et al, 2006) was commissioned to review the functions and contribution of educational psychologists in England and Wales in light of *Every Child Matters: Change for Children*. The implementation of the Children Act (2004) and associated guidance (DfES, 2004), commonly referred to as the *Every Child Matters* (ECM) agenda, aims to improve multidisciplinary working, integrated planning, commissioning and delivery of services and outcomes for children. A range of implications and recommendations were highlighted in the review report:

■ The impact of educational psychologist's work should be assessed against the five ECM outcomes. The role of educational psychologists is to improve outcomes for children and this may require a radical reorientation of service evaluation efforts which have often focused on school staff satisfaction rather than child outcomes.

- There should be a shift in the focus of service delivery from school to community.

- There should be renewed emphasis on multi-agency involvement and specialist educational psychology input.

- In defining the distinctive contribution of educational psychologists there should be an emphasis on psychology.

- The future possible integration of educational and child clinical psychology professions and training should be investigated.

One final word about the fourth of the above points is necessary. It was argued that identification of the distinctive contribution that educational psychologists, as opposed to other professionals can make, should drive decisions about the balance of activities they undertake.

> *The general view that the EPs' distinctive contribution lies in their psychological skills and knowledge would suggest that agreed clarity of the EP role should be focused around the particularly psychological function within it (Farrell et al, 2006:102).*

It is interesting that almost exactly the same conclusion was reached almost 40 years earlier, in the Summerfield Report:

> *The particular contribution of psychologists in education services derives from their specialized study of psychological science and its application to education and to other aspects of human development. It should be the main criterion in determining their work (DES, 1968: xi)*

A major implication is that as aspects of psychology and their applicability to education change, so an impetus should be provided for development and change in educational psychology (see Cameron, 2006). So, for example, over the next decade we might expect to see the realization of some of the current promise of neuroscience in this respect (Blakemore and Frith, 2005; Goswami, 2006).

Educational psychology practice today: A case study

In this section of the chapter we present a case study, which illustrates the integrated way in which different core activities and levels of work may be incorporated in the educational psychologist's everyday practice. The starting point for this case study is a request from a school for advice on an individual pupil who is causing concern, made to the educational psychologist during one of their regular visits to the school. This is a very common starting point. Almost 50 per cent of educational psychology work is carried out on school premises (Imich, 1999; DfEE, 2000b) and further time is spent writing reports, making home visits and liaising with other agencies in relation to the work in school.

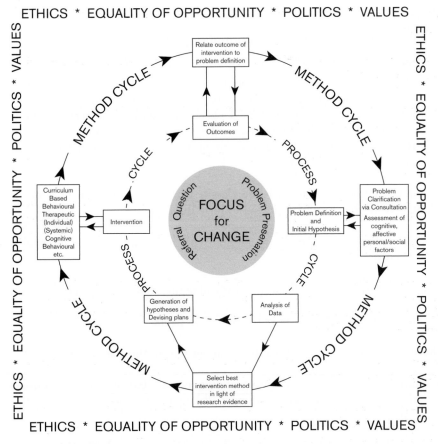

ETHICS * EQUALITY OF OPPORTUNITY * POLITICS * VALUES

ETHICS * EQUALITY OF OPPORTUNITY * POLITICS * VALUES

ETHICS * EQUALITY OF OPPORTUNITY * POLITICS * VALUES

ETHICS * EQUALITY OF OPPORTUNITY * POLITICS * VALUES

METHOD CYCLE

METHOD CYCLE

METHOD CYCLE

METHOD CYCLE

CYCLE

PROCESS

CYCLE

PROCESS

Referral Question

Problem Presentation

FOCUS for CHANGE

Relate outcome of intervention to problem definition

Evaluation of Outcomes

Curriculum Based Behavioural Therapeutic (Individual) (Systemic) Cognitive Behavioural etc.

Intervention

Problem Clarification via Consultation

Assessment of cognitive, affective personal/social factors

Problem Definition and Initial Hypothesis

Generation of hypotheses and Devising plans

Analysis of Data

Select best intervention method in light of research evidence

Figure 1.1 DECP Framework for psychological assessment and intervention.

While the specifics of policy and practice vary between local authorities, educational psychology practice in responding to requests of this kind is guided by the framework for psychological assessment (see Figure 1.1) contained in the BPS Division of Educational and Child Psychology (DECP) Professional Practice Guidelines (BPS, 2002). The process cycle contained in this model is essentially a problem-solving process, and it has been argued that the applied psychology professions are, at their core, problem-solving professions (Pearson and Howarth, 1982). The method cycle to which it links describes stages in a **consultation** between an educational psychologist and adults concerned about a child's progress. A widely accepted definition of consultation makes this link clear '. . . an indirect problem-solving process between a [consultant] and one or more [consultees] to address concerns presented by a client . . .' (Sheridan et al, 1996: 341–342). Models of consultation commonly used by educational psychologists in the USA (Gutkin and Curtis, 1999) and the UK (Woolfson et al, 2003) utilize a closely similar set of stages. The psychologist in this case study used a six-stage problem analysis framework (Monsen and Frederickson, in press).

Emilio – case study

Phase 1: Collect background information, clarify role and expectations

On one of the educational psychologist's regular visits to a primary school, a teacher requested advice on how to manage the learning and behaviour of Emilio, a 6-year-old pupil in her Year 1 class. She had been concerned about Emilio for some time and had obtained written consent from Emilio's parents to consult the educational psychologist about him, in line with the *BPS Code of Ethics and Conduct* (BPS, 2006).

During the initial meeting with the class teacher the main areas of concern highlighted were that Emilio appeared to have difficulty in:

- Initiating and sustaining verbal interaction with adults and peers in a range of social situations.

- Engaging in turn-taking and sharing of learning materials with peers.

- Communicating needs and views to adults and peers.

- Behaving in a positive, non-disruptive manner within the classroom.

In addition, some background information was collected, for example Emilio lived with both his parents and a younger sibling and the first language of the home is Spanish.

At the end of the initial consultation meeting it was agreed that this was an appropriate case for educational psychologist involvement and that an intervention would be considered successful if Emilio could:

- Speak up more frequently within class and social settings.

- Engage in appropriate turn-taking behaviour.

- Share things with his peers.

Phase 2: Initial guiding hypotheses

On the basis of the information collected from the consultation with the teacher the educational psychologist begins to generate tentative initial guiding hypotheses, drawing both on the unique details of the presenting problem situation and the knowledge base within the discipline of psychology, as can be seen below.

1. A range of environmental contingencies could be maintaining and reinforcing inappropriate social behaviour (Spence, 2003)?
2. There could be insufficient motivational factors in class to encourage verbal interaction (Gresham, Watson and Skinner, 2001)?
3. Emilio's expressive and receptive language skills could be delayed (Conti-Ramsden and Botting, 2004)?

4. Emilio's temperament could predispose him to behave in a shy and introverted manner (Crozier and Alden, 2005)?
5. Emilio's social problem-solving skills could be delayed (Webster-Stratton and Reid, 2003)?
6. There could be insufficient social opportunities for modelling/teaching of appropriate social behaviours (Spence, 2003)?
7. English as an additional language could be a factor (Snow, 2002)?

Initial guiding hypotheses focus and direct subsequent assessment activities, whose purpose is the collection of data to test the applicability and relevance of these hypotheses to the problem situation surrounding Emilio. In this case the educational psychologist and class teacher agreed that the educational psychologist would carry out structured classroom observations, arrange an interview with Emilio's parents and conduct some assessments of language competencies and social cognition with Emilio. The teacher agreed to keep a record of specific behaviours, together with information about events occurring before and after the behaviour.

Phase 3: Identified problem dimensions

From the assessment information collected, the following were identified as the main features of relevance in understanding the situation for Emilio.

1. There were insufficient motivational factors within the classroom context to encourage verbal interaction. The teacher tended to ask a series of questions to which Emilio could respond by nodding or shaking his head. Also, other pupils often responded on his behalf.
2. There was a range of environmental contingencies that appeared to be maintaining inappropriate social behaviour. From the behavioural record being kept by his teacher, it was apparent that her attention was often secured by disruptive behaviour and that Emilio was sometimes able to retain and use resources which he had snatched from others or refused to share with them.
3. Emilio presented in many social situations as shy and reserved.
4. Emilio's expressive and receptive language skills were below average for his age.
5. Emilio's social skills and social problem-solving skills appeared delayed.

These aspects, along with strengths and assets, would be used to inform intervention planning. A particular relevant strength was Emilio's good oral comprehension skills, despite some vocabulary difficulties.

Phase 4: Problem analysis

This is the case conceptualization or formulation that attempts to integrate the problem dimensions and represent relationships between them. In this case it was argued that the following three within-pupil factors could all be acting to form barriers to Emilio's social participation: shy personality, limited knowledge of what is appropriate within social situations and delayed expressive language skills. It was anticipated that the limited level of social contact would further perpetuate Emilio's difficulties by limiting opportunities to model and practise appropriate social skills (Spence, 2003). In addition to these within-child factors, the presence of insufficient environmental factors to motivate Emilio's oral communication (Gresham, Watson and Skinner, 2001) and the presence of environmental contingencies that reinforced competing inappropriate social behaviours (Spence, 2003) were contributing to the low occurrence of verbal social communication and the higher than average levels of inappropriate social behaviour. This can be represented visually on an **interactive factors framework** (see Figure 1.2) which also assists in the formulation of intervention plans.

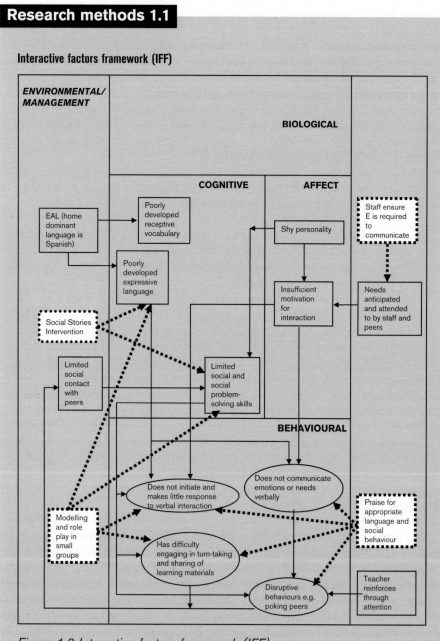

Figure 1.2 Interactive factors framework (IFF).

The IFF (see Frederickson and Cline, 2008) was developed from the Causal Modelling Framework (Morton and Frith, 1995; Morton, 2004). The IFF displays all of the problem dimensions identified, together with other relevant aspects of the problem situation for which there is evidence. The integrating hypothesis/es are shown via arrows indicating the connections between the behavioural, cognitive, affective, environmental and biological level variables as argued in the Integrating Statement. As can be seen from the dotted lines in Figure 1.2, the IFF diagram also represents the anticipated effects of suggested interventions on the priority problem dimensions.

Phase 5: Agreed action plan

Table 1.3 summarizes the actions that were discussed and agreed in an intervention planning meeting between the educational psychologist and the class teacher, Emilio's parents, and the school Special Educational Needs Coordinator (SENCO), who is responsible for managing arrangements within the school to meet pupils' special educational needs.

Priority problem dimensions	Objectives
Social interaction and problem-solving skills	To teach explicitly appropriate responses in various social situations using: ▪ Social stories (Smith, 2003) ▪ Modelling To promote a positive and cooperative class environment to encourage socially appropriate behaviour
Expressive language in social situations	To increase the need for verbal communication by altering environmental contingencies

Table 1.3 Agreed action plan for Emilio

Phase 6: Monitoring and evaluation of outcomes

Table 1.4 shows how outcomes were evaluated in relation to two of the intervention goals for Emilio. It can be seen that the educational psychologist again interviewed the class teacher and again carried out observation in the classroom using interval sampling (where the presence or absence of a particular target behaviour within each of a number of short time intervals is noted). In addition, **goal attainment scaling (GAS)** was used. GAS was developed by clinical psychologists in the USA to evaluate the outcomes of mental health interventions (Kiresuk and Sherman, 1968; Kiresuk et al, 1994). It involves identifying indicators for expected outcomes of intervention goals and then scaling these so that levels more, much more, less and much less than expected

Aims of intervention	Pre-intervention measures	Post-intervention measures	Interpretation
Sitting on carpet with hands and feet to self (does not poke peers)	**GAS** (Kiresuk et al, 1994): *Pre-intervention* 60% of time on carpet *Target set* 80% of time on carpet	**GAS** (Kiresuk et al, 1994) *Post-intervention* 100% of time on carpet	E's targeted inappropriate behaviour was extinguished. E exceeded the initial target set for him
	Teacher interview *Pre-intervention* E pokes his peers	**Teacher interview** *Post-intervention* E sits with a straight back and keeps his hands and feet to self. E does not poke his peers any more	
Increase frequency of verbal interaction in class to peers and teacher	**Teacher interview** *Pre-intervention* E tends to be quiet in class. Compared to the rest of the class, he talked less to his peers and to the teacher	**Teacher interview** *Post-intervention* E had began to respond more to her, would initiate questions and answers and would talk about his work	E has shown improvement in his targeted behaviour
	Interval sampling (with attempts at establishing social validity by observing E along with two randomly selected classmates, one girl [G] and one boy [B]) *Pre-intervention*	Interval sampling (with attempts at establishing social validity by observing E along with the same two other pupils in class) *Post-intervention*	
Initiates conversation with teacher	E (0) G (2) B (1)	E (4) G (1) B (4)	
Responds to teacher	E (2) G (7) B (1)	E (1) G (2) B (1)	
Initiates conversation with peers	E (7) G (17) B (19)	E (13) G (13) B (11)	

Table 1.4 Evaluation of outcomes

are also specified. When review meetings are held, actual outcomes can be located on the scales. GAS can assess change produced by any kind of intervention and has been used widely in health and education. Examples of its use include the evaluation of behavioural consultation (Sladeczek et al, 2001) and a behaviour support service led by educational psychologists in Essex (Imich and Roberts, 1990).

While this is a thorough evaluation, concerns are often expressed that this is an aspect of educational psychology practice that is given insufficient attention (Leadbetter, 2000). Kratochwill and Stoiber, writing in an American context, suggest that, due to pressure of work, 'school psychologists may fall into "crisis routines", rather than follow systematic procedures for intervention planning, monitoring and evaluation' (Kratochwill and Stoiber, 2000: 247). Educational psychologists have an ethical duty to evaluate the outcomes of their advice for the children and young people concerned so that effectiveness can be maximized and any unanticipated negative outcomes in individual cases identified and rectified. In addition, successful work at the individual level can lead to invitations by schools to undertake organizational level work that can efficiently impact on the learning and development of a larger number of pupils. For example, following work with Emilio, the educational psychologist was asked by the SENCO to deliver training on the social stories intervention approach to the whole staff. (More information on the social stories intervention approach can be found in Chapter 8.) The head teacher was very interested in the awareness the class teacher had developed about ways in which she and Emilio's classmates had unwittingly been reinforcing undesirable behaviour. As a consequence the educational psychologist was invited to a school senior management team meeting to discuss the possibility of carrying out a systems project in the school on 'behavioural awareness', involving staff and pupils. (More information on systems work by educational psychologists at a whole school level can be found in Chapter 13.)

Educational psychologists as scientist-practitioners

The central role of **hypothesis testing** in practice frameworks such as the problem analysis framework described above demonstrates how educational psychologists function as scientist-practitioners. In keeping with other applied psychologists, this is a role to which educational psychologists have frequently aspired, often finding themselves acting as 'mid-wife' to the contribution of science to complex social problems (Lane and Corrie, 2006). Or, as Elliot (2000) puts it '. . . the educational psychologist represents an important link between the worlds of academic psychology and education'.

At its simplest level, and a simplistic one at that as it turns out, the term 'scientist-practitioner' might conjure up notions of an expert researcher, or an expert conversant with pertinent research, who is able to draw on this knowledge to advise others or engage directly in various activities designed to help others, especially those in some form of need. And this was indeed a conceptualization to which early practitioners attempted to adhere.

The origins of the scientist-practitioner

The idea of the applied psychologist as a scientist-practitioner originated from the Boulder Conference, held in Colorado in 1949 in an attempt to forge the identity of the new profession of clinical psychology, which was felt to be engaged in an 'erratic process of expansion'. Basically, this professional group was faced with a choice between allying itself somehow to psychiatry and other therapeutic approaches or establishing itself as a separate profession built upon academic and research-based psychology. As a result of that conference it chose the latter.

No sooner had this decision been taken, however, than a fundamental tension began to reveal itself, a pull between two positions that is still felt to this day and is exemplified by the two quotes in Focus box 1.1 that illustrate extreme ends of a spectrum:

Focus 1.1

An example of a competing pull on the priorities of the applied psychologist as scientist-practitioner

. . . we must be careful not to let social need interfere with scientific requirements (Eysenck, 1949)

. . . even after 15 years, few of my research findings affect much of my practice. Psychological science per se *doesn't guide me one little bit . . . My clinical practice is the only thing that has helped me in my practice to date. (Matarazzo, cited in Bergin and Strupp, 1972)*

Further dilemmas and challenges for educational psychologists as scientist-practitioners

Other tensions and competing pulls became apparent as educational psychologists, who also adopted an identity as scientist-practitioners, attempted to develop this role and to deal with the increasing demands and expectations placed upon them by wider society (see Miller and Frederickson, 2006). Some of these issues, which recur in different forms throughout this book, are now briefly introduced.

Unidirectional or bidirectional influences?

In many successful fields of human endeavour, such as medicine and engineering, there is a well-established tradition that 'basic research' (in laboratories) informs 'applied research' (in 'simplified' field settings) that in turn, after a period of development, informs professional practice (Tizard, 1990). Can we automatically assume that this unidirectional influence will also hold for psychology? Or might we equally, or more plausibly even, look to the everyday problems brought to the attention of applied psychologists as the starting points for the investigations of academic research psychologists? After all, the study of cases of acquired neurological problems has been valuable in learning about normal neurological processing (e.g. Shallice and Warrington, 1975) and the study of cases of atypical development in seeking to learn about normal development (e.g. Snowling and Hulme, 1989).

Generalizable results and idiographic problems

A major goal of psychological research is to arrive at a generalized account of some underlying psychological process or processes (Clarke, 2004). In order to do this, research is usually carried out with groups of participants where only a few 'variables' are subjected to study. For educational and other applied psychologists the situations where their help is being sought – either with individuals, groups or organizations – are usually idiographic and complex in nature. Significant findings from group studies offer an indication of likely efficacy, not a prescription. For children and adolescents with all kinds of psychological problems the 'best available' treatment does not work in up to one-third of cases and some children deteriorate in response to intervention (Carr, 2000). Therefore 'evidence-based practice' is necessary but not sufficient. Careful evaluation in individual cases is also required.

The systemic context of individual problems

Individual problems of learning or development are typically embedded within a complex pattern of cause and effect inside a system where changing one aspect can potentially affect others. This dynamic context to many problems means that interventions aimed at an individual may stand no chance of success if other interfering organizational features cannot also be controlled or modified. Traditionally, most academic research has been conducted outside such contexts, leading to possibly successful outcomes in the research context but poor transfer into a child's everyday environment. Within developmental psychology Bronfenbrenner (1974) argued that development should be studied in its ecological context and criticized ' the study of the strange behaviour of children in strange situations for the briefest possible period of time'. Instead the developmental systems approach apparent in the bio-ecological model of human development incorporates investigation of process (activity engagement that promotes development), personal attributes of the people involved, context in which development is taking place, and time (see Bronfenbrenner and Morris, 2006). It promotes the use of structural equation modelling and other statistical techniques that have been developed to handle this kind of complexity

Statistical sophistication is not the same as rigorous scientific method

Historically educational psychologists have been closely associated with the use of norm-referenced psychometric tests, especially 'intelligence tests'. While such tools appear to lend a high degree of sophistication to assessments, permitting fine discriminations to be made, and the performance of individuals to be closely compared to that of much larger groups, they are not usually well suited to informing interventions or evaluating their impact. There have been repeated calls for more rigorous evaluation of interventions at both group and individual levels. At a group level there is a demand for the systematic evaluation of local innovatory programmes and local implementations of national initiatives generated by an increasing focus on accountability requirements and evidence-based practice in education (Sebba, 2004). At an individual level Kratochwill and Stoiber argue that 'concerted effort should be given to developing viable resource tools that permit flexible and adaptable use of empirically supported interventions and that incorporate progress monitoring strategies as part of the evaluation process' (Kratochwill and Stoiber, 2000: 247).

'Giving psychology away' – what if some people do not seem to want it?

Many educational psychologists responded enthusiastically to George Miller's classic injunction to 'give psychology away' (Miller, 1969). The needs of young people were too many and too widespread and the potential benefits to them, their teachers and parents too substantial not to adopt this approach. As an academic subject with practical applications, psychology was being incorporated into the training of teachers, social workers and child care professionals. Likewise, many educational psychologists appreciated the potential advantages of putting useful elements of their own knowledge and practice into the hands of, and then supporting, frontline professionals and parents, who were in regular contact with young people. It came as a shock therefore to find that advice was sometimes not followed and recommended interventions not implemented. However, instead of construing these responses as 'non-compliance' or 'resistance', educational psychologists were moved to an exploration of the barriers to the implementation of psychological advice and interventions, a field of study now often incorporated within the rubric of 'consultation' (Noell et al, 2005; DuPaul et al, 2006).

The 'political' context of educational psychologists' work

A final challenge for educational psychologists attempting to work as scientist-practitioners lies in the political context in which they operate, political in the sense that their time is a scarce resource that is inevitably distributed in favour of a few, however those particular recipients come to be selected. How educational psychologists spend their time remains a preoccupation. In advising local authorities on how to distribute their equally finite amounts of money and support professional time, there is a danger that educational psychologists can become seen or used by their employers and others as 'street level bureaucrats' (Lipsky, 1971). In the light of expectations such as these, it can take a determined effort from within the educational psychology profession itself in order to maintain and promote the benefits of practice as scientist-practitioners. The recent recognition of the centrality of psychological science in determining the educational psychologist role (Farrell et al, 2006) should be helpful in this regard.

Training as an educational psychologist

In all branches of applied psychology in the UK the requirements for **chartered status** with the BPS are an undergraduate degree in psychology that confers the **graduate basis for registration (GBR)** with the BPS followed by a three-year postgraduate programme of supervised training and practice accredited by the BPS. In educational psychology the arrangements in Scotland are different from those in the rest of the UK. In Scotland, two universities, Dundee and Strathclyde, offer a two-year accredited masters programme, following which trainee educational psychologists obtain a post in an educational psychology service accredited by the BPS to provide a final year of supervised practice. In England, Wales and Northern Ireland three-year doctoral training programmes are offered by the following higher education institutions: Birmingham University, Bristol University, Cardiff University, Exeter University, the Institute of Education in London, Manchester University, Newcastle University, Nottingham University, Queens University Belfast, Sheffield University, Southampton University, the Tavistock Clinic in London, UCL and the University of East London.

The three-year doctoral programmes of professional training in educational psychology were introduced in September 2006. Prior to that the training in England, Wales and Northern Ireland required the completion of a teaching qualification, two years qualified teaching experience, a one-year accredited masters programme and a year of practice, supervised by a chartered educational psychologist or equivalently qualified practitioner (essentially only two years of postgraduate training and practice in psychology). In recent years in the UK we have been moving towards statutory regulation of applied psychologists, to replace the current voluntary system run by the BPS. It is proposed that statutory regulation and professional training course accreditation will be run by the Health Professions Council.

Teaching experience is no longer a requirement for training as an educational psychologist in any part of the UK. However the application process is highly competitive (a programme might typically receive 200 applications for 10 funded places) and applicants are unlikely to be successful in obtaining an interview unless they can demonstrate relevant experience of working with children within educational, childcare or community settings. Examples of settings in which relevant experience is likely to be gained include work as: a graduate assistant in an Educational Psychology Service, a school teacher, a Learning Support Assistant, an Educational Social Worker, a Learning Mentor, a Speech and Language Therapist, a Care Worker, a worker in early years settings. Voluntary experience of various kinds over a number of years may assist applicants in demonstrating a breadth of relevant experience. Whatever kind of work has been done, universities will be primarily interested in what applicants have learnt from their experiences that is relevant to work as an educational psychologist, and how they have been able to apply the knowledge of psychology gained through their first degree.

Funding is available for educational psychology training and different models currently operate in different parts of the UK. In Wales and Northern Ireland three-year bursaries are available, whereas in England bursary funding covers the first year and trainees need then to obtain posts in Educational Psychology Services where they are paid salaries for the two remaining years of training. Readers who are interested in training as an educational psychologist are advised to visit the BPS website (www.BPS.org.uk/) and the websites of the training providers, listed above, for up-to-date information. Educational psychology also has its own trade union, the Association of Educational Psychologists (AEP), and you will be able to find information on the AEP website (www.aep.org.uk/) about a wide range of issues including pay and conditions of educational psychologist. The AEP, in collaboration with the publishers Taylor and Francis, also produce the most widely read UK professional journal for educational psychologists, *Educational Psychology in Practice*, which you would be well advised to read if you are thinking of applying for educational psychology training.

The content of professional training as an educational psychologist

The course centres listed above all offer BPS-accredited training as a professional educational psychologist and therefore all offer, with distinctive individual variations, a three-year programme that address the BPS required learning outcomes for such training. Looking through the range of topics covered in this book and intended primarily for final year undergraduates, the casual observer might wonder why a further three years of postgraduate study is necessary before a person can qualify to practise as an educational psychology. In answer to such a query it must first be acknowledged that, due to space constraints, these chapters are selective in their breadth of coverage and restricted in their depth of coverage. Second, there are many more school-focused topics requiring study than are covered in this volume. Examples include working with pupils deemed to have attention deficit disorder, the special strengths and needs of deaf children, and working with the staff and students of schools that have experienced violent or tragic events. Finally, there are important areas of educational psychology practice that are not addressed in the rest of this book: for example, work specifically focused on the child below school age, on children in their families, on work with parents and carers in home and community settings, on work with multidisciplinary teams such as Child and Adolescent Mental Health Services, and on young people post school or in the juvenile justice system.

However, training as an effective and highly skilled professional requires considerably more than an intensive period of advanced knowledge acquisition. This is only one of three strands to the BPS accreditation requirements; a high level of research training and a minimum of 300 days supervised professional practice are the other two. So, aspiring educational psychologists have to study advanced research methods and carry out a major piece of empirical research, in order to acquire and demonstrate the knowledge and skills expected from a postgraduate researcher. In doing so, they will usually be contributing as scientist-practitioners to the development of policy and practice in the local authorities where they carry out their supervised professional placements and, hopefully, to a wider national agenda for ensuring that all children do meet the five outcomes stipulated within the ***Every Child Matters*** programme (be healthy, stay safe, enjoy and achieve through learning, make a positive contribution to society, achieve economic well-being).

Finally, all elements of the training will need to integrate, with the whole representing more than the sum of the parts. It is in the professional placements in particular that trainees are expected to demonstrate a high level of what might be termed 'professional artistry' (Schon, 1987) – interpersonal skills, agile problem-solving abilities and a self-questioning reflective stance. No amount of knowledge can improve outcomes for an abused, or a seriously failing, or a painfully anxious young person, if this knowledge cannot be utilized appropriately, communicated effectively, tailored to the contexts and understandings of those in the best position to help, and conceptualized within a set of values that are truly humanistic and person-centred. This is what constitutes the training challenge – a challenge which if met places applied psychology in a position where it can make major contributions to the education, welfare and safety of all children and young people.

Summary

■ Educational psychologists carry out a range of activities aimed at promoting the learning and development of children and young people (0 to 19 years), through the application of psychology. They spend most time working with schools and other education providers but also work in pre-school settings, and with children and their families and with other agencies.

■ The first educational psychologist in the UK was appointed in London in 1913 and fulfilled a broad role including work with individual children experiencing problems and research and development work across the local authority. However there has long been a tension between providing detailed assessments of special educational needs for a small number of pupils and engaging in prevention, intervention and training that can benefit a whole school community.

■ The distinctive contribution of educational psychologists derives from their specialist knowledge of psychology. However their role, both historically and currently, has also been determined by political imperatives and the availability of other staff to carry out key functions.

■ Educational psychologists' consultation, assessment and intervention work is carried out with regard to the BPS Division of Educational and Child Psychology professional practice guidelines. Underpinning these is a problem-solving process model which involves hypothesis generation and testing as a central activity.

■ Like other applied psychologists, educational psychologists are conceptualized as scientist-practitioners. A number of the tensions and issues surrounding this conceptualization are identified and discussed.

■ Professional training in educational psychology in the UK requires a three-year undergraduate degree in psychology that confers graduate basis for registration with the BPS followed by an accredited three-year postgraduate programme of supervised training and practice.

Key concepts and terms

British Psychological Society
  (BPS)
Chartered status
Consultation
Educational psychology
Every Child Matters (ECM)
Goal attainment scaling (GAS)
Graduate basis for registration
  (GBR)

Hypothesis testing
Interactive factors framework (IFF)
Psychometric testing
School psychology
Statement of special educational
  needs

Sample essay titles

- To what extent can educational psychologists be described as scientist practitioners?
- Select any psychology course from the first two years of your degree and critically evaluate its applicability to educational psychology practice.
- Identify any area of psychological theory and research which you think is relevant to the practice of educational psychology and which is not featured in a chapter of this book. Produce an up-to-date review of the literature in this area and outline its implications for educational psychology practice.

Further reading

Books

Farrell, P., Woods, K., Lewis, S., Rooney, S., Squires, G., and O'Connor, M. (2006). *A Review of the Functions and Contribution of Educational Psychologists in England and Wales in light of* 'Every child matters: Change for Children'. Nottingham: DfES Publications.

Miller, A., and Frederickson, N. (2006). 'Generalisable findings and idiographic problems: Struggles and successes for educational psychologists as scientist-practitioners.' In: D. Lane and S. Corrie (Eds) *The Modern Scientist-Practitioner: Practical Approaches to Guide How Professional Psychologists Think*. London: Routledge.

Squires, G., and Farrell, P.T. (2007). 'Educational psychology in England and Wales.' In: S.R. Jimerson, T.D. Oakland and P.T. Farrell (Eds) *The Handbook of International School Psychology*. London: Sage, 81–90.

Topping, K.J., Smith, E., Barrow, W., Hannah, E., and Kerr, C. (2007). 'Professional educational psychology in Scotland.' In: S.R. Jimerson, T.D. Oakland and P.T. Farrell (Eds) *The Handbook of International School Psychology*. London: Sage, 339–350.

Journal articles

Cameron, R.J. (2006). Educational psychology: The distinctive contribution. *Educational Psychology in Practice*, 22, 289–304.

Leadbetter, J. (2000) Patterns of service delivery in educational psychology services: some implications for practice. *Educational Psychology in Practice*, 16, 449–460.

Woolfson, L., Whaling, R., Stewart, A., and Monsen, J.J. (2003). An integrated framework to guide educational psychologist practice. *Educational Psychology in Practice*, 19, 283–302.

1 | Cognition, learning and instruction

2 What use is 'intelligence'?

Tony Cline

The concept of **intelligence** has been influential in psychology, and that influence has often been portrayed as malign. This chapter will analyse how ideas about intelligence have developed in recent years among the general public and within psychology. Applications of these ideas in education will be illustrated by examining two specific areas:

- The identification of **moderate and severe learning difficulties**.

- The notion of **multiple intelligences**.

The chapter ends with a discussion of the changes that have occurred over time in the role that the assessment of intelligence has played in the practice of educational psychologists.

Learning outcomes

When you have completed this chapter you should be able to:

1. Outline how views of the concept of intelligence have changed over time among teachers and the general public and discuss reasons for these changes.
2. Explain and evaluate selected theoretical approaches to conceptualizing intelligence within psychology.
3. Describe some of the ways in which psychologists' ideas about intelligence have been applied in education and discuss the possible value of current applications.

Views of the concept of intelligence among teachers and the general public

If someone is described to you as 'intelligent', what might you expect to notice about them when you meet them? When teachers in various countries have been asked questions like this about the pupils they work with, they have tended to list sets of abilities such as:

■ Going beyond the given.

■ Seeing connections between different ideas.

■ Seeing patterns in data.

■ Applying concepts to new contexts.

■ Thinking logically.

■ Applying knowledge from one context to another.

■ Demonstrating deep understanding of a concept (Adey et al, 2007).

But Adey and his colleagues note a paradox: 'These responses explicate professional, intuitive, experienced-based conceptions of general ability. But as soon as you try to suggest that a good word to describe this general ability is "intelligence", you encounter resistance' (Adey et al, 2007: 75–97). The term had broader public acceptance in western countries in the 1940s, but after that time there appears to have been a steady erosion in confidence about how intelligence quotient (IQ) tests measure intelligence. This is reflected in Table 2.1, which records some of the changes found by Shipstone and Burt (1973) who repeated a survey originally conducted by Flugel in 1947. Those participating in such surveys within western cultures would generally agree that some notion of general mental ability is important in the judgements they make about other people. That does not mean that they are all comfortable with the ways in which psychologists have treated this construct. The image of professional practice in educational psychology suffered for many years from an association with the regular administration of intelligence tests. This image became inaccurate over time. Successive surveys by Farrell and Smith (1982), Farrell et al (1989) and Woods and Farrell (2006) recorded slow change within the profession from the routine use of global **intelligence scales** to their highly selective use within a much broader range of assessment strategies. An outline of the rise and fall of educational psychologists' engagement with psychometric practices and with the notion of global intelligence is presented in the final section of this chapter.

Particularly sceptical views on the value of the construct of intelligence have been expressed by commentators on school education. These views covered a range of issues:

	Percentage disagreeing with the proposition in 1947	Percentage disagreeing with the proposition in 1973
This sort of measurement of 'general intelligence' would help find the right man for the job	22	41
Intelligence tests are better than ordinary examinations for finding out the brains a person was born with (as distinct from what he has been taught)	16	27
If a child's intelligence is measured when he is between 8 and 10, we can get an idea of how intelligent he will be when he is grown up	41	52

Table 2.1 Changes in public opinion recorded by Shipstone and Burt (1973)

■ Theoretical – scepticism that a single construct can explain as much variation in children's learning as had originally been suggested. This view gained empirical support when, for example, the contribution of general verbal abilities to predictions of young children's progress in reading was shown to be less than that of some specific reading-related skills (Blatchford et al, 1987).

■ Practical – doubts about whether intelligence can be measured reliably in a sufficiently fine-grained way to provide useful information for planning how to adapt teaching to the needs of individual children (Resing, 1997).

■ Moral – concern that the measurement of intelligence may be inequitable in its treatment of the performance of children who have had limited access to learning opportunities during early childhood (Scarr, 1984).

■ Ideological – worries about racist interpretations of some 'scientific' ideas on group differences in measured intelligence (Tomlinson, 1982).

■ Pedagogic – concern that the concept of intelligence suggests that children have a fixed level of ability and that this will discourage teachers from trying to develop untapped **potential** (Adey et al, 2007).

In the face of such extensive concerns why have some psychologists continued to employ the construct of intelligence and try to develop new theories of intelligence and new ways of measuring it? To understand this it is necessary to examine first how they have conceptualized the construct – their answers to the question 'What is intelligence?'.

The concept of intelligence in psychology

Cultural influences on how psychologists conceptualize intelligence

Throughout history the conceptualization of human abilities in each society has been influenced by the cultural values of that society. This means that there is great variation in the way in which intelligence is described across periods of history and across regions of the world. For example, in classical Chinese traditions the Confucian image of an intelligent person included a moral perspective, emphasizing the use of abilities in the service of 'benevolence' and highlighting the possibility that an individual can enhance their potential through effort. In the Taoist tradition, on the other hand, the concept of intelligence incorporates not only a capacity for effective action but also humility and the flexibility to be able to respond to changed circumstances. Yang and Sternberg (1997) studied conceptions of intelligence among heterogeneous samples of adults in two major cities in Taiwan and showed that their ideas about what characterizes an intelligent person had different emphases from those typically

ANTHROPOMETRIC LABORATORY

For the measurement in various ways of Human Form and Faculty

This laboratory is established by Mr Francis Galton for the following purposes:

1. For the use of those who desire to be accurately measured in many ways, either to obtain timely warning of remediable faults in development, or to learn their powers.

2. For keeping a methodological register of the principal measurements of each person, of which he may at any future time obtain a copy under reasonable restrictions. His initials and date of birth will be entered in the register, but not his name. The names are indexed in a separate book.

3. For supplying information on the methods, practice, and uses of human measurement.

4. For anthropometric experiment and research, and for obtaining data for statistical discussion.

Charges for making the principal measurements:
THREEPENCE each to those who are already on the register.
FOURPENCE each to those who are not

Figure 2.1 Galton's Anthropometric laboratory.

Source: Flanagan and Harrison, 2005: 4.

found in western populations and reflected values associated with the cultural legacy of Confucianism and Taoism.

Working within the framework of scientific method, early psychologists tried to base their ideas about intelligence on empirical investigation. The first strategy was to collect systematic data on how a wide range of people performed on a range of short mental tests. Inevitably the design of their studies was influenced by cultural expectations within their society. Examine the advertisement in Figure 2.1 which was circulated on a handbill in London in 1884 by Francis Galton (1822–1911), an energetic polymath from a wealthy Victorian family. On this evidence alone, what aspects of his approach do you think are in line with what would be expected today in terms of ethical requirements and methodology, and what aspects deviate from today's standards?

That handbill was circulated when Galton established his first laboratory at a Health Exhibition in London. When it closed a year later, he opened another nearby. Eventually he collected data on approximately 17,000 individuals (Johnson et al, 1985). The large battery of tests that he used included physical measures such as length and breadth of the head and functional measures such as breathing capacity. Among the functional measures was one that later played a significant role in the development of experimental psychology, participants' **reaction times** to visual and auditory stimuli. As we will see, this also later featured in theoretical analyses of the nature of intelligence. However, Galton's own conceptualization of intelligence was based on a misunderstanding of the operation of perception and cognition that led him to stress the value of measuring sensory acuity as a basis for analyzing individual differences in mental ability: 'The only information that reaches us concerning outward events appears to pass through the avenue of our senses; and the more perceptible our senses are of difference, the larger the field upon which our judgment and intellect can act' (Galton, 1883, cited by Wasserman and Tulsky, 2005).

This biological emphasis, along with his interest in the role of heredity in individual differences, illustrates ways in which Galton's historical and cultural position influenced his ideas about intelligence. The study of intelligence since his day has benefited from advances in scientific method but may be no less subject to the cultural and social factors that influence thinking generally at any time.

Factorial theories of intelligence

The early psychometricians developed a wide variety of mental tests, many of which have stood the test of time and continue in use today. Examples include:

- A *vocabulary* test in which the participant is presented with a list of words one at a time and has to provide a definition of each one to the interviewer.

- A *block design* test in which the participant is presented with a number of wooden or plastic blocks that have sides that are either all white or all red sides or a mix of red and white. They are required to arrange them according to a two-dimensional pattern that they are shown in a booklet, and they are timed on this task.

Figure 2.2 The block design test.
Source: Will & Deni McIntyre/Science Photo Library.

Charles Spearman (1863–1945) was a pioneer of factor analysis and emphasized the high correlations that are found between mental tests. He concluded that what matters in human intelligence is some form of mental energy that is captured by a general factor in these correlations which he called '*g*'. The notion of *g* was thus based on statistical analysis and highlighted the shared variance that had been found when examining the results of a wide range of mental tests. This core finding has proved remarkably robust. Thus, over ninety years after Spearman's initial reports on the subject, Jensen (1998) reviewed studies of correlates of *g* including:

- A record of creative accomplishment in arts and sciences.

- Job performance in a wide range of occupations.

- Scholastic performance.

- Success in training programmes.

However, from a very early stage there were competing views. For example, Louis L. Thurstone (1887–1955) developed a technique of multiple factor analysis which made it possible to extract separate 'group factors' when analysing matrices of correlations. On that basis he argued that too much importance had been given to the notion of a general factor and highlighted the role of what he called **primary mental abilities** in explaining the variance in scores on a battery of mental tests. The 'separate and unique' abilities that he identified were word fluency, number facility, verbal comprehension, perceptual speed, associative memory, spatial visualization and inductive reasoning. At the time that he developed this model Thurstone denied the validity of Spearman's general factor, but by the end of his life, after evolving factor analytic techniques further so as to give more attention to higher order factors in a matrix, he was ready to acknowledge the possible existence of *g* at a higher order level (Wasserman and Tulsky, 2005). Thurstone's emphasis on the importance of separate and unique abilities has been echoed in recent years by an influential theory of '**multiple intelligences**' (Gardner, 1983) which will be discussed later in this chapter.

Spearman and Thurstone had each made important contributions to the development of the statistical techniques of factor analysis, but in their day this was a laborious process involving extensive manual calculations. Carroll (1993) undertook a major re-analysis of more than 460 data sets from earlier studies of intelligence, employing contemporary factor analytic techniques and taking advantage of the advances in computer technology that had occurred in the interim. Many of his data sets were from earlier pioneers of intelligence assessment, including Thurstone. The 'three-stratum theory of cognitive abilities' which emerged from his work is a hierarchical model in which there are three types of ability:

■ First order abilities which are narrow in scope and highly specialized, such as absolute pitch, phonetic coding, spelling ability. These are subsumed by

■ Second order abilities which are broader in scope and subsume a number of first order abilities. Examples include general memory and learning, broad visual perception, broad cognitive speediness. These are subsumed by

■ A third order general intelligence.

The notion of intelligence as a general core plus special abilities thus has a substantial evidence base, and this model has been well received. Carroll (2005) outlined what he saw as the implications for the practical assessment of individuals by groups such as educational psychologists. While ideally all the

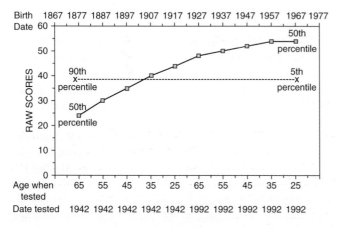

Figure 2.3 Adults'scores by age when a non-verbal reasoning test (Raven's Progressive matrices) was standardized in 1942 and re-standardized in 1992. This figure is adapted from Flynn (1999) who pointed out that the bottom 90 per cent born in 1877 fall within the same range of scores as the bottom 5 per cent born in 1967.

abilities in his extensive lists should be tested, that would be impractical. But it needs to be recognized that, if only g is assessed and this policy is followed strictly, 'many abilities that are important in particular cases would probably be missed' (Carroll, 2005: 75).

There is one assumption that has often been associated with the concept of g, although it is not a necessary corollary of it. This is that intelligence is a fixed, inherited quality which cannot be enhanced or increased. That assumption has been discredited over the last 40 years, because it has been shown that mean IQ in a society tends to increase over time with increases in affluence or educational opportunities (Flynn, 1999 – see Figure 2.3), that the measured IQ of deprived children often increases following adoption (O'Connor et al, 2000) and that mean intelligence measures in a general school population may increase following long-term intervention programmes in school such as cognitive acceleration (Adey et al, 2007).

Process-based and biological theories of intelligence

Factorial theories of intelligence highlight ways in which human abilities are organized or structured but do not explain how they work. Another approach to investigating the detailed working of cognitive abilities is to break down intelligence test tasks to their basic components and analyse the micro-level cognitive processes that underlie cognitive abilities. The findings of cognitive psychology are applied to this analysis so that the focus shifts over time with changes in the focus of interest in cognitive psychology and in the instrumentation that is available. This can be illustrated by considering the progress over time of research on the relationship between intelligence and what at one point was termed 'cognitive speed'. In western cultures people who are seen as intelligent are often described as 'quick'. Does **speed of information processing** offer an explanation of individual differences in intelligence?

Initially it was shown that speed of reaction on a simple decision-making task (e.g. pressing a button when a light comes on) did not correlate highly with performance on a range of problem-solving tasks. But if the task was made more complex (e.g. if participants had to react as quickly as possible to one or another of several stimuli), then the correlations with measures of cognitive ability increased significantly. However, the amount of variance in ability test performance that can be explained in this way is limited, as correlations rarely exceed 0.4. In addition, it emerged that the apparently simple **reaction time (RT)** task was more complex than had been assumed. To do well on an RT task a participant did not just have to respond quickly to a stimulus, they also had to focus their attention on the target and maintain it there, and they had to move quickly to make a response. Studies of the decline of performance with ageing suggested that it was not speed of processing in itself that explained the correlation between reaction time and ability measures but a decline in the ability to focus and maintain attention over time (Horn and Blankson, 2005). In Research Methods box 2.1 you will find an account of an alternative experimental paradigm which was designed to provide a simpler and 'cleaner' test of cognitive speed – **inspection time**.

Research methods 2.1

Inspection time and intelligence

In a typical experiment on inspection time, participants are shown two parallel, vertical lines, one of which is longer than the other. The two lines are joined at the top by a horizontal bar. In one form of the stimulus the long line is on the right and in the other it is on the left. The difference in length is sufficient so that people with normal vision can discriminate between the longer and shorter lines easily: with sufficient inspection time, they give an error-free performance on every occasion. But what happens if the task is made more difficult? One way of achieving that is to allow participants to view the lines for only a very limited period of time. Another way is to prevent participants from processing information that is available in iconic memory after the stimulus has been removed. This can be done by presenting a visual mask of some kind immediately after the target stimulus.

In order to measure a participant's 'inspection time' the target stimuli are presented randomly so that the long line is equally likely to appear on the left or the right side. The duration of the stimuli's appearance on screen will vary, e.g. between 10 and 300 milliseconds. Each time it appears participants are required to state whether the long line appeared on the left or on the right. They are told to try to judge it correctly and have no instruction to work quickly. Their accuracy is plotted against the length of exposure of the stimulus. Typically the longer the figure appears on the screen, the more accurate participants' judgements about it are. Some participants achieve high accuracy scores with much shorter periods of exposure than others: they show themselves able to process simple sensory input relatively quickly. It turns out that these individuals tend also to obtain higher scores on cognitive ability tests. (For a review see Deary and Stough, 1996.) The aim of the experimental paradigm was to reduce the effect of all other variables such as movement speed or iconic memory to a minimum so that individual differences in performance on the task could be attributed almost entirely to a single variable – inspection time (IT). It was hypothesized that, 'if IT does measure the time required to make a single observation of the sensory input, then such a quantity seems likely to operate as a basic factor limiting perceptual and cognitive performance in general' (Vickers and Smith, 1986, cited by Deary and Stough, 1996: 603). For an example of a major theory of intelligence that emphasizes the importance of speed of information processing and draws on the results of inspection time studies, see Anderson (1992).

Research on inspection time and intelligence showed that people who obtain high scores on intelligence tests (especially non-verbal intelligence tests) also tend to have the ability to make more accurate judgements when stimuli are visible for very brief periods. Perhaps, then, a fundamental characteristic of intelligence is that it is associated with variation in the speed with which people take in and process very simple stimulus information. There must be some doubt about so sweeping a claim, however, first because theorists can point to more 'fundamental' processes at the biological level, and second because complex information processing seems to rely on other cognitive components besides speed of processing for its successful completion. We will look at each of these points briefly in turn.

First, can individual differences in intelligence be explained at the biological level? The rapid technical advances made in recent years in neuroscience have meant that we are closer now to understanding the nature of the challenge in this field than we were even a decade ago. We know, for example, that intelligence is not localized in the frontal lobes of the brain as was once thought. Colom, Jung and Haier (2006) used structural magnetic resonance imaging to study the brains of adults who had different patterns of scores on various intelligence tests. They found that measures of verbal and non-verbal g (i.e. vocabulary and block design) correlated with the amount of regional grey matter across the frontal, parietal, temporal and occipital lobes and not just in the frontal lobes. But what do such correlations mean? Deary and Caryl (1997) pointed out that, even when stable associations are shown between measures of intelligence and aspects of brain activity, it is difficult to articulate the constructs that are being assessed by the neuroscience techniques. In addition, like any other correlational research, these studies on their own cannot determine the direction of causation: it is not clear from this research whether the operation of intelligent activity in everyday life influences the development of brain structure or vice versa.

A further possibility is that the critical characteristic of more intelligent people is not that their brains differ structurally from those of others but that they operate in a more efficient manner. This hypothesis was triggered by the finding that there is a *negative* correlation between glucose uptake across the brain and performance on mental tests such as Raven's Progressive Matrices (a non-verbal ability test closely related to g). It was argued that, if those who do well on such tests consume less sugar during their performance, they are expending less effort on the task. This was taken further, and it was shown that, if participants in an experiment learn a complex task (such as a task involving visuospatial skills) and then practise it, the brightest of them not only show lower overall glucose metabolism in the brain but show higher levels in those specific brain areas that are important to the task that has been learned: they focus their mental efforts more efficiently (Haier, 1993).

Second, is speed of information processing the most important component of cognitive activity in determining intelligence? In the West we tend to think of clever people as being quick people. In some cultures it is assumed that a wise person will take time to think. Research on complex information processing found evidence to support the latter view as well as the former: when the time people take to solve a problem is broken down, it is found that those who obtain higher scores on intelligence tests tend to take longer on planning how to tackle the problem and then compensate for that by

Activity 2.1

How to improve intelligence: A modern fairy tale

In the latter half of the twenty-first century the citizens of the UK became disillusioned with the cult of celebrity, which had been so influential in their culture for the previous two generations. They ceased to want to read about the wives and girlfriends of leading footballers in their magazines; they ceased to want to watch TV games featuring celebrity contestants; they ceased to want to buy products just because they were endorsed by celebrities. Economists and other members of the intellectual elite in Europe became very worried. The void that had been left by the loss of interest in celebrity must be filled. A special commission was set up and took evidence on what might best replace the cult of celebrity. They rejected many suggestions such as a cult of physical strength and a cult of temperamental calm because they did not appear to offer economic advantages over other national groups. The proposal they decided to take forward was that the UK should develop a cult of intelligence. Instead of every child hoping to become famous, the pressures within British culture should inspire every child to try to become more intelligent. But how could this be achieved?

The Commission issued an open invitation to any person in the kingdom to come forward and present their ideas on the steps to be taken to enhance the national level of intelligence. A dietician suggested changing the national diet and was sent away for lack of evidence that their method would work. A geneticist suggested building up a stem cell bank from the brain material of Fellows of the Royal Society and was sent away because of ethical objections. As the time limit that the Commission had set was approaching, they had no viable ideas to take forward. At last three wise sages from the discipline of psychology asked to address them. Unfortunately they had different ideas about what intelligence comprises. The first psychologist had a factorial theory of intelligence and emphasized the importance of identifying which ability factors were weakest in any individual's repertoire and which were strongest. The second psychologist had an information processing theory of intelligence and emphasized the importance of processing speed. The third psychologist had a biological theory of intelligence and emphasized the importance of efficiency.

If you had the theoretical views of each of those psychologists, what advice would you expect to give the Commission about how to improve the national level of intelligence?

The ending of our modern fairy tale was lost when the Commission's computer crashed. You may like to speculate about how it ended.

completing the final stages of problem solution more quickly (Sternberg, 1981). Subsequently Naglieri and Das (1997) developed an ambitious theory of intelligence that highlighted the role of planning in cognitive activity alongside attention or arousal, simultaneous processing and successive processing – the PASS theory.

For an educational psychologist the greatest challenge from psychological theories of the basis of intelligence is to tease out what their implications might be for education.

If we have an idea about what intelligence is, does that help us to plan how to improve it? Before you turn to the next section about the applications of the concept of intelligence in education, reflect on what the possibilities might be by tackling the task in Activity box 2.1.

Applications of ideas about intelligence in education

There have been many applications of ideas about intelligence in education. In the past intelligence tests have been used to identify children who were 'subnormal', children with exceptional gifts and talents and children who might be suitable for an academic style of selective education in grammar schools. During the second half of the twentieth century confidence in the reliability and validity of these methods was steadily eroded. Curriculum-based testing and close classroom observation were seen as providing a more secure basis for key educational decisions (Sutherland, 1990; Freeman, 1998), and intelligence was seen as only one component of giftedness (Sternberg and Grigorenko, 2002). In addition, the influence of a notion of fixed and unchangeable intelligence came to be seen as fostering a sense of helplessness in teachers and students alike: if intelligence is seen as something that you are born with there is nothing you (or your teachers) can do to break out of the limitations it places upon you. In the first part of this section we will examine the application of a factorial theory of intelligence to the identification of learning difficulties. In the second part we will consider recent attempts to apply process-based theories of intelligence to support effective education across the ability spectrum.

The identification of moderate and severe learning difficulties

In 1904 the Minister of Public Instruction in France appointed a commission to investigate options such as special classes for educating the group of children who were then called 'defective'. One challenge for those involved was how to decide which children needed to be admitted to the new classes. That was not easy because there was no agreement about what constituted mental subnormality and no standard method of testing children to identify it. The Commission relied heavily on the work of a psychologist, Alfred Binet, and a psychiatrist, Henri Simon, to overcome this problem. Unlike Galton in England,

Binet and Simon played down the importance of psychophysical tests. They thought of intelligence as involving higher order, more complex skills, including judgement, comprehension and reasoning ability. These early scales were relatively simple and crude, and Binet himself had serious reservations about them. Nonetheless they were seen as achieving their main objective – enabling those responsible for provision for the mentally retarded to identify who needed their services. A historian of psychology has observed:

> If the criteria that authorities were forced to rely upon up to that time are taken into account, the eager welcome given to the Binet–Simon scale does not appear excessive. Some physicians had struggled bravely to devise a way of differentiating between the idiot and the imbecile along the lines suggested by Pinel, who claimed that an idiot's attention was 'fugitive' whereas an imbecile's attention was 'fleeting' . . . Some frankly acknowledged that their judgments were uncertain. Dr. Walter Fernald, head of the Massachusetts School for the Feebleminded, regretted that the best that he had been able to do for the classification of children was to depend on observations of their posture and motor coordination when they stepped from the vehicle that brought them to his institution. Others insisted they could tell more about a child based on feelings about the child or on the twinkle, or lack of a twinkle, in the child's eye than could ever be learned from mental testing. But these voices were drowned in the chorus of approval. In Belgium, Germany, Italy, England, and the United States great interest in Binet's work was aroused. Here at last seemed to be an objective means of classification and a convenient device upon which could be placed the greater part of the responsibility for making decisions. (Reisman, 1991: 60).

During the period since then there have been significant technical advances in the structure of intelligence tests. For example, they no longer rely on a concept of 'mental age', a description of a child's intellectual level as the chronological age for which their overall performance on an intelligence scale is average or typical. This had proved an unreliable and misleading statistic. In addition, they give more attention to non-verbal skills in parallel with verbal skills. However, the most remarkable feature of the subsequent history of

Notional IQ range	0–25	26–50	51–70
1913	Idiot	Imbecile	Feeble-minded or High-grade defective
1944	Educationally subnormal (severe)		Educationally subnormal (mild)
1981	Severe and profound learning difficulties		Moderate learning difficulties

Table 2.2 Official terminology for describing children with learning difficulties

intelligence testing has been its conservatism. The first American version of Binet's scales was published by Terman in 1916. Almost 100 years later, when an updated and revised fifth edition of the *Stanford–Binet Intelligence Scale* was published, Binet himself would have recognized many of its features, both the format of some individual items and the procedure for interviewing a testee (Roid, 2003).

That continuity is surprising because the language used to describe learning difficulties and the ways in which such difficulties are conceptualized have changed radically during that period. The shift in official terminology in the UK is illustrated in Table 2.2. The changes, of course, signify a rejection of terms and phrases that were seen to have negative connotations. But the shift goes further than that: the earlier terminology implied that the groups who were listed in each column were in completely different mental categories, while the more recent terminology places individuals on a dimension which differs only in the severity of the difficulties that they encounter.

Table 2.2 provides a notional range of IQs for each of the groups. In the past it would have been expected that children whose IQs were less than 50 would attend one type of special school (for those with severe or profound learning difficulties) and those whose IQs were in the range 51–70 would attend another type (for those with moderate learning difficulties). However, studies over an extended time period showed that not all children within those intelligence brackets were required to attend the 'appropriate' type of school. Those who appeared to have moderate learning difficulties on the basis of IQ might continue to attend a mainstream school if their reading attainment level was higher (Rutter et al, 1970) or if they showed relatively fewer behaviour difficulties (Simonoff et al, 2006). Separate placement in a special school has been becoming less and less common as a result of policies of educational inclusion. But that is not the only reason why educational decisions about children with learning difficulties are no longer taken mainly on the basis of assessments of intelligence.

Dissatisfaction with cultural bias in intelligence tests undermined confidence in the validity of the tests for educational purposes (Gipps and Murphy, 1994: Chapter 3). More fundamentally, however, the categorization of learning difficulties by IQ was undermined by the finding that there is no simple relationship between differences in measured intelligence and patterns of learning behaviour. Knowing the IQ of a child with moderate and severe learning difficulties does not give a teacher useful information about whether they are likely to learn in a particular way or to experience particular learning problems. More attention needs to be paid to motivational and attitudinal factors (Zigler, 1999). Adaptations of pedagogy and curriculum content are more likely to be successful when they are based on a broader analysis of the children's approaches to learning in naturalistic settings as well as their current knowledge and understanding (Porter, 2005). Concerns of this kind led many educational psychologists to advocate a more balanced approach to assessment with less reliance on norm-based **intelligence scales** (Lokke et al, 1997).

Multiple intelligences and special abilities

Thurstone's early work on special abilities has been taken forward in recent years in the form of a theory of 'multiple intelligences' that was developed by Howard Gardner. Like Thurstone, Gardner argued that human intelligence is not a single complex entity and does not involve a single, integrated set of processes. His model envisaged several relatively autonomous ability sets, which he called, in the plural, intelligences. Each individual is thought to have a unique profile of these intellectual capacities. They are described as developing out of 'a biopsychological potential to process information that can be activated in a cultural setting to solve problems or create products that are of value in a culture' (Gardner, 1999: 33). Thus he rejected the notion of intelligence as fixed and innate. He drew on empirical data to identify the cognitive abilities that were to be included in the list of multiple intelligences, but the data sets on which he relied were not just from psychological research. He also drew on the results of studies in biology and cultural anthropology. There were explicit criteria for identifying an area of ability as a separate and distinct 'intelligence'. They included, for example, biological criteria: 'An intelligence should be isolable in cases of brain damage, and there should be evidence for its plausibility and autonomy in evolutionary history' (Chen and Gardner, 2005: 78). The set of multiple intelligences he listed in his 1983 book included:

- *Linguistic intelligence* (used in reading, writing, understanding what people say).

- *Logical-mathematical intelligence* (used in solving maths problems, checking a supermarket bill, logical reasoning).

- *Spatial intelligence* (used in reading a map, packing suitcases in a car so that they all fit).

- *Musical intelligence* (used in playing a musical instrument, appreciating the structure of a piece of music).

- *Bodily-kinesthetic intelligence* (used in imitating gestures, dancing, running).

- *Interpersonal intelligence* (used in relating to other people, e.g. in understanding another person's behaviour or feelings).

- *Intrapersonal intelligence* (used in understanding ourselves and how we can change ourselves).

He emphasized that that was not a definitive list and added to it later. Further, while he thought of these distinct abilities as functioning somewhat independently of each other, he noted that, when we observe intelligent behaviour, it is usually the result of an interaction between intelligences.

This formulation proved popular with educators. It was seen as egalitarian in that everyone might have an area of intelligence in which they showed strengths even if they did not do well on tests of *g*. It highlighted the value of teaching outside the core academic skills of literacy and numeracy. It stimulated experiments in pedagogy that were designed to draw on and enrich different 'intelligences' (Klein, 1997). To that end there were initiatives to develop assessments based on multiple intelligence theory that would assist teachers to select instructional strategies and materials that would be appropriate for each individual child (Chen and Gardner, 2005).

However, there have been multiple criticisms of Gardner's multiple intelligences. Critics within education have argued that the theory is too broad to be useful for detailed curriculum planning and presents a static view of student competence (Klein, 1997). The justification for the criteria used to define separate intelligences has been criticized as muddled and reliant on individualistic judgements (White, 2004). Critics from within psychology have pointed out that Gardner's intelligences correlate positively with *g* and so, like Thurstone's primary mental abilities, are best thought of as factors of general intelligence (Brand, 1996). Analysts of expert performance have highlighted evidence that outstanding results in a particular field do not simply reflect specific innate abilities but rely significantly on skills that are acquired through deliberate practice (Ericsson and Charness, 1994).

Educational psychologists' involvement in the assessment of intelligence

As concepts of intelligence and the tools for investigating intelligence have developed, what involvement have educational psychologists had in this activity? Early accounts of the work of educational psychologists in child guidance clinics refer to 'a room for the psychologist and his various kinds of test' (Burke and Miller, 1929, quoted by Sampson, 1980: 4). At around the same time an American commentator was protesting: '. . . it must be borne in mind that the psychologist in the Child Guidance Clinic does a great deal more than the estimating of intelligence quotients by the Binet-Simon and other tests' (Hardcastle, 1933, quoted by Sampson, 1980: 10). However, an account of a Scottish clinic in that period located the expertise and responsibilities of the psychologist centrally in this field: 'The psychologist is a person trained in the measurement of intellectual capacity and in educational methods . . . He is responsible for the accurate measurement of the child's intelligence and also for an estimation of latent capacity, specific disability and any abnormality of temperament that may appear during the testing of the child' (Dickson, 1938: 24).

As psychological science broadened its scope, psychologists came to see their role in quite different terms. Advances in this aspect of their practice reflected the advances that were made in conceptualizing children's cognitive development and mental abilities. When a government committee reported on the work of educational psychologists 30 years after Dickson's publication, they emphasized that:

. . . efforts have been made by psychologists to supplement general types of assessment with more detailed investigations designed to throw light on ways in which problems are solved and the kinds of difficulty that occur. While it remains invaluable to have accurate and reliable information about a child's intelligence, information is also needed about its underlying constituent processes . . . There are several reasons for this added emphasis. First, many intelligence tests provide little information about the nature of problem solving activities and skills and 'all-or-none' methods of scoring are regarded as too insensitive by many who use these tests. If a child fails a particular item, a psychologist can usually only guess at the reasons for his failure, and cannot necessarily assume that the child is incapable of solving all similar problems. Conversely, success in a particular solution does not mean that it has necessarily been arrived at by the most efficient route. Secondly, more detailed diagnostic study can lead to distinctions between a child's intellectual strengths and weaknesses, and hence to knowledge which could enable a psychologist to help a teacher to devise an appropriate remedial programme for the child. In this way, remedial methods might be planned more scientifically in order to place children who need this kind of help in environments for learning which are adapted to their needs. (Summerfield Committee, 1968: 8)

The Summerfield Committee's survey of how educational psychologists allocated their time indicated that psychological assessment formed an important component. Recent reports by a DfEE Working Group (DfEE, 2000c) and a DfES-appointed research team (Farrell et al, 2006) make clear that the assessment of individual children remains a major element of educational psychologists' work, but in these reports there is no mention of intelligence testing as a key part of that task and assessment is tied to consultation and leads to intervention. The use of intelligence scales features in the professional literature when there is a specific reason for undertaking an assessment of general mental ability, e.g. when there has been traumatic brain injury (Bozic and Morris, 2005). But even in these situations the assessment of general mental ability is likely to make only a modest contribution to an effective investigation of the presenting problems. In the practice of educational psychology, as in education more generally, the use of intelligence as a concept is now considered of limited value. There is much greater investment in developing dynamic approaches to assessment (Elliott, 2003) and methods of assessing specific functions that relate closely to academic achievement such as **working memory** (Alloway et al, 2005a, b).

Summary

- Teachers tend to agree on how they identify general ability in their pupils, but they are often resistant to using the word 'intelligence' to describe that.

- Scepticism about the value of a construct of intelligence is based on a range of concerns – theoretical, practical, moral, ideological and pedagogic.

- Psychologists' ideas about intelligence are moulded, in part, by cultural influences.

- From the early years of the twentieth century psychologists developed competing views of the factorial structure of intelligence which have a continuing influence today.

- While a factorial theory of intelligence can suggest how human abilities are organized, it cannot explain how they work.

- The analysis of basic components of intelligent activity has highlighted the significance of cognitive speed.

- An alternative account focuses on the efficiency with which those with higher tested intelligence focus their mental efforts, measuring efficiency in terms of glucose metabolism.

- When ideas about intelligence have been applied in education, their influence has been seen as negative in some respects.

- Today the identification of moderate and severe learning difficulties depends less on the use of intelligence assessment than it has done in the past.

- The theory of multiple intelligences has proved popular in educational applications but has also attracted damaging academic criticism.

- Educational psychologists rely on global intelligence scales in their assessment work less than they did in the past.

Key concepts and terms

Cultural influences
Factorial theories of intelligence
g
Inspection time
Intelligence
Intelligence scales
Moderate and severe learning
  difficulties

Multiple intelligences
Potential
Primary mental abilities
Reaction time
Speed of information
  processing
Working memory

Sample essay titles

- 'Psychological theories of intelligence reflect the social and cultural values of their society.' Discuss.
- Evaluate the strengths and weaknesses of factorial theories of intelligence.
- To what degree do psychological research and theory support the use of the word 'quick' to describe someone who is intelligent?
- What are the advantages and disadvantages of defining moderate and severe learning difficulties in terms of intelligence?
- Educational psychologists are reported to have turned away from the use of normative intelligence scales. Evaluate reasons why they might have chosen to do so.

Further reading

Books

Cianciolo, A.T., and Sternberg, R.J. (2004). *Intelligence: A Brief History*. Oxford: Blackwell.

Flanagan, D.P., and Harrison, P.L. (Eds) (2005). *Contemporary Intellectual Assessment: Theories, Tests and Issues*, (2nd Ed.). New York: Guilford Press.

Journal articles

Adey, P., Csapo, B., Demetriou, A., Hautamäki, J., and Shayer, M. (2007). Can we be intelligent about intelligence? Why education needs the concept of plastic general ability. *Educational Research Review*, 2, 75–97.

Sternberg, R.J. (1999). Successful intelligence: finding a balance. *Trends in Cognitive Sciences*, 3, 436–442.

3 Raising educational achievement

What can instructional psychology contribute?

Andy Miller

In this chapter you will learn about the various ways that educational psychologists have attempted to employ 'instructional psychology' to help raise educational attainments in schools, especially with pupils whom teachers have traditionally found to be the hardest to teach. We will begin by looking at the different ways that educationalists in general have used the term 'underachievement' and at a range of interventions by which educational psychologists have attempted to help raise the attainments of low- and under-achieving children and young people. The term 'instructional psychology' is variously used and in this chapter refers to factors in a young person's **learning environment**, and particularly to actual teaching style and methods, such as the use of **behavioural objectives**, **task analysis**, **direct instruction** and **precision teaching**. Each of these will be examined and the basic tenets of such approaches illustrated by case examples. Finally, the results from larger-scale applications of instructional psychology aimed at lower-achieving children across a number of classrooms and schools will be examined.

Learning outcomes

When you have completed this chapter you should be able to:

1. Explain and evaluate the evidence for the efficacy of instructional psychology.
2. Critically evaluate the relative merits of construing low academic attainment as a form of special educational need and as a challenge for instructional methods.
3. Analyse data recording methods within instructional approaches in order to draw conclusions about teaching effectiveness.

Introduction

One major impediment to achieving government targets to raise educational standards in schools is the seemingly stubborn 'tail of underachievement' – the phenomenon whereby the least academically talented in our schools seem to be the hardest to reach in terms of raising their attainments. Educational psychologists have, throughout the history of their profession, been active in attempts to rectify this, both through more traditional individual casework approaches and latterly through larger-scale educational interventions.

Changing conceptions of 'underachievement'

The term 'underachievement' has long been found within the everyday discourse of educational psychologists although its field of reference and its popularity as an explanatory construct has passed through a number of fashions and phases in the past half century.

When, historically, the practice of IQ testing amongst educational psychologists was at its zenith, the notion of 'underachievement' was applied to circumstances where a child or young person was found to be attaining in a core academic area at a level below that which 'might be expected' given their IQ. In the parlance of the time, youngsters identified by such means were often described as 'not reaching their potential'. If the academic area in question was literacy, and it almost always was, then the existence of norm-referenced reading and spelling tests allowed psychologists and others to make precise statements about the extent to which the measure of one differed from the other in terms of the statistical likelihood of the occurrence of that degree of difference. By such means, the extent to which a young person might be deemed to be underachieving could be stated not only in terms of the delay in acquiring some academic abilities (e.g. 'three and a half years behind his expected level in reading') but also in terms of the probability of this occurrence (e.g. 'a disparity of this magnitude or greater is likely to be found in only 1.7 per cent of pupils of his age'). Furthermore, a central ingredient in the diagnosis of such conditions as dyslexia and, later, specific literacy difficulties was usually a discrepancy between some measure of literacy difficulties and an IQ test result.

The concept of underachievement implies a level of performance that is less than, or *beneath* that of something else and the criterion for selecting that comparison has shifted over time. In the early days of the expansion of sociological studies within education much attention was paid to social class. So, Willis (1977) for example, in a classic ethnographic study, argued that the curriculum in what were then secondary modern schools was designed to meet the political and social need for a large workforce engaged in manual labour. In this sense, it was argued that many working class youngsters underachieved in comparison to their more advantaged and affluent middle class counterparts. Other studies have posited an underachievement of girls against boys before 1970 or so and then, since 1988 or thereabouts, of boys against girls (Marks, 2000) and of children from ethnic minority groups (Gilborn and Mirza, 2000) against white youngsters.

By the mid 1990s, the comparison that was galvanizing action on the part of the newly elected New Labour government was between British pupils and their counterparts in other countries. In a defining study that brought the term 'the long tail of underachievement' to the fore, Brookes, Pugh and Shagen (1996) investigated the reading performance of 9-year-olds in the UK and compared these results to those obtained on the same tests from children of the same age across 27 countries. These researchers discovered that the proportion of children in the UK scoring in the upper and middle ranges compared favourably with the highest attaining countries. The UK, however, was found to have a greater than average proportion of children who achieve poorly. At around the same time, the *Third International Mathematics and Science Study* reported equally gloomy results for mathematics when compared to 45 other countries (Beaton et al, 1996). In addition to this tail of underachievement being judged too long, it was also characterized as 'stubborn', as being resistant to modification, leading to concerns that not only were individual educational achievements under threat but also the country's very future, in terms of economic competitiveness.

In an attempt to rectify this, the government set targets for children at age 11 years, in terms of levels of attainment on existing standard assessment tasks allied to the National Curriculum. In this way, not only were individual youngsters who did not meet the 'expected' level for their age group identified as underachieving, schools themselves could also earn this designation and all its attendant negative publicity if too great a proportion of its students were deemed to be individually underachieving. Subsequent developments have employed increasingly sophisticated forms of data manipulation in order, for instance, to determine the degree of improvement, or 'value added', that might be due to school rather than pupil factors or to beam in more particularly on discrete subgroups of pupils whose scores are relatively depressed. In all these developments though, the central organizing principle is that the concept of underachievement is to be understood as a shortfall, whether for the individual or the organization, against a centrally prescribed expectation.

Educational psychologists and underachievement

Educational psychologists have made a range of contributions to the alleviation of low attainments and underachievement. Within the Special Educational Needs Code of Practice (Department for Education and Science, 2001), for example, they have been required to carry out assessments of young people deemed to have learning difficulties and to have not progressed after the school has employed a number of specially targeted interventions. If the assessments carried out by educational psychologists and other professionals within and outside of school conclude that the young person does have a special educational need then the Local Authority is required by law to produce a Statement of Special Educational Need (SEN). Within this Statement, in addition to a full assessment of the child's special educational needs, the Local Authority must stipulate the provision that is judged necessary to meet these needs.

While these legislative arrangements may have benefited many young people, they have also proved to be a continuing source of contention and disappointment for some. Among many educational psychologists there has been a growing feeling that the concept of SEN has focused too heavily upon individual differences to the detriment of considerations of the range of environmental demands to which children may or may not have been subject (Frederickson and Cline 2008).

Jonathan Solity, a major proponent of the view that educational psychologists should attend to factors in the learning environment, and particularly to actual teaching methods and style, states that '. . . the key to ensuring that children make progress is what and how they are taught rather than the availability of additional resources, parental support or one-to-one teaching' (Solity et al, 2000).

Instructional psychology

Solity et al (2000) and others have advocated for an **instructional psychology** that attempts to raise the attainments of all children and young people with low achievements, whether designated as having SEN or not, by applying psychological principles of teaching, learning and curriculum design across a whole school. Within the work of some educational psychologists, a number of contributory elements of such an instructional psychology – such as behavioural objectives, task analysis, direct instruction and precision teaching – may be found and the remainder of this chapter examines each of these in greater detail.

Behavioural objectives

The first major contribution of instructional psychology to British practice was probably made by Ainscow and Tweddle (1979) who challenged dominant thinking about special educational needs by calling for an approach based on curriculum (or task) analysis and the generation of learning objectives. By placing an emphasis on 'behavioural objectives', these authors argued for a much greater focus upon factors over which teachers had some control.

Behavioural objectives have two main characteristics: they contain an action and they are observable. So, 'writes down the numbers 1 to 10 from a model', would meet these criteria whereas 'knows the sounds of the letters a to j' does not, the latter not being expressed as an observable action. Ainscow and Tweddle argued that a major advantage of behavioural objectives was that teachers who acquired the skills involved in writing these were subsequently far better able to plan their teaching activities with an explicit goal for the learner in mind. While this may seem rather obvious and simplistic, it should be remembered that the pupils they were specifically concerned with were those who had failed to progress very much with less 'precise' methods where a reasonable degree of incidental or vicarious learning might have been required. Case Study box 3.1 presents an example of such a pupil.

This case study demonstrates that a 15-month period of teaching based specifically upon instructional psychology principles was able to produce rates of reading improvement far in excess of that gained by following standard SEN procedures that involved small classes, expert help and formal reviews (and red filters). This explicit attention to task-analysed small steps, the fine grain of teaching and learning arrangements and the motivational consequence of

Case study 3.1

Using behavioural objectives with Michael

Michael was a 13-year-old student in a secondary school who was referred to the author because his parents wanted to know whether he might be better placed in a small unit for young people with dyslexia/specific literacy difficulties. He had been experiencing difficulties with reading and spelling throughout his school career and, upon transfer to secondary schooling, he seriously struggled with the subject-based academic curriculum and especially with homework, despite the best efforts of a skilled special needs support department.

Michael had a Statement of Special Educational Need that identified his specific literacy difficulties but was very reluctant to be withdrawn from some lessons into the special needs department, to which he attached great stigma. In conversation, it was apparent that he was an articulate and thoughtful young person and tests showed his level of verbal comprehension to lie within a high average range for his age.

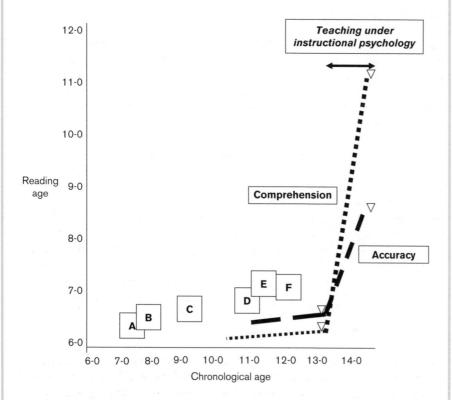

Figure 3.1 Michael's reading ages at 13 years 2 months and 14 years 5 months, his extrapolated course of development since 6 years and the various educational interventions made during this period.

Key:

A. Michael is in a class of 32 children with 2 teachers. His parents request 'an assessment' of his abilities at age 7-1 when he is about to transfer to Junior School/Key Stage 2.

B. Michael is transferred to a 'special teaching facility' based in a local junior school at age 7-9.

C. The Local Authority issues a Statement of Special Educational Need when Michael is 9-0 and among its recommendations are the development of 'sight vocabulary and phonic skills' and 'a sympathetic approach to self-esteem'.

D. A red filter (transparent plastic overlay) is temporarily introduced over reading materials when Michael is aged 11-0. Some suggest this aids reading by reducing glare and/or facilitating visual processing.

E. At an annual review of his Statement, at age 11-5, his teachers and parents minute that he has 'mood swings' and is 'obstreperous and uncooperative at home and school' and 'appears very depressed'.

F. After transfer to secondary school, at age 12-0, it was recorded that Michael and his parents were very concerned about his ability to access and carry out the work required of him at this new phase of schooling.

When Michael was tested at age 13 years 2 months (13-2) using the Wechsler Objective Reading Dimensions he obtained a reading age for reading accuracy of 6-6 and for reading comprehension of 6-3. This test has a basal level of 6-0 for both measures. So, in Figure 3.1 these scores are partially extrapolated back to a chronological age of 6-0, where normally developing youngsters would be predicted to obtain reading ages of around 6-0 for both accuracy and comprehension, indicating just how little reading progress Michael had made in seven years of schooling, some of this as the recipient of the special attention paid him as the subject of a Statement of SEN.

At around the time of this testing, Michael's case file was also scrutinized in order to ascertain any types of special provision of teaching approaches that had been applied and these are represented by boxed capital letters and explained in the key.

It was clear that various interventions over a seven year period had failed to make any substantial impact on his levels of reading and hence on Michael's ability to access whole areas of the curriculum.

Consequently, and with the agreement of everybody involved, it was decided to devise a concerted programme based on instructional psychology, and on the use of behavioural objectives and knowledge of results in particular. A set of resource materials – Alpha to Omega – was selected as this represents a graded sequence of phonic exercises aimed particularly at young people with specific literacy difficulties. Then a small book was devised and on each of the first 10 pages was written a behavioural objective with spaces for a start date and a finish date. So, the very first page contained:

Task 1: Recite after a model the first 8 letters of the alphabet, A–H (for two days running)

Start date:

Finish date:

Figure 3.2 Specimen entry for a behavioural objective.

The remaining nine pages each contained a behavioural objective, ending with 'Task 10: Recite the 5 vowels'. The tasks were sequenced to include writing tasks as well as reciting.

Michael's teachers were encouraged to use whatever teaching methods they favoured in order to enable Michael to carry out and achieve the objective. It was also explained to Michael that, although some of the early exercises would feel very elementary, they were part of a long sequence that would be approached 10 at a time. At the beginning of each daily (or, where possible, twice daily) teaching session Michael was *always* shown the current 10 pages of objectives, with those already achieved and those still to be worked upon being emphasized. No more than 10 objectives were ever set in advance but, as the teaching progressed, the ever-growing set of those already mastered was always revisited at the beginning of each session.

Michael and his teachers responded positively and persevered with this system for 15 months with later objectives concerned with writing sentences from dictation, spelling words conforming to specific rules and solving anagrams. After this period Michael was again tested on the same reading test and his impressive achievements are also presented in Figure 3.1.

unambiguous feedback concerning success enabled Michael to become more settled into his secondary school, to subsequently achieve a number of GCSE passes and eventually to enrol for a full-time course in computing at a college of further education.

In Michael's case example, the task (or curriculum) analysis was achieved fairly easily by sequencing the objectives so that they corresponded closely with the *Alpha to Omega* materials. Proponents of these approaches also paid considerable attention to aspects of task analysis such as the 'step size' between objectives, their correct ordering and the links to overall teaching goals (Ainscow and Tweddle 1979).

Critics of the approach argued that, if spread across a pupil's whole curriculum, a behavioural objectives approach would deliver an extremely restricted and excessively dull educational diet. Advocates, on the other hand, replied that, as in Michael's case study above, a regular approach for a small part of every day could produce considerable gains in essential skills. The logical and organizational absurdity of extending the use of behavioural objectives too far, however, could be seen at the other end of the educational spectrum in the example of a US university medical school that in the 1970s had produced a list of curriculum objectives that ran to 880 pages! (Harden, 2003).

Direct instruction

Direct instruction (DI) is a highly teacher-directed and prescribed approach to teaching first outlined by Bereiter and Englemann in their 1966 book *Teaching*

Focus 3.1

Direct instruction and controversy

This report of the High/Scope Preschool Curriculum study traces the effects on young people through age 15 of three well-implemented preschool curriculum models – the High/Scope model, the Distar model, and a model in the nursery school tradition . . . The three preschool curriculum groups differed little in their patterns of IQ and school achievement over time. According to self reports at age 15, the group that had attended the Distar preschool program engaged in twice as many delinquent acts as did the other two curriculum groups, including five times as many acts of property violence. The Distar group also reported relatively poor relations with their families, less participation in sports, fewer school job appointments, and less reaching out to others for help with personal problems. These findings, based on a small sample, are by no means definitive; but they do suggest possible consequences of preschool curriculum models that ought to be considered. (Schweinhart et al, 1986.)

This conclusion, stated in alarmist terms, has been widely disseminated in the news media. Of course, it is an alarming conclusion – sufficiently alarming that it threatens in one stroke to undo the extensive and well-documented case for the educational benefits of direct instruction. Under close examination of the facts that are provided, however, the damning evidence quickly evaporates . . . In its mythic role, however, (Bereiter's 1966 book with Englemann) has stood for a host of dark forces that many educators imagine to be lurking in the background of early childhood education. Actually reading the book, which very few of the myth makers appear to have done, would go a long way toward dispelling such phantasms. (Bereiter, 1986.)

N.B. Bereiter's rebuttal attacks the methodology employed by Schweinhart et al (1986), in particular the use of a self report approach which he claims is 'distressingly silent on matters of procedure'.

Disadvantaged Children in the Preschool. It is fair to say that since that time the approach has generated – and continues to generate – strong feelings within some in the educational world (see Focus box 3.1, where Distar is the direct instruction approach).

In DI approaches, the period of instruction is tightly organized and aims to maximize for students their '**academic engaged time**', even if this is to occur for only one or two minutes each day. In order to do this, the teacher employs a pre-prepared script and a set of materials containing a task analysed sequence of objectives. The teacher's delivery emphasizes clarity and lack of ambiguity, building in rhythm, pacing, intonation and pointing. The teaching technique employs a **Model–Lead–Test** sequence which has been seen by its critics as controlling, robotic and/or boring whereas its advocates emphasize the security

	Teacher	Pupil
Introduction	We are going to learn to read this list of words today. I'll go first then we'll do them together and then you can have a go on your own.	
Model	Ready. This word says house.	
Lead	Let's do it together. Ready. This word says . . . house.	house
Test	Now you try it. This word says . . .	house
Correction after Test (only if needed)	This word says 'house'. You say it.	house

Table 3.1 An example of a portion of a 'teaching trial' for single word recognition

provided for the learner and the inclusion of '**errorless learning**'. An example extract is provided in Table 3.1.

The teacher keeps very closely to the script, avoiding extra comment and ensuring that a brisk pace is maintained. Within the approach, teachers' additional utterances, even when intended as helpful or reassuring, are seen as distractions from academic engaged time and interruptions to the learning. Each run through, or 'trial', as above is completed quickly with its outcome – either 'correct' or 'correct with correction' recorded – before the next trial is commenced. The correction option ensures 'errorless learning' in that the student always finishes with a correct response. Sequences of objectives move the learning from these early acquisition skills onto fluency building using such methods as **precision teaching** (see below). Within reading, subsequent objectives would also address reading passages of prose, developing phonic skills and the comprehension of passages.

Large-scale evaluation of direct instruction

During the 1960s, the US government undertook a huge initiative – the Headstart Project – that aimed to provide cognitive and affective enrichment to disadvantaged pre-schoolers in the inner cities. Despite some considerable successes, one hugely disappointing finding was that the gains, the 'head start', made by these young children during this preschool intervention, were not maintained through their first few years of formal schooling with the children slipping back to a level that might have been predicted had no additional help being provided in the first place.

Consequently, a second major initiative – **_Project Follow Through_**, dubbed at the time the largest educational experiment ever – was funded over a nine year period and aimed to compare the effects of a range of different educational interventions carried out during the first three years of schooling (Carnine, 1979). In total, 75,000 children spread across 139 sites were tested in terms of basic academic skills (e.g. word recognition, spelling, maths computation), cognitive skills (e.g. reading with comprehension, maths problem solving) and affective measures (e.g. self-esteem, degree of taking responsibility for academic successes and failures, etc.).

One of nine different interventions, which ranged from highly teacher-directed approaches such as direct instruction, through to the child-centred and discovery-learning ethos of the then highly fashionable British 'open classroom', was employed in each of the participating institutions, with each supported by a university department sympathetic to the particular approach.

The main findings relevant to the topic of this chapter that emerged from *Project Follow Through* were:

■ Direct instruction was the only intervention to produce positive outcomes in basic skills, cognitive skills and affective measures (i.e. outcomes beyond that which would have been predicted had no intervention taken place and where individual children each provided their own baseline comparison measures).

■ Only four interventions produced positive outcomes in any categories.

■ The more child-centred approaches particularly failed to produce positive measures.

In terms of affective measures, it was particularly surprising to some both that direct instruction produced positive responses and that the open classroom failed to do so. A prevalent feeling at the time was that direct instruction might be able to encourage the 'rote learning' of very basic skills but it would not be able to develop higher-order, cognitive skills or happier, more confident learners. These latter areas were seen as the province of a more child-centred ethos.

Echoes of the Follow Through research can still be found, for instance in an experimental study by Klahr and Nigram (2004) that attested to the effectiveness of direct instruction approaches compared with discovery learning in the area of science education, both in terms of learning basic procedures for designing and interpreting simple experiments but also with subsequent transfer and application of this basic skill to the more diffuse and authentic context of scientific reasoning.

Swanson (2000) captured a major element of this long-running disagreement 'there has been some lively debate . . . as to whether instruction should be top-down via emphasising the knowledge base, heuristics and explicit strategies, or a bottom-up emphasis that entails hierarchical instruction at the skill level' and attempted to summarize and distil the effects of DI by carrying out a meta-analysis of 3,164 studies. The major finding from Swanson's review was that a combined programme of DI and strategy ('top-down') instruction yielded higher effect sizes (0.84) than DI (0.68) or strategy alone (0.72). The conclusion drawn was that a combined model of DI and strategy instruction can positively influence children with learning difficulties, with regression analysis showing several components (e.g. sequencing, daily testing, segmentation and synthesis) yielding particularly high effect sizes.

Haring and Eaton's instructional hierarchy

In the hypothetical DI example above, we imagined a pupil who might be learning to read a set of common words 'by sight' (rather than, say, by phonic analysis). Of course, teachers of young children, especially those with learning difficulties, will point out that these pupils will usually have considerable difficulty in retaining their learning so that, when returning to the task the next day or whenever, it is likely that the young person may not be able to read those words, leading either to soul-destroying repetition for the child (and teacher) or to a search for other teaching methods, or to the abandonment of this particular teaching objective. It is in these circumstances that Haring and Eaton's (1978) **instructional hierarchy** can prove a very useful explanatory framework.

Acquisition	Learners become able to perform a skill accurately for the first time
Fluency	The learner becomes able to perform the new skill fluently as well as accurately
Maintenance	Accuracy and fluency are maintained even in the absence of periods of direct teaching of the skill
Generalization	Learners become able to apply the skill across different contexts
Adaptation	Learners are able to make novel adaptations to the skill in order to solve new problems

Table 3.2 Haring and Eaton's (1978) five stages of instruction and learning

Haring and Eaton (1978) proposed five stages of instruction and learning, see Table 3.2. Within this framework, the child who learns something one day and has forgotten it the next – a common cry from teachers of youngsters with learning difficulties – has only reached an acquisition stage for that skill, in our example, the reading of a list of words. His or her learning will not be maintained unless an explicit strategy aimed at ensuring fluency is also devised. This is where precision teaching comes in.

Precision teaching

Precision teaching was developed by Lindsley (1971) in the USA as a method for improving learners' fluency, making daily assessments of progress and providing immediate feedback to both learners and teachers. It was taken up and enthusiastically promoted by a number of educational psychologists in the West Midlands in the early 1980s, most notably Booth and Jay (1981), Raybould and Solity (1982) and Williams and Muncey (1982).

Although Kessissoglou and Farrell pointed out in 1995 that early interest did not seem to have been maintained, at least in publications within the profession, a renaissance was triggered by the British Psychological Society's

1999 working party report *Dyslexia, Literacy and Psychological Assessment*. Among its conclusions was the recommendation that precision teaching (and single-subject experiments) offer '. . . a set of strategies for carrying out focused assessments of pupil performance over time and for recording progress in a way that facilitates judgements about accuracy and fluency of performance' (BPS, 1999: 55).

Using precision teaching with Roop – a case example

The graph shown in Figure 3.3 is taken from an intervention in which a Learning Support Assistant is teaching small groups of high frequency words to a girl called Roop and illustrates a number of the features of the precision teaching approach (Raybould, 2004). Once an acquisition level with a group of

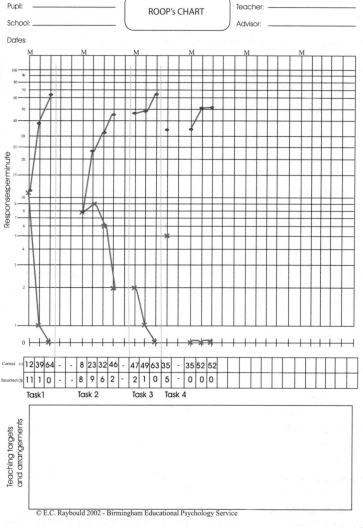

Figure 3.3 A chart demonstrating Roop's increasing fluency in reading four sets of high frequency words.

these words has been reached, Roop is presented with a 'probe sheet' consisting of these words repeated over and again in irregular sequences and asked to read as many as she can within one minute. Each of these one minute sessions, each 'trial', is recorded on a frequency chart with the number read correctly signified by a dot and the number of errors by a cross, as shown.

The y-axes for frequency charts are represented as a semi-logarithmic rather than a linear scale so that similar *rates* of progress, for example, doubling a success rate from, say, 5 to 10 correct per minute has the same gradient as doubling the rate from 20 to 40 per minute – or any other doubling.

In this example, Roop has spent three trials on task 1, a small group of words, and increased her success rate from 12 to 39 to 64 per minute while

---

Activity 3.1

Using fluency charts to make decisions about teaching

Look at the four fluency charts below and then attempt to match each of these with a statement from the list of possible interpretations. Then, try to make the further link between each of these and a related teaching implication.

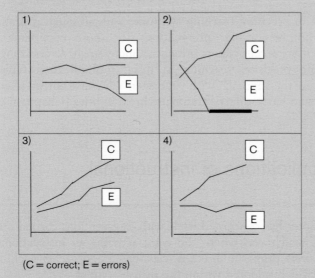

(C = correct; E = errors)

Figure 3.4 Fluency charts.

Possible interpretations

1. The task is appropriate, learning is taking place and the error rate has been reduced.
2. Learning is taking place but the error rate is not reducing.

3. Learning is not taking place.
4. Learning is taking place but the error rate is increasing.

Teaching implications

1. Change the emphasis of the teaching to focus specifically on the items leading to errors.
2. Re-emphasize the need for accuracy and encourage the child to go more slowly for a while.
3. Move to the next task in the sequence if the pre-selected success criterion has been achieved.
4. Reduce the size of the task, change the teaching method or increase incentives.

simultaneously reducing her errors from 11 to 1 to none. Criteria for progressing to the next task in terms of success and error rates will have been set in advance. By being able to read these words very fluently in this manner, White and Eaton's hierarchy predicts that the learning will be retained, allowing instruction for maintenance and beyond to be considered, and for new skills to be built upon this foundation.

The growing interest in precision teaching continues and, although it is still not making a major impression on interventions for those experiencing educational difficulties, more recent papers present an increasingly diverse range of accounts from using precision teaching to teach multiplication tables (Gallagher, 2006) to using the approach with youngsters who have autism (Kerr et al, 2003) and those who have suffered traumatic brain injuries (Chapman et al, 2005).

Larger-scale applications of instructional psychology

In the main, this chapter has concerned itself with interventions carried out with individual pupils, which was where the early activities of instructional psychology enthusiasts were primarily directed, class-based approaches such as Distar not having been widely adopted within the British context.

However, Miller et al (1985) developed a larger-scale system that aimed to train teachers in direct instruction and precision teaching, using teaching methods to address each of Bruner's (1966) three modes in which knowledge is represented – enactive, iconic and symbolic – as well as, at the same time, supporting these teachers as they carried out individualized interventions within their classrooms with pupils previously identified as experiencing serious literacy difficulties. In this way, three educational psychologists were able to support 95 children and their teachers across a large geographical area and over a period of a year. Upon evaluation after this period, 84 per cent of participating teachers completed questionnaires that indicated that 289 direct instruction and 187 precision teaching programmes had been successfully completed with these children.

An even larger-scale application can be found in the *Early Reading Research* carried out by Solity et al (2000) in six experimental and six comparison schools and involving a total of 370 children followed for two years from reception age. The relevant experimental school teachers were trained in distinctive instructional principles to teach their children 'through distributed rather than massed practice three times a day for ten to fifteen minutes; how to generalise their skills and, through a process known as interleaved learning which minimises forgetting' (Solity et al, 2000: 115). Detailed attention was also paid to other aspects in a 'framework for teaching reading' informed by instructional psychology resulting after two school years in the experimental school children outperforming the comparison school children on all measures of literacy – word reading, comprehension, letter sounds, synthesis, segmentation and spelling – but not rhyming, which was deliberately not taught. Solity et al (2000) also found that their approach had made a significant impact on the learning outcomes of both lower and higher achieving pupils and concluded that there are '. . . alternative ways of making provision for lower achieving pupils than through the legislative and administrative approaches promoted within the field of special education'.

Conclusion

We have seen that teaching approaches that derive from instructional psychology can help to overcome **educational underachievement**, this conclusion being supported by case studies employing single case designs as well as larger-scale experimental approaches. These studies can also be seen to address many of the various conceptualizations of underachievement. The implementation of such approaches has, in turn, focused attention upon a range of disparate questions such as the effectiveness of formal arrangements for addressing special educational needs, the relationship between basic and higher-order skills and self-esteem, the uneasy perceptions of control and prescription within teaching, assessment of progress and queries about the most productive forms of feedback. Given that instructional psychology impinges on so many educational concerns, it is perhaps not surprising that it has generated its enthusiastic supporters as well as its sceptical critics, with strong feelings and contentious debate frequently flaring up between these two camps.

Summary

- Educational 'underachievement' has been conceptualized in varying ways, including the notions that some individuals do not reach their 'potential', that some groups – girls, boys, members of ethnic minorities – achieve at a lower level than others, that some schools achieve less pupil progress than comparison schools, and that some countries are less successful than others in terms of key academic skills.

- The UK has been found to have a longer tail of underachievement, i.e. more young people obtaining low scores in reading and mathematics, than many other countries.

- Educational psychologists have a legally prescribed role in contributing to that minority of low-achieving young people who are seen as having special educational needs. Others have argued that teaching based on instructional psychology can address the far wider group of low achievers and is the key to ensuring that all these children progress.

- Carefully sequenced behavioural objectives can provide motivation and successful learning opportunities.

- *Project Follow Through* compared the relative effectiveness of nine different teaching approaches to the progress of socially and economically deprived youngsters in the first three years of schooling in the USA. **Direct instruction** was found to be the most effective approach in terms of basic skills, cognitive skills and affective measures.

- A five-stage instructional hierarchy developed by Haring and Eaton, with stages of acquisition, fluency, maintenance, generalization and adaptation, has helped to account for some of the difficulties commonly experienced by slower learning children and their teachers.

- Precision teaching approaches have been promoted in the UK by some educational psychologists and can be used to make daily assessments of learning and to improve learners' fluency levels.

- Some educational psychologists have provided examples of larger-scale applications of successful teaching interventions deriving from instructional psychology.

Key concepts and terms

Academic engaged time
Behavioural objectives
Direct instruction
Early Reading Research
Educational underachievement
Errorless learning
Instructional hierarchy

Instructional psychology
Learning environment
Model–lead–test
Precision teaching
Project Follow Through
Task analysis

Sample essay titles

- Can instructional psychology help eradicate the long tail of educational underachievement?
- Instructional psychology encourages teaching approaches that focus on dull rote learning and only the most basic of skills and knowledge. Discuss.
- How might instructional psychology challenge common conceptualizations of 'special educational needs'?
- Direct instruction approaches have generated scathing attacks from various educationalists. Why have some educational psychologists persisted in promoting these and other aspects of instructional psychology?

Further reading

Books

Frederickson, N., and Cline, T. (2008). *Special Educational Needs, Inclusion and Diversity. A Textbook* (2nd Ed.). Buckingham: Open University Press.

Swanson, H.L. (2000). 'What instruction works for students with learning disabilities? Summarizing the results from a meta-analysis of intervention studies.' In: R. Gersten and E.P. Schiller (Eds), *Contemporary Special Education Research: Synthesis of the Knowledge Base on Critical Instructional Issues*. Mahwah, New Jersey: Lawrence Erlbaum Associates.

Journal articles

Bereiter, C. (1986). Does direct instruction cause delinquency? *Early Childhood Research Quarterly*, 1, 289–292.

Chapman, S.C., Exing, C.B., and Mozzoni, M.P. (2005). Precision teaching and fluency training across cognitive, physical, and academic tasks in children with traumatic brain injury: a multiple baseline study. *Behavioural Interventions*, 20, 37–49.

Klahr, D., and Nigram, M. (2004). The equivalence of learning paths in early science instruction: effects of direct instruction and discovery learning. *Psychological Science*, 15, 661–667.

Solity, J., Deavers, R., Kerfoot, S., Crane, G., and Cannon, K. (2000). The Early Reading Research: the impact of instructional psychology. *Educational Psychology in Practice*, 16, 109–129.

4 Is inclusion for children with special needs psychologically defensible?

Norah Frederickson

This chapter will examine controversies surrounding the prevailing international policy of **inclusion** in mainstream schools for children who have **special educational needs (SEN)**. It will review research on the efficacy of integrated versus segregated schooling, illustrating the range of methodological issues encountered in research of this type in applied settings. It will investigate the claim that psychological theory has been conscripted to support arguments on both sides of the debate and examine the contribution that psychological theory has made, and could make, to this area of social policy and educational psychology practice.

Learning outcomes

When you have completed this chapter you should be able to:

1. Critically evaluate the arguments that are made for and against inclusion and identify their socio-political or scientific bases.
2. Discuss the research evidence on the efficacy of inclusion, its methodological limitations and the methods that can be used to collate and appraise this evidence.
3. Describe the different strands of psychological theory that have contributed to research on the social outcomes of inclusion.

What is inclusion?

The most basic definition of the policy of inclusion is that it involves educating children with special educational needs (SEN) in mainstream schools with normally achieving peers, rather than in separate special schools or classes. Over the last 15 years, inclusion has been embraced by many countries as a key educational policy. The Salamanca Statement, which was signed by the representatives of 92 countries, called on governments 'to adopt the principle of inclusive education, enrolling all children in regular schools unless there are compelling reasons for doing otherwise' (UNESCO, 1994: 44). National legislation in many countries including the USA (IDEA, 1997) and the UK (DfEE, 2001) has promoted 'inclusive education' for pupils who have special educational needs or disabilities.

The UK Special Educational Needs and Disability Act states that children who have a Statement of Special Educational Needs must be educated in a mainstream school unless this would be incompatible with parental wishes or with the provision of efficient education for other children (DfEE 2001: Section 324). Statements of Special Educational Needs are required to access additional resources beyond those normally available to mainstream schools and are produced by means of a statutorily regulated multi-agency assessment, to which an educational psychologist must contribute their advice. The issue of inclusion is one which has a high profile in the work of educational psychologists. Much of this work is carried out at an individual child level, in terms of consulting with parents and teachers, advising the local authority and supporting schools in developing skills and strategies to meet a broader range of needs. However, educational psychologists are also involved with development, research and evaluation in inclusion initiatives in local authorities.

Thomas, Walker and Webb (1998) report that the term '**integration**' (or '**mainstreaming**' in the USA) which pre-dated 'inclusion' is often used synonymously with it. However some, like Ainscow (1995), draw a sharp conceptual distinction between integration and inclusion. Integration is seen as a process of assimilation where the onus is on providing a child who has SEN with additional teaching or resources to enable them to 'fit in' and succeed in a mainstream school. By contrast, inclusion is seen as a process of accommodation where the mainstream school restructures itself to be better able to meet the needs of all pupils. As Lindsay (2007) points out, this conceptual distinction is not always clear in practice and a wide variety of definitions of inclusion are in use, as is illustrated in Focus box 4.1.

Focus 4.1

. . . the provision of services to students with disabilities, including those with severe impairments, in the neighbourhood school in age-appropriate general education classes, with the necessary support services and supplementary aids (for the child and the teacher) both to ensure the child's success – academic, behavioral and social – and to prepare the child to participate as a full and contributing member of the society. (Lipsky and Gartner 1996: 763)

. . . the process by which a school attempts to respond to all pupils as individuals by reconsidering and restructuring its curricular organisation and provision and allocating resources to enhance equality of opportunity. Through this process the school builds its capacity to accept all pupils from the local community who wish to attend and, in so doing, reduces the need to exclude pupils. (Sebba and Sachdev, 1997: 9)

. . . to be fully included they [children with SEN] should take a full and active part in the life of the mainstream school, they should be valued members of the school community and be seen to be integral members of it. (Farrell, 2000: 154)

Activity 4.1

Case study

Read the following case study and decide whether this would be regarded as 'inclusion' on each of the three definitions provided above.

Tom is a 7-year-old who has Down's syndrome. His parents are committed to him receiving his education in his local mainstream school with his siblings and neighbouring children who play with him at home. He has attended his local nursery/infant school since the age of 3, spending two years in the nursery class, and last year and this year in the reception class. Tom's self-help skills (dressing, feeding, toileting) are similar to most of the other children in the reception class. However, his language skills are more typical of a 3–4-year-old in that he will talk in short (on average 4–5 word) 'telegraphic' sentences which leave out connecting words, e.g. 'Where Lego box?'. He has no particular friends, but his classmates (especially Vikki, Emma and Sarah) will include him in their play. He clearly enjoys this interaction, although he is always given dependent and subservient roles – the baby, the patient. He loves picture books but does not seem to be aware of the function of print in conveying the story. However, he can recognize his own name and produce simple representational drawings.

His school receives a visit one afternoon per week from a specialist teacher who advises his class teacher and sometimes works with Tom. He has a Learning Support Assistant (LSA) with him each morning, as stipulated on his Statement of Special Educational Needs. He works in his classroom for 80 per cent of the week, and is withdrawn to work in a quiet room with his LSA for the other 20 per cent. However, he has his own learning programmes in everything, except project work and PE/games. His teachers fear that he will not be able to make a successful transition to junior school next year. They feel that Tom is making some progress in the reception class, which would probably be disrupted if he were moved to the Year 2 class in preparation for transfer to junior school. They also fear that he may be bullied in junior school and feel that his needs might be best met through placement in a school for children with moderate learning difficulties.

Should children with special educational needs be educated in mainstream schools?

Tom's teachers in Activity box 4.1 have some doubts that he should be educated in a mainstream school but his parents are committed to this. While his teachers focus on actual or possible outcomes (academic progress and bullying), his parents focus on being part of his family and local community. Fundamental differences in view are apparent also in debates between researchers. Whereas the question asked at the start of this section would be regarded by many as capable of empirical resolution, to some it would be regarded not merely as unanswerable, but unaskable. Lindsay (2003) provides a review of the arguments on both sides of this debate. On the one hand he considers the view that the efficacy of inclusive education in achieving improved outcomes for children with SEN is a justifiable area for scientific enquiry. On the other, he explores the position that the adoption of inclusion as a public policy is properly regarded as a matter of rights and morality, to which evaluations of efficacy are largely irrelevant.

There are problems with both the 'rights' position and with efficacy research in this area (which will be covered in more detail later in this section). Farrell (2000) nicely illustrates some of the dilemmas that may occur when different sets of rights conflict: the right to inclusion, the right to an effective education, the rights of parents, the right to choice, the rights of other children.

> *A parent may feel that their child has a right to be educated in a mainstream school but an objective assessment of the child might indicate that his/her rights to a good education could only be met in a special school. Whose rights should take preference in cases like this, the parents or the child? In addition, what if placing a child with SEN in a mainstream school seriously disrupts the education of the other pupils? Surely they have a right to a good education as well? (Farrell, 2000: 155)*

Strong advocates of the 'rights' position also recognize such dilemmas:

> *. . . there are also situations in which some choose exclusion – the deaf community comes to mind immediately. Few would argue against their right to choose to be educated together in a school other than their local neighborhood one, despite concerns that segregation may serve to perpetuate the prejudices that make separate schooling desirable in the first place. To argue categorically against the right to make such choices can therefore be seen as an arrogant denial of another's fundamental right to self-determination. (Gallagher, 2001: 638)*

The problems with research in this area are also substantial and well documented (Madden and Slavin, 1983; Siegel, 1996; Lindsay, 2007):

- Difficulties in specifying the independent variable. The definitions in Focus box 4.1 indicate the variety of different arrangements that might be considered to be inclusion. The amount of time children with SEN spend in mainstream classes can also vary greatly.

- Poor matching of participants across group. There are often systematic differences between 'integrated' and 'special school' groups, such that the latter typically have a range of additional problems.

- Differences between the curriculum being followed in each setting, with greater emphasis being placed on academic subjects in mainstream settings and on self-help and social education in special schools and classes. There may be differences in the sampling of these domains by the outcome measure used.

- Differences between the qualifications and experience of the teachers in mainstream and special placements.

Nonetheless, most reviews of efficacy research over the last three decades and using a range of methods have reached fairly similar conclusions. Early narrative reviews highlighted the inconclusive nature of the evidence but tended to come down marginally in favour of inclusion, with some qualifications. Madden and Slavin (1983) concluded that there appeared to be some advantage to integrated placements in relation to both academic and social progress, but only if a suitable individualized or differentiated educational programme was offered. Hegarty (1993) argued that it was difficult to justify maintaining segregated provision if it is no better. During the 1980s and 1990s a number of meta-analyses were also conducted. These more structured approaches aim to reduce the possibility of reviewer bias by using statistical summary techniques on the numerical results of the reviewed studies. Baker, Wang and Walberg (1994–5) summarized three such studies (see Table 4.1). **Effect sizes** were calculated to provide a measure of the strength of the findings that was relatively independent of different study sample sizes. The positive effect sizes reported indicated a small to moderate benefit of inclusion on both academic and social outcomes.

Author(s)	Carlberg and Kavale	Wang and Baker	Baker
Year published	1980	1985–6	1994
Time period	Pre-1980	1975–84	1983–92
Number of studies	50	11	13
Academic effect size	0.15	0.44	0.08
Social effect size	0.11	0.11	0.28

Table 4.1 Results of meta-analyses on effects of inclusive placement.
Source: Baker et al, 1994–5.

Odom et al (2004) conducted a systematic review of articles in peer-reviewed journals and data-based chapters, published between 1990 and 2002, on 3–5-year-olds with disabilities and their typically developing peers in inclusive classroom-based settings. The results were reported using a theoretically based structure capable of accommodating both scientific and social policy issues, Bronfenbrenner's **bio-ecological model** (Bronfenbrenner and Morris, 2006). The nested systems within which children are thought to develop were mapped on to particular areas of the research literature as follows:

- Biosystem: child characteristics.

- Microsystem: classroom practices.

- Mesosystem: interactions among participants (family members, multi-professional teams).

■ Exosystem: social policy.

■ Macrosystem: cultural and societal values.

■ Chronosystem: changes in variables over time.

Conclusions from the first two areas were comparable to those from other reviews. Overall a range of positive developmental and behavioural outcomes were identified although children with SEN were not as socially integrated as their typically developing peers.

Lindsay (2007) reported a target journal review of published inclusion efficacy studies between 2000 and 2005. Eight journals in the field of SEN were targeted and 1373 papers considered. Of these only 1 per cent were found to address efficacy issues, either comparing the performance of children with SEN in special and mainstream settings or comparing the performance of children with SEN in mainstream with typically developing schoolmates. As with the pre-2000 evidence, the weight of evidence from this review was only marginally positive overall. The review concludes that there is a need to research more thoroughly mediators and moderators, in particular those drawn from psychological theory, that support optimal education for children with SEN.

Similar conclusions have emerged from a number of reviews over the last 10 years that have focused on social and affective outcomes of inclusion. Interest in these areas has been particularly strong because of predictions, which claimed a basis in psychological theory, that inclusion could be expected to increase social interaction, peer acceptance and positive social behaviour of children with SEN. Initial findings failed to support these expectations and showed that children with SEN were less socially accepted and more rejected by their mainstream classmates. This led some authors to question 'Is integrating the handicapped psychologically defensible?' (Stobart, 1986) or express concern that placement of children with SEN in mainstream without appropriate preparation constituted 'misguided mainstreaming' (Gresham, 1982). Two more recent reviews in this area will be discussed: a review of social competence and affective functioning of children with high incidence SEN such as moderate learning difficulties and behavioural difficulties, attention deficit hyperactivity disorder and dyslexia (Gresham and MacMillan, 1997c) and a review of children's attitudes towards those with intellectual and physical difficulties (Nowicki and Sandieson, 2002).

Gresham and MacMillan (1997c) concluded that the research on the social position of children with moderate SEN was very clear. Compared with their mainstream classmates, they were more poorly accepted and more often rejected, had lower levels of social skills and higher levels of problem behaviours. However, findings in the affective area of **self-concepts** were less clear. Some studies reported lower self-concepts for children with SEN, while some reported higher self-concepts, and still others failed to find any differences between pupils with SEN and their peers. Drawing on social comparison theory, it was found that much of the research could be interpreted by considering the social group with which children were comparing themselves in different situations. A child's self-concept was usually higher when it was assessed in a special education classroom than when it was assessed in a mainstream classroom, where the achievement of the other children was higher.

Nowicki and Sandieson (2002) also reported some clear findings on children's attitudes from a **meta-analysis** of publications between 1990 and 2000. Overall, children without disabilities were preferred to children with either physical or intellectual disabilities, however inclusive classrooms had a medium-sized effect on facilitating positive attitudes. No consistent effect of type of disability was identified. However, there were indications that context–disability interactions might have been operating to shape attitude. For example, Tripp, French and Sherrill (1995) found that attitudes towards hypothetical children with physical difficulties, assessed by questionnaire during a physical education class, were more favourable in non-inclusive classes. By contrast, attitudes to children with learning difficulties did not differ between inclusive and non-inclusive PE classes. In apparent contradiction to **contact theory**, the experience of contact with children who have physical difficulties in these physical education lessons of 9–12-year-olds appeared to have had a negative impact. It indeed appears, as Lindsay (2007) argues, that more detailed consideration of the contribution of psychological theory would be of value in developing optimal educational experiences for children with SEN.

How can psychological theory contribute?

In this section we will examine four psychological theories that have been applied to understanding and changing children's attitudes and behaviour towards peers who have SEN:

■ **Theory of planned behaviour**.

■ Contact theory.

■ Labelling/**Attribution theory**.

■ Social exchange theory.

According to the theory of planned behaviour (Ajzen, 1991) there are three major influences on behaviour, such as positive interaction with classmates with SEN (see Figure 4.2), attitude towards the behaviour (own positive or negative view of the behaviour), **subjective norm** (perception of the views of other significant people, e.g. parents, teachers, friends), and perceived behavioural control (**self-efficacy** in relation to the behaviour). These three factors combine to account for the strength of the intention to perform the behaviour in question, which is the major determinant of whether the behaviour is actually carried out. In addition, actual behavioural control may directly impact on ability to carry out the behaviour. To the extent that children are aware of the barriers to carrying out the behaviour, the measure of perceived behavioural control can serve as a proxy for actual control and this is represented by the dotted line in Figure 4.1. For example, a child may have difficulty carrying out their intention to interact

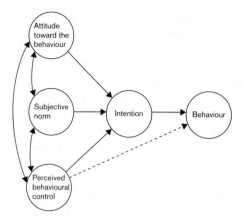

Figure 4.1 Theory of planned behaviour.

Source: Ajzen, I. (1991). The theory of planned behavior. Organizational Behavior and Human Decision Processes, 50, 179–211.

with a classmate with SEN because of organizational arrangements in the classroom, such as teacher-determined groupings. This theory suggests that both attitudes towards classmates with disabilities and the balance of environmental facilitators and barriers will be important determinants of behaviour towards children with disabilities, and that intervention efforts are likely to need to address both aspects.

A small number of studies have used the theory of planned behaviour to investigate the attitudes and behaviour of children towards peers with SEN included in mainstream schools. Consistent with the theory, Roberts and Lindsell (1997) found that 8–12-year-old children's attitudes towards peers with physical disabilities strongly predicted their intentions to interact positively with them. Additionally, children's attitudes correlated significantly with those of their teachers and mothers (the subjective norm). Roberts and Smith (1999) found that children's attitudes towards peers with physical disabilities and their perceived behavioural control were significant predictors of their behavioural intentions to interact with and befriend such peers. In addition, intentions predicted the amount of time children reported spending with their classmates with physical disabilities in the classroom and playground.

Contact theory was identified by Stobart (1986) as one of the theories that at an early stage had been 'conscripted to handle the psychological implications of the policy of inclusion' (Stobart, 1986: 1) and it has continued to influence research in inclusion. The original theory holds that interaction between groups can change attitudes of in-group members (e.g. pupils who do not have disabilities, majority ethnic group pupils) towards out-groups (e.g. pupils who have disabilities, minority ethnic group pupils) and can reduce stereotyping and prejudice if four conditions are met: equal status between the groups in the contact situation, common goals, no competition between groups, and authority's sanction of the contact (Allport, 1954). It is not difficult to see that these conditions are unlikely to have been met in the physical education classes in the study by Tripp et al (1995), described earlier.

Both contact theory and the theory of planned behaviour were used by Marom, Cohen and Naon (2007) in designing an intervention for children aged 10–12 years to improve disability-related attitudes and self-efficacy for interacting with children with disabilities. The intervention was a direct contact programme between students with disabilities who attended special education schools, and students without disabilities who attended mainstream schools. A control group of students who were not receiving the intervention were also recruited. The intervention had two phases: a) children in the intervention group received specific information from special school staff about the disabilities of the students they were going to meet, together with general information about people with disabilities; b) children met and interacted directly with pupils with disabilities via joint, non-competitive, activities, such as music, art and social games. The meetings were held weekly to fortnightly throughout one school year. Improvements in attitudes and specific self-efficacy were found for the intervention but not the control group. The authors acknowledge the limitations of using existing groups that are neither randomly assigned nor matched on key variables of interest. A further limitation is that it was not possible to evaluate separately the two phases of the intervention.

A number of other studies which have drawn on contact theory have reported positive findings. Newberry and Parish (1987) found that, for 8–11-year-old scouts and guides, social interaction with children who have disabilities fostered more favourable attitudes, but only when the disabilities were relatively apparent (severe learning difficulties, physical disabilities, hearing difficulties, visual difficulties, but not specific learning difficulties). Maras and Brown (1996) reported that children from a mainstream primary school who were involved in an integration programme with children from a school for children with severe learning disabilities (SLD) showed more positive social orientation towards the pupils with SLD over time, while the control group showed little change.

However, there are also some less positive findings. Maras and Brown (2000) did not find attitudes to pupils with SEN to be significantly more positive in schools where various kinds of integration were occuring than in control schools that did not have integrated provision. The authors raise questions about the extent to which the contact in some of these schools met Allport's (1954) conditions for success, given large class sizes and limited use by teachers of cooperative learning activities. Nonetheless this study set out to investigate generalization of effects from contact with one or more members of an out-group to the whole group. Two contrasting models of contact were tested:

1. The **decategorization model** (Brewer and Miller, 1984) which holds that generalization will be facilitated by a focus on enabling in-group members to get to know out-group members as individuals and minimizing the salience of category distinctions.
2. The 'intergroup' contact model (Hewstone and Brown, 1986) which holds that generalization will be facilitated by a focus on maintaining the salience of 'in-group' and 'out-group' boundaries and emphasizing the typicality of the 'out-group' members met so that attitudes will readily transfer to those not met.

Maras and Brown (2000) selected schools operating integration approaches that related to the two models of contact:

1. Where children with SEN were not clearly identified by the schools to their mainstream peers as being members of a wider group.
2. Where children with SEN were clearly identified by the schools as members of a group of similar others who were taught separately for all or part of the time. In addition mainstream children were given information about the children with SEN and how to interact with them.

Children in the **intergroup contact model** schools were found to have more sharply differentiated attitudes across groups and relatively less positive attitudes to children with than without SEN. However, the hypothesis that the intergroup contact model would facilitate generalization received support from the finding of stronger correlations between sociometric preferences for known and unknown peers with SEN in the categorized than in the decategorized schools.

The intergroup contact model also proved more effective than the decategorization model in an 'extended contact', as opposed to an actual contact intervention (Cameron and Rutland, 2006). The **'extended contact effect'** or 'indirect cross friendship hypothesis' suggests that vicarious experiences of friendship, for example knowledge of in-group members being friends with out-group members, might be effective in reducing prejudice. The intervention was designed for 5–10-year-olds in UK primary schools. Once a week for six weeks stories were read about friendships between non-disabled and disabled children and discussed in small groups. In some stories, the protagonist's disability category membership was de-emphasized and their individual attributes highlighted (decategorized model), in other stories category membership was emphasized and the child's typicality highlighted (intergroup contact model). In this study intended behaviour showed positive change in both conditions while attitudes also showed change in the intergroup condition.

The Cameron and Rutland (2006) study also indicated that 'extended contact' can be effective and some advantages over direct contact have been identified. For example, extended contact may avoid negative affect, such as anxiety, that might be elicited by direct contact. Extended contact might also be useful where there is little opportunity for direct contact, and as a preparation for direct contact, for example prior to the arrival of a child with SEN in a particular mainstream class.

Labelling and attribution theory

The implications of recent research on the contact hypothesis would seem to be that more positive attitudes towards children who have SEN can be fostered if their 'special' category membership is clearly apparent to other children. This appears contradictory to the critiques of labelling that played an important role in advocating integration. Dunn argued that labels such as 'mentally retarded', in common use then, served as a 'destructive, self-fulfilling prophecy' (Dunn, 1968: 8). However, even research on labelling as such has consistently shown that peer group attitudes are more influenced by a child's behaviour than by a categorical label. For example, videotapes of children engaging in positive or negative behaviours were shown to 8–12-year-old viewers, half of whom were told that the child was in a 'special class for the retarded' (Van Bourgondien, 1987). The child's social behaviours, but not the label, had a significant effect on the viewers' attitudes towards them.

More recently the attitudes and behavioural intentions of 11–12-year-old children towards hypothetical peers with attention deficit hyperactivity disorder (ADHD) were assessed through response to vignettes (Law et al, 2007). Attitudes towards the characters in the vignettes were found to be mainly negative and there was a significant relationship between attitudes and willingness to engage in social, academic and physical activities, suggesting that the behaviour of children with ADHD could lead to substantial exclusion by classmates. However, diagnostic/psychiatric labels had no additional influence upon attitudes or behavioural intentions.

There is some evidence that a categorical label may sometimes have a protective effect in terms of helping to ameliorate negative attitudes held by mainstream peers towards children with SEN who exhibit poor social behaviour (Bak and Siperstein, 1986). Children aged 9–12 years viewed a video of a child reading. Conditions varied in terms of whether the child was labelled 'mentally retarded' and whether they were depicted as socially withdrawn or aggressive. Assessment of the viewers' attitudes suggested that the label had a protective effect, in that attitudes were less negative with the label when the child was withdrawn. However this did not hold when the behaviour exhibited was aggressive, when only a weak effect was apparent.

Attribution theory (Weiner, 1985) has proved useful in examining the relationship between perceived deviance and negative peer reactions. A key concept is perceptions of responsibility. A negative or an unexpected event triggers attributional processes in a search for explanation. Someone who is perceived to be responsible (for example someone who fails an exam because they do not bother studying) is likely to elicit anger from other people, whereas a person who is not held responsible (someone who fails an exam because they have been very ill) is likely to evoke sympathy. Juvonen (1991) suggested that reactions to 'deviant' individuals are amenable to attributional analyses, as encounters with such individuals may be regarded as negative or non-normal events that elicit a search for explanation.

Sigelman and Begley (1987) investigated links between the personal controllability of problems and peers' evaluations of blame among 5–6-year-old and 8–9-year-old children. They were told about peers who were either in a wheelchair, obese, learning disabled or aggressive and were either given no causal information or given information about the cause (controllable or uncontrollable) of each problem. Children in both age groups were responsive to the causal information provided, and assigned blame in proportion to ascribed responsibility. When causal information was lacking, the children tended to hold all but the child in the wheelchair responsible although, with age, increasing emphasis was placed on external causes.

The idea that children spontaneously identify deviance among peers and attribute responsibility in ways that lead to particular affective reactions and accepting or rejecting behaviour was investigated by Juvonen (1991). Twelve-year-olds were asked to identify classmates they considered different to themselves and describe how they were different. They also completed a sociometric measure assessing peer acceptance and rejection. Six categories of deviance were identified: rule breaking (including aggression), social image (including bragging), activity level, low achievement, social withdrawal and physical condition. The more children perceived a classmate as different, the more likely they were to reject that classmate. Juvonen (1991) also investigated mediating processes both in judgements of hypothetical children and judgements of actual classmates. In both cases, perceptions of responsibility for the deviance predicted interpersonal affect (anger and sympathy) and how liked or disliked the deviant child was. These, in turn, predicted social consequences, such as rejection and social support. Figure 4.2 in Research Methods box 4.1 shows the results obtained with actual classmates.

Research methods 4.1

Interpreting structural equation models

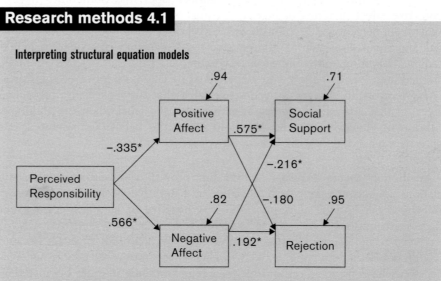

Figure 4.2 Path diagram of perceived responsibility, general affect and social consequences for deviant classmates.

Source: Juvonen, J. (1991). Deviance, perceived responsibility, and negative peer reactions. Developmental Psychology, 27, 672–681.

Structural equation modelling (SEM) is increasingly used in educational psychology research because it allows complex mediational and other relationships between combinations of variables and factors to be analysed. It is considered to be better than simpler analytical techniques in dealing with the complexity and interactivity involved in many priority research areas in applied settings such as schools. It is used to test a theory or model of the relationships between variables, shown by connecting arrows (the single arrows pointing at the variables are error terms).

The co-variances among the variables in the predicted model are compared with the observed data and goodness-of-fit between the two sets of co-variances estimated. There are different programmes that are used for SEM such as LISREL, AMOS and EQS (used by Juvonen, 1991). In EQS the fit of the model is statistically evaluated with a chi-square statistic which tests the similarity of the co-variances of the predicted model and the observed data. If the chi-square value is *non*-significant, there is a good fit between the model and the data. In this case the chi-square value was statistically non-significant, $X^2_{(2, N = 114)} = 0.43$, $p = .81$.

Here is how Juvonen (1991: 678) explains the main findings shown in the figure:

All path coefficients but one were significant. The more responsible classmates were perceived to be for their deviance, the more negative affect ($\beta = .566$) and the less positive affect ($\beta = -.335$) they elicited. The more negative affect the deviant classmates elicited, the more likely they were to be rejected ($\beta = .192$) and the less likely other children were to give them social support ($\beta = -.216$). On the other hand, the more positive affect the deviant classmates elicited, the more likely they were to get social support from their classmates ($\beta = .575$). These data did not, however, support the path between positive affect and rejection. Thus, according to these results, positive affect for a deviant classmate does not necessarily predict lack of rejection. There were no direct paths between perceived responsibility and social consequences.)

Activity 4.2

Why do you think that the path between positive affect and rejection was not supported? What findings have been reported in this chapter so far that might be relevant? Record the reasons you consider most important at this point. As you read the rest of the chapter consider other possibilities and review at the end the reasons you have recorded.

Social exchange theory (Thibaut and Kelley, 1959; Kelley and Thibaut, 1978)

We have seen from research on attribution theory that non-normative behaviour may receive a more supportive response from classmates where the perpetrator is identified as having SEN or other 'non-blameworthy' difficulties. Comparable findings have been obtained from research on social exchange in children's interpersonal relationships. Social exchange theory holds that desire for affiliation with others relates to the sum of the perceived costs and benefits of interacting with them, set against some minimum level of expectation – the comparison level. The comparison level may be different for children who have SEN.

A number of studies have found that different behavioural norms are associated with peer group acceptance and rejection for children who have SEN than for their mainstream school classmates (Taylor et al, 1987; Roberts and Zubrick, 1992; Nabuzoka and Smith, 1993; Frederickson and Furnham, 2004). The majority of children who were rejected by classmates scored high on costly social behaviours (e.g. aggression) and low on beneficial social behaviours (e.g. cooperation) (Newcomb et al, 1993). The opposite pattern of scores, high on beneficial and low on costly behaviours, was found for well-accepted children. By contrast, children with SEN who were rejected did not show a symmetrical pattern; they had low scores on beneficial behaviours, but did not have high scores on costly behaviours (Frederickson and Furnham, 1998). Asymmetry was also apparent in differentiating high from average acceptance. For children with SEN, beneficial behaviours were not characteristic of good peer acceptance, only low levels of costly behaviours.

These findings can be considered in terms of the distinction drawn between **exchange relationships** and **communal relationships** (Clark and Mills, 1979, 1993). The symmetrical behavioural assessments received from classmates by normally developing children are consistent with the application of exchange relationship norms. The asymmetrical assessments received by children with SEN suggest a special responsiveness to their social needs, consistent with the application of asymmetrical communal norms (Clark and Mills, 1993). Many case studies of relationships between children with SEN and their typically developing classmates also support this conceptualization. For example, 'Although there is undeniable warmth between the children, most of the comments and non-verbal interactions reflect a helper-helpee relationship, not a reciprocal friendship' (Van der Klift and Kunc, 2002, p.22) and 'The interactions, although tending to be highly positive, had the feel of a parental type of role on the part of the children without disabilities' (Evans et al, 1998: 134).

In an experimental test of these ideas, Frederickson and Simmonds (in press) investigated the way in which children aged 8–9 years and 10–11 years distributed rewards jointly earned for work done with classmates who were acquaintances or children with SEN. Among the older, but not the younger children, findings supported the characterization of relationships with acquaintances as exchange relationships and with children who have SEN as asymmetrical communal relationships.

Social exchange theory can also predict features of the social environment likely to affect intention to interact with classmates who have SEN. For example, Frederickson and Furnham (1998) predicted that the costs, as opposed to benefits, of interaction would be higher in classes that are less cohesive. They also hypothesized that in classes where mainstream peers perceive their work to be difficult, perceived similarities with children who have SEN will be increased and the relative costs of working with them reduced. In line with these predictions, high levels of classroom cohesiveness (in addition to low levels of disruptive behaviour) were found to be associated with peer acceptance towards children with SEN. On the other hand, rejection of this group was lower both when they were rated by peers as 'cooperative' and where the majority of children in the class found the work difficult.

The influence of school ethos factors on pupils' attitudes to peers with SEN was also investigated by McDougall et al (2004). Using a structural equation modelling approach, they found that positive student relationships at the school level and a school goal task structure that promoted learning and understanding for all, rather than social comparison and competition among students, had significant associations with positive attitudes. They suggest that school-wide, ecologically based initiatives aimed at modifying the environment to create a supportive school ethos should be an important element of any effort to enhance attitudes towards students with disabilities.

Inclusion: Implications from psychological theory and research

In this section we have reviewed a number of strands of psychological theory that have been applied in investigating and endeavouring to enhance inclusive practice. There are two consistent findings. First, aspects of the school social environment can have a predictable and important influence on pupils' attitudes, intentions and actions. Second, for many children with SEN in many school contexts, clearly acknowledging differences, as well as what they have in common with their classmates, appears more likely to facilitate their inclusion than appearing not to recognize or address the differences that exist. This may appear counter-intuitive to some in the field of education. However, it has long been known that even at relatively young ages children notice and react to atypical behaviours in other children (Coie and Pennington, 1976; Maas et al, 1978). Rather than leave classmates to make their own (often rather negative) attributions, more positive outcomes are likely to result if adults provide advance information, ongoing explanations and appropriately structured and supported opportunities for contact. An illustration of how this might be done is provided in Activity box 4.3.

Activity 4.3

Read the following description of the inclusion team from the perspective of an educational psychologist who has been asked to advise on its operation, development and evaluation.

1. What features can you identify that are consistent with recommendations from psychological theory and research?
2. What further developments would you suggest? Draft a paragraph on each, providing a rationale from the knowledge base in psychology.
3. How might the following aspects be investigated: the social competence and affective functioning of the children with SEN, and the attitudes and behaviour of their classmates towards them?

The Foxwood Inclusion/Outreach Team (adapted from Frederickson et al, 2007)

This team was created to effect a phased and supported transition to a mainstream placement for pupils who had been educated in Foxwood Special School from the age of 2 years as part of an early identification and intervention programme for children with moderate/severe learning difficulties. One lead teacher and two teaching assistants were identified to support an initial cohort of 23 pupils across 18 primary schools. Individual pupil contracts were established with mainstream schools local to their homes in terms of the type and the initial amount of inclusion appropriate for each individual pupil. However, the ultimate target was that all 23 pupils should be full time in a mainstream school with continuing support within a two-year period.

Detailed discussions took place with the mainstream school and with parents so there was clarity about the aims and objectives of the programme. There were some children who initially attended a primary school for purely social reasons, while others joined for national curriculum subjects. The individual programmes then developed according to the child's needs. Social and affective aspects were carefully considered throughout. Perhaps one of the most significant factors in the child being successfully included was that they wore the same uniform as their peer group. Alongside this symbol of belonging, another important element of the process was peer preparation. It was recognized that peer acceptance was an essential feature of an inclusive school and as a result a peer group package was developed. It comprised workshop activities, delivered by an inclusion team member and the class teacher together and aimed at introducing the child with SEN to their new classmates and promoting supportive pupil interaction in mainstream settings.

Summary

- Inclusion involves providing education in mainstream schools for all children and contrasts with the provision of separate special schools or classes for children with SEN.

- The role of scientific research in shaping the social policy of inclusion is disputed. Neither rights considerations nor research evidence are clear cut. Conflicting rights can create ethical dilemmas, and methodological problems with the research evidence can render clear conclusions elusive.

- Reviews of efficacy research using different methodologies have generally identified a marginal advantage of inclusive placements on academic and social outcomes. However, the position of children with SEN on measures of social and affective adjustment is less positive than for their classmates who do not have SEN.

- Four strands of psychological theory addressing aspects of social perception and attribution, interpersonal relationships and group relations were identified and their contribution to promoting the social inclusion of children with SEN examined.

Key concepts and terms

Attribution theory
Bio-ecological model
Communal relationship
Contact theory
Decategorization model
Effect size
Exchange relationship
Extended contact effect
Inclusion

Integration
Intergroup contact model
Mainstreaming
Meta-analysis
Self-concept
Self-efficacy
Special educational needs
Subjective norm
Theory of planned behaviour

Sample essay titles

- What are the implications from psychological theory and research for the design of programmes to promote the social inclusion of pupils with SEN?
- Is labelling always a bad thing? Discuss with reference to the inclusion of children who have SEN.
- The conditions set by contact theory cannot realistically be met in mainstream schools for most children with severe SEN. Discuss.

Further reading

Books

Frederickson, N., and Cline, T. (2008). *Special Educational Needs, Inclusion and Diversity. A Textbook* (2nd Ed.). Buckingham: Open University Press. (Especially Chapter 4).

Journal articles

Frederickson, N., Simmonds, E., Evans, L., and Soulsby, C. (2007). Assessing Social and Affective Outcomes of Inclusion. *British Journal of Special Education*, 34, 105–115.

Gresham, F.M., and MacMillan, D.L. (1997c). Social competence and affective characteristics of students with mild disabilities. *Review of Educational Research*, 67, 377–415.

Lindsay, G. (2003). Inclusive education: A critical perspective. *British Journal of Special Education*, 30, 3–12.

Lindsay, G. (2007). Educational psychology and the effectiveness of inclusive education/mainstreaming. *British Journal of Educational Psychology*, 77, 1–24.

Marom, M., Cohen, D., and Naon, D. (2007). Changing disability-related attitudes and self-efficacy of Israeli children via the Partners to Inclusion

Programme. *International Journal of Disability, Development and Education*, 54, 113–127.

Odom, S.L., Vitztum, J., Wolery, R., Lieber, J., Sandall, S., Hanson, M.J., Beckman, P., Schwartz, I., and Horn, E. (2004). Preschool inclusion in the United States: a review of research from an ecological systems perspective. *Journal of Research in Special Educational Needs*, 4, 17–49.

Siegel, B. (1996). Is the emperor wearing clothes? Social policy and the empirical support for full inclusion of children with disabilities in the preschool and early elementary grades. *Social Policy Report, Society for Research in Child Development*, X (2 and 3), 2–17. Available to download at: www.srcd.org/documents/publications/spr/spr10-2_3.pdf

5 Effective communication in school

Do teachers and students talk the same language?

Tony Cline

The effective use of language is fundamental to school learning, but the language of school is very different from the language that many children acquire within their families. School pupils have to learn to vary their use of language in different environments. This chapter will review how children learn to communicate in infancy and will examine how the language they learn at that stage differs from the language that they will later need at school. Do differences between home talk and **classroom talk** inhibit students' engagement with the curriculum? In the final section of the chapter we will see how ideas from socio-cultural theory based on the work of Vygotsky have been applied to help teachers to overcome these challenges. The chapter will include an illustration of how educational psychologists have drawn on research findings in this field to provide support in schools.

Learning outcomes

When you have completed this chapter you should be able to:

1. Describe key features of the development of children's language and other modes of communication before they start school.
2. Evaluate the claim that some children find school learning more difficult because the language and communication skills they have learned at home have not prepared them well for the demands that are made at school.
3. Analyse key features of different forms of classroom talk, employing a well-researched socio-cultural approach.

Activity 5.1

Laurie Lee, the writer, described his first day at school in his autobiography, Cider with Rosie, and recalled that his teacher told him to 'Wait there for the present'. He went home at the end of the day bitterly disillusioned because he was not given one *(Perera, 1981: 4)*.

In a nursery school in London a teacher was talking to a 4-year-old girl whose mother, she knew, was from America.

Teacher: *Were you born in America? [No reply.] Or were you born in England? Do you know?*

Child: *I was . . . I was born in my mummy's tummy. (Tizard and Hughes, 1984: 207)*

A 9-year-old Portuguese child who had recently arrived in the United States was struggling to finish copying a homework assignment from the board when the teacher started erasing it. *'Stop it!'*, called the child emphatically, using a phrase she had learned from her classmates in the playground. The teacher looked surprised. *(Menyuk and Brisk, 2005: 87)*

The actor, Stephen Fry, recalled going up to his older brother, Roger, at his new prep school and calling him by his name. He was told off for doing so: *'You call me bro here. Bro. Understood?'* Only surnames were used: Roger was Fry, R.M. and Stephen was Fry, S.J. *(Fry, 1997: 2)*.

When Harry Potter met his future friend, Ron Weasley, on the train going to the Hogwarts School at the beginning of his first term there, he tried to explain that he had grown up in an ordinary Muggle family and felt quite ignorant about everything to do with wizardry:

'. . . and until Hagrid told me, I didn't know anything about being a wizard or about my parents or Voldemort.'
Ron gasped.
'What?' said Harry.
'You said You-know-who's name!' said Ron, sounding both shocked and impressed. *(Rowling, 1997: 75)*

In each of those episodes a child misunderstood something or made what counted as a mistake. Can you explain exactly what the problem was in each example and how it occurred? What does your analysis tell you about the challenges children face when they move from the **language environment** of their home to a different setting such as the language environment of a school?

The early development of language and communication skills

The initial experiences that lay the foundations for language development

The main questions addressed in this chapter concern how children use the language and **communication skills** that they have developed in early childhood once they start school. In order to tackle those questions it is necessary to review key features of pre-school language development. The foundations are laid from the very beginning. If infants are given a choice shortly after birth between listening to speech sounds and non-speech sounds that are equally complex, they show a preference for the speech sounds (Vouloumanos and Werker, 2007). At the outset they themselves produce sounds that simply relate to their physical state – reflexive vocalizations such as crying and sneezing. But within two months they move on to cooing and gurgling, sounds that appear to express a wider range of moods and needs. This activity evolves through experimenting with sounds, playing with their vocal tract and producing squeals, hoots and some vowel-like sounds. As they experience others' reactions to them and eventually observe their caregivers' modelling of effective communication, infants are stimulated towards the development of language themselves.

There is a good deal of evidence that the basic structures of this development are built into humans' genetic make-up. Those structures are stimulated by caregivers' behaviour – the constant use of the names of objects that an infant can see or hear and the verbal description of actions and events as they are happening in the infant's vicinity. When the child makes clear what they want by pointing or looking or touching, they are reinforced by obtaining gratification and receiving others' attention. As they hear more and more talk from their family, they begin to babble selectively, making increasing use of the sounds that characterize the languages of those who speak to them. Eventually they acquire the languages, dialects and accents that they hear around them. The roots of effective communication are simple and adaptable (Jaswal and Fernald, 2002).

In trying to understand how these early developments lay the foundation for effective communication in school it is helpful to consider the ideas about language development associated with the **socio-cultural theory** of Lev **Vygotsky**. He tried to show how the **culture** in which a person is brought up influences the course of their development. He used the term 'culture' broadly to describe the customs of a particular people at a particular time – the learned traditions and aspects of lifestyle that are shared by members of a society, including their habitual ways of thinking, feeling and behaving. Speech was seen as having the role of containing and transmitting culture, since language stores social experience from the past and makes it available to others in the future. Through language a person can be not only an active agent who is immersed in what they are doing at this moment but also 'a reflexive agent' who is distanced from their immediate context (Valsiner, 2000).

Culture has a material aspect in the environment and the objects that people create, and also a symbolic (or semiotic) aspect in the language that they use to describe these things to others. Vygotsky saw culture as having a key formative role in development, as it is transmitted both through social interaction and through speech. Thus he envisaged the development of language as forming the basis for the development of thinking. The foundation of that process is an infant's social interaction with those around them. This is expressed in what he called 'the general, genetic law of cultural development':

> *All the basic forms of the adult's verbal social interaction with the child later become mental functions . . . Any function in the child's cultural development*

appears twice, or on two planes. First it appears on the social plane and then on the psychological plane. First it appears between people, as an interpsychological category and then within the child, as an intrapsychological category. (Vygotsky, 1978: 73)

There is little direct empirical evidence for this theoretical construction of how the process might operate, but it has had a great deal of influence. We will discuss later in the chapter ways in which researchers with a background in education and psychology have suggested that teachers can draw on Vygoskian ideas to help pupils overcome the challenges that they face in effective classroom communication. One aspect of those challenges is that the initial experiences that provide the foundations of language development vary greatly between children. In many parts of the world children are exposed to more than one language during their early years and grow up as bilingual speakers. It is estimated that between a half and two-thirds of the world's population are bilingual or multilingual (Baker, 2001). But that is not a universal experience, and some countries, such as England, are mainly monolingual.

Even within the same language or dialect there may be differences in **socio-economic status (SES)** or ethnic background that will lead to variations in children's language experiences at home. For example, when Hart and Risley (1992) made regular observations for a period of just over two years in the homes of 40 families in a mid-Western city in the USA, they found marked differences in the frequency of different kinds of utterances by parents in high and low SES homes. In the families with lower SES a substantial proportion (up to 20 per cent) of parent utterances to children functioned to prohibit the children's activities within the home, whereas discouraging prohibitions of that kind were rarely heard in families with higher SES. Instead the children in higher SES families were more likely to hear questions (up to 45 per cent of parent utterances) and more frequent repetitions and elaborations of their own topics (up to 5 per cent of parent utterances). Similar findings on SES group differences in the use of language by parents to their children have been reported in other countries, including the UK, and have led to the use of such terms as 'verbal **deprivation**' to explain differences in school performance between children from different SES backgrounds. Other research (e.g. Tizard and Hughes, 1984) has indicated that the picture of socio-economic differences is more complex than that summary implies, but it is important to keep the impact of such differences on children's language experiences in mind when considering the subsequent development of their communication skills at school.

Non-verbal communication and pragmatic skills

When young children speak their first word, most parents celebrate what they see as an important milestone in development. Doherty-Sneddon has pointed out that they tend not to recognize key milestones in non-verbal communication in the same way: 'we seldom hear parents report when their children first began pointing to ask for something, or when they first used an action like flapping their hands to represent a bird' (Doherty-Sneddon, 2003: 9). She argues that people underestimate the importance of such steps in the development of children's overall communicative competence. Just as infants are attuned to recognize and seek out speech sounds, they are also sensitive to some forms of non-verbal communication such as smiling and pointing.

This ability to read the non-verbal signals communicated by those around them is mirrored by an ability to develop the use of many forms of **non-verbal communication** themselves. Young children learn to direct their eye gaze at what they want others to know they are interested in. They also develop increasingly sophisticated ways of communicating their feelings and desires through facial expressions. They learn the conventional meanings that different hand gestures have in their society so that they can convey agreement or dissent with their hands alone. They learn to illustrate their speech with gestures to support the message they want to put over, e.g. by drawing a visual picture in the air or pointing at something while talking about it or beating out the rhythm of their speech to emphasize particular words as they are spoken. Eventually they can draw on the full range of their communication resources, non-verbal and verbal, to understand others and to convey their own meaning and intentions. What they do not learn at this stage are the conventions of non-verbal communication that hold sway at school. The foundations are laid, but the specific expectations of teachers and peers in that setting will be learned later.

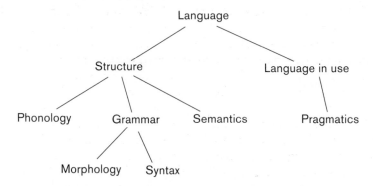

Figure 5.1 Aspects of language. (Adapted from Crystal, 1988.)

Source: Introduction to Language Pathology, D. Crystal (1988). With permission John Wiley & Sons Limited.

In order to be a competent user of a language a child must develop knowledge and skills relating to its structure and key components:

- Its sound system (phonology), e.g. which sounds normally occur in words and which do not.

- Its structural rules at the level of the word (morphology), e.g. how the form of a noun changes when it is plural (*dogs* as opposed to *dog* in English).

- The ways in which words may be combined together to form sentences (syntax), e.g. the rule that states that the object of a verb comes after the verb in English (*The dog gnawed the bone* rather than *The bone gnawed the dog*).

■ The ways in which words and sentences convey meaning (semantics), e.g. the link between the word *dog* and the 'meaning' of the word, *a four-legged, domesticated animal of a particular type*.

It is not enough, however, to have a grasp of the key components of a language. In addition, a person who is to use the language effectively for the purposes of communication with others needs to know *how* it is used – they require **pragmatic skills**. For example, they need to appreciate and follow the conventions of turn taking in conversation, and they need to understand when a change in the tone of a person's voice means that a question is really a command, e.g. when a child's mother says 'Aren't your toys in an awful mess?'.

Pragmatic rules may vary between social and ethnic groups within a society as well as between societies. For many children the move from home to nursery or school is made more challenging because the pragmatic rules they have learned at home lead them to misinterpret communications from others in the new setting or to communicate a meaning they do not intend. They may fail to make eye contact when it is expected and thus give the inaccurate impression of being sullen and unwilling to talk. Like the Portuguese girl who was quoted in Activity box 5.1, they may put requests in a direct way ('I want . . .') when an indirect form is considered more polite and respectful ('Can I have . . .'). Like Harry Potter, they may unselfconsciously use a word or name that is normally considered taboo in their new environment.

Entering the new language environments of nursery and school

Conversations between adults and children

When children leave the domestic environments of early child care for the larger-scale, more institutional settings of nursery or school, new language demands are made of them. They encounter a wider range of different people from a greater variety of speech backgrounds, they are involved in a new set of social routines requiring different types of language, and they must learn to use the **vocabulary** and syntactical forms associated with the demands of school subjects. They bring multi-faceted communication skills to these new challenges. For example, Flewitt (2005) conducted a longitudinal, ethnographic study of 3-year-old children in playgroups and nurseries and showed how they employed what she termed 'multimodal' forms of communication when interacting with others. She described adults and peers co-constructing meaning through words, gaze, facial expression and body movement. In one collaborative session at a playgroup, for example, Michael drew on the support of George, a work experience student, to build a house with Lego based on a published illustration. At first they worked alongside each other on separate models. Then, after some time, Michael asked George for help with his house, initially asking indirectly and then directly. Focus box 5.1 presents Flewitt's account of what happens.

Focus 5.1

Conversation between a child and a helper in a playgroup (Flewitt, 2005)

Line	Time code	Participant	Language	Action
18	00:36	Michael	it doesn't fit	glance to George
19		George	let's see	gaze from bricks in box to Michael's model
20	01:00	Michael	can you try (?)	
21				George helps to fit piece on, Michael watching closely
22	01:17	Michael	#that's righ#t	reaching for model takes model, 10 seconds play with model, making engine noise, gaze to George
23		George		watching Michael, smiling
24	01:29	Michael	isere isere nov' one?	shows George model
25	01:31	George	I'll see	looks in box for piece
26	01:52	Michael	I need (?) I nee' two two of #dem	watching George look in box leaning forwards to look in box glance to George watches George looking in box, plays with pieces in his hand
27		George and Michael		both look for piece, first in box, then on floor
28	02:11	Michael	oh #dere #dus' #dere (?) #de doggy (?)	reaches for brochure and shows it to George points to picture points
29		George	a dog?	looks in box, finds dog, passes to Michael
30	02:31	Michael	dere's a pu#ssy an' a dog	fixes dog in 'kitchen'
31		George		starts to sort through pieces in box
32	02:45	Michael	#look! der'e a pu' cat dere's a (?) look an anover one	closely watching pieces as George moves them around in box, sees something and reaches into box takes out piece and fits it to puzzle

This symbol indicates that, when the person making the transcription was listening to the audiotape, they found the sound at this point non-standard or unclear.

This extract illustrates Michael's ability at the age of 3 to use a combination of means of communication in order to achieve his objectives in his interaction with George. Flewitt pointed out that George's ability to play his part was crucial. He

> . . . acted as Michael's equal in status, paying close attention to his purposive play and fully cooperating with his requests without directing him. This approach allowed Michael to construct a highly complex model from an illustration, with modifications that reflected his interpretations of houses from home (a low decorative wall in the garden, cat in the kitchen), from playgroup (with flowers and butterflies – recent curriculum foci) and from elsewhere (drive with car). The activity was interrupted after 23 minutes when 'tidy-up time' was called, whereupon Michael dismantled the model and tidied away the pieces. (Flewitt, 2005: 218–219)

As we will see later, a child is unlikely to achieve their full potential for communicating with others unless the people they are talking to are able to play an active role in interpreting, repairing and augmenting what they are trying to say. All too often at nursery and at school that support is not available or is given in a less sensitive and responsive way than George was able to do in that extract.

Many teachers believe that the key determining factor in children's success in negotiating the linguistic challenges at school lies in pre-school preparation at home. For example, a teacher from Bridgend in South Wales responded to a survey on the subject by suggesting: 'Often parents do not know any songs or rhymes and have little idea of how to talk to and play with their children' (Basic Skills Agency, 2003: 18). Such views might be reinforced by evidence that children from seriously disadvantaged backgrounds show delayed language development, compared to national norms, when they enter nursery at 3–4 years old, even if their overall cognitive abilities are within the average range (Locke and Ginsborg, 2003).

At the same time there have been research reports on nurseries and schools that would make less comfortable reading for teachers who attribute the problems to children's **language environment** at home. Observational research in the past has sometimes indicated that early years settings may stimulate less extensive and less wide-ranging talk in young children from all backgrounds than they show when at home with their parents. For example, a study of a small group of 4-year-old girls in London in the 1980s indicated that they had relatively few encounters with adults in the child-centred play environment of their nursery schools and classes. The most common theme of their brief conversations with staff was their own play, in contrast to the much greater variety of topics that were touched on in the course of everyday conversations at home. The staff asked them many questions about what they were doing, questions that they answered briefly or not at all. Beyond that 'they rarely asked the staff questions of their own, or made the kind of spontaneous remarks that keep a conversation going' (Tizard and Hughes, 1984: 198).

Findings of this kind led to serious efforts to improve communication practices in early years settings. But recent studies have shown that early years staff still very often manage their daily conversations with children in ways that are unlikely to foster rich language development. For example, Siraj-Blatchford et al (2002) conducted extensive classroom observation in 12 early years settings that had been selected as exemplars of good practice. Out of 1967 questions that staff asked of children during their recordings, 60.8 per cent were unclassified, 34.1 per cent were closed questions and only 5.1 per cent were open questions. The researchers pointed out that open-ended questioning is more likely to provide significant encouragement for children to take the initiative in a conversation and to stimulate sustained, shared thinking (Siraj-Blatchford et al, 2002: 55). There is some survey evidence that the initial training of teachers and other staff who work in early years settings in England may not prepare them adequately in the area of speech and language development (Mroz and Hall, 2003). Brief in-school training at a later stage of their career may not be enough to change established poor practice in staff questioning in the classroom. That at least was the finding of a group of educational psychologists in London in a project that will be described later in the chapter (Bickford-Smith et al, 2005).

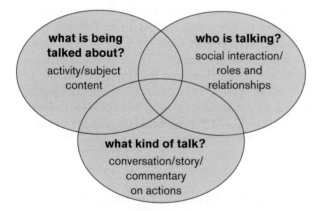

Figure 5.2 Key features of spoken language at school.
Source: DfES, 2003.

Bridging the gap between home and school

Bridging the gap between home and school is a major challenge for all those involved – children, parents and teachers. Children's play sometimes focuses on bridging a specific gap that is relevant to this chapter – the language gap between school and home. A key feature of nurseries and other early years settings is the provision for free play where children can participate in activities that represent lifelike situations such as cooking and cleaning a 'house' or driving a 'car'. When they play a role in these situations, children often imitate the more mature language they have heard from adults engaging in those activities. They not only practise the kind of language that accompanies these activities but also further their knowledge of how to participate in different kinds of conversation (Menyuk and Brisk, 2005: Chapter 4).

The learning process extends beyond the school when they take school language home while playing 'school' in the home setting. Children import the vocabulary, syntax and tone of their classroom when playing the role of teacher with younger siblings at home. For example, Gregory (2005) presents an excerpt from a maths 'lesson' in which 11-year-old Wahida took the role of teacher and her 8-year-old sister Sayeda was pupil. Sayeda had solved one problem successfully.

Wahida:	So, I'm going to put some sums on the board for you, OK? Ready?
Sayeda:	Yes.
Wahida:	The first sum's going to be – OK Sayeda do you remember to write the date first?
Sayeda:	Yes, Miss.
Wahida:	Well done! Now I'm going to write the sums. The first sum is 30655? If you want to do lattice, you can. Or you can do your own way, you can or you can do in your mind, but I would love to see some working out.

Gregory points out that Wahida models her use of language on that of her teacher both in her choice of lesson-related words and in the way that she structures her speech, e.g. referring to her requirements using indirect rather than direct speech (that she would love to see some working out) (Gregory, 2005: 228). Sayeda cooperates readily and also adopts the conventions of school speech. When psychologists highlight the gap between the language of home and the language of school in some social groups, they often focus on the language models provided by parents. Gregory argues that 'playful talk' provides a bridge between the two domains, and she has shown that siblings and grandparents may play a role in such talk as well as parents.

The impact of schooling on children's language

Key features of language development in the middle years of childhood

Attending school on a full-time basis leads to a significant increase in the range of sources of input to children's language learning. Their vocabulary and what they try to say encompasses new kinds of abstraction and ambiguity. During this developmental stage, there are also dramatic developments in their pragmatic competence as they become more able to take the perspectives of other people with whom they are talking. These major trends are summarized in Table 5.1.

As the child's vocabulary grows, the structural features of their speech change. They speak in longer and more complex sentences, and they use the morphological options in the language more extensively, e.g. adding prefixes and suffixes to familiar words such as *displeased* and *excitement*. Their increasing literacy skills transform the range of language to which they are exposed and make available to them models and sources that encompass specialist vocabulary and formal syntax outside the scope of everyday conversation. When they come across unfamiliar words in a story, they soon add them to their growing lexicon.

	Young children	School-age children and adolescents
Types of input	Learn language through listening and watching	Learn language through listening, watching and reading
Level of awareness	Absorb language unselfconsciously from those around them	Often learn through reflecting on and analysing language as an entity in itself influenced by increasing metalinguistic awareness
Level of abstraction	Add words to their vocabulary that generally have concrete referents (e.g. traffic lights, Peugeot, motorway)	Also add words to their vocabulary that represent abstract concepts (e.g. welfare, relevance, democracy) and words or phrases that are interpreted metaphorically (e.g. 'skeleton in the closet')
Level of ambiguity	Tend to interpret what they hear literally	Appreciate and come to enjoy word play in puns, riddles, jokes and advertisements
Awareness of the perspectives of others	Adjust their linguistic style to the person they are speaking to only to a limited extent	Are increasingly aware of the thoughts, feelings and needs of whoever they are speaking to and adjust the content and style of their speech accordingly

Table 5.1 Critical processes in early and later language development. (Adapted from Nippold, 1998: 4–6)

Robbins and Ehri (1994) showed that children who already have larger vocabularies may be more likely to learn new words from listening to stories than children with meagre vocabularies. This is one example of the **Matthew Effect** which seems to operate often in formal education (cf. Stanovich, 1986). This derives from the parable of the talents in the New Testament: 'For unto every one that hath shall be given, and he shall have abundance: but from him that hath not shall be taken away even that which he hath'
(The Gospel according to Matthew, King James' Version, XXV, 29).

It is not necessary to accept this outcome as inevitable. In one intervention designed to counteract the Matthew Effect, Bickford-Smith et al (2005) responded as educational psychologists to a request for help from the head teacher of a London school in an area of high social and economic deprivation. They trained members of the nursery staff to deliver an intensive 10-week vocabulary learning programme to selected groups of pupils. The approach was partly based on earlier research which had shown that visual cues, including manual signing, can support early speech and language development. They taught the staff to introduce a set of target nouns, verbs and concepts to the children by modelling them. The words were also visually reinforced through use of signs, symbols, real objects and photographs. This enabled the children to match each word to an object or activity and eventually to use the target word in carefully managed conversations. Staff were encouraged to use the target words during other parts of the working day at school, and an attempt was made to help them develop a 'language rich' environment in the nursery. The evaluation showed that, while not all parts of the project were successful, the children who took part in the intensive teaching programme did improve their scores on a standardized language scale significantly when compared to a control group who did not participate in it.

It may be that some of the children who are referred to educational psychologists as having 'special educational needs' have difficulties that are exacerbated because of differences they experience in the use of language at home and at school. Problems of phonological processing or social skills that are discussed in later chapters may be further exacerbated by this factor. However, the most important conclusion from the work of teams such as Bickford-Smith, Wijayatilake and Woods is perhaps that we do not need to be resigned to the Matthew Effect. In the next section we will examine an initiative at a later stage of schooling that is firmly based on that kind of determination.

Reviewing the rules of classroom talk

What is the best way of running a whole class discussion so that all the children articulate their ideas about the topic that is being discussed? Traditionally the teacher stands at the front of the classroom and asks a series of questions. Pupils who know the answer to a question put up their hands, and the teacher chooses one of them to tell the class what they think the answer is. It has recently been suggested that this practice is unhelpful. It is a well-established way of managing a lesson, and almost all of us will have experienced it as pupils. What can possibly be wrong with it? Critics have highlighted many limitations:

1. Some children who know the answer will not put up their hands for fear that they will look foolish if they are wrong or that they will be labelled as 'geeks' or 'swots' if they are right.
2. Some who do not know the answer will put their hands up eagerly anyway because they cannot bear to be left out.
3. The procedure may be undermined by teacher bias that leads to children from particular groups rarely being given the chance to contribute.
4. The exercise addresses only the teacher's agenda and risks overlooking important questions and concerns that some children have.
5. If a substantial proportion of the teacher's questions are closed questions and they rarely ask open-ended questions, the children will be given limited practice in articulating more complex ideas on the topic. With a closed question the task may simply become guessing what the teacher has in mind.
6. Those children in the class who are learning English as an additional language or who hear few models of sustained, reasoned argument at home, will not be given sufficient opportunities for oral practice of the construction of sentences in which words such as 'because' and 'if' and 'why' are used successfully.

There are many alternative ways of organizing classroom discussion that have been proposed to overcome these problems. Most involve some form of discussion in pairs or small groups which is sometimes followed by plenary discussion with the whole class or by a presentation of each group's conclusions to their peers or some combination of these. But it would be wrong to assume that discussion in small groups necessarily leads to children practising worthwhile communication skills. They may often be unclear about what exactly they are expected to do, and they may have little idea of what would constitute a good, effective discussion. After all, for many of them school will be the only place where they experience such discussions. Focus box 5.2 presents an extract illustrating the kind of unproductive talk that can result if a group of 9–10-year-old children are set a discussion task with little training or preparation. This extract was collected by Mercer et al (2004) as part of a larger-scale study. It was recorded by a group who were working through a computer-based task on the soundproofing qualities of various materials:

Focus 5.2

Transcript 1: Control school group who are working on 'Keep it Quiet' (from Mercer et al, 2004: 368–369)

Hannah: (reads from screen) Keep it Quiet. Which material is the best insulation? Click 'measure' to take a sound reading. Does the pitch make a difference?

Darryl: No we don't want clothes. See what one it is then. *(Points to screen)*

Hannah: No it's cloth.

Darryl: Oh it's cloth.

Hannah: Go down. This is better when Stephanie's in our group.

Darryl: Metal?

Hannah: Right try it.

Deborah: Try what? That?

Hannah: Try 'glass'.

Darryl: Yeah.

Deborah: No one.

Hannah: Now.

Darryl: *(interrupts)* Measure.

Hannah: Now measure. Hold. *(Turns volume control dial below screen)*

Darryl: Results, notes.

Hannah: Results. We need to go on a different one now. Results.

Darryl: Yeah, you need to go there so you can write everything down.

Hannah: I'm not writing.

Focus box 5.3 presents an extract from the discussion of a group who had received training designed by Mercer and his colleagues on the basis of socio-cultural principles which had been derived initially from Vygotsky's theoretical ideas on the development of language and cognition.

Focus 5.3

Transcript 2: Target school group who are working on 'Blocking out light' (from Mercer et al, 2004: 369)

Ross:	OK. *(reads from screen)* Talk together about a plan to test all the different types of paper.
Alana:	Dijek, how much did you think it would be for tissue paper?
Dijek:	At least ten because tissue paper is thin. Tissue paper can wear out and you can see through, other people in the way, and light can shine in it.
Alana:	OK. Thanks.
Alana:	*(to Ross)* Why do you think it?
Ross:	Because I tested it before!
Alana:	No, Ross, what did you think? How much did you think? Tissue paper. How much tissue paper did you think it would be to block out the light?
Ross:	At first I thought it would be five, but second –
Alana:	Why did you think that?
Ross:	Because when it was in the overhead projector you could see a little bit of it, but not all of it, so I thought it would be like, five to block out the light.
Alana:	That's a good reason. I thought, I thought it would be between five and seven because, I thought it would be between five and seven because normally when you're at home if you lay it on top, with one sheet you can see through but if you lay on about five or six pieces on top you can't see through. So that's why I was thinking about five or six.

One of the team's training strategies was to ask pupils to draw up a set of 'ground rules' for making effective, productive, discussion happen during a joint activity. Here is one example developed by a group of trainee teachers:

- Seek contributions from all group members, ensuring that everyone has a chance to speak.

- Actively listen and stay involved.

- Be positive and open to new ideas.

- Question others about their ideas.

- Respect and value other people's opinions and feelings.

- Explain your ideas concisely but clearly.

- Give clear reasons for your opinions, and expect them from others.

- Challenge and discuss points if you disagree.

- In case of alternative proposals, decide together which is supported by the best reasons.

- Keep to the subject.

- Be ready to compromise and reach agreement if possible. (Mercer, 2005: 19)

Activity 5.2

Distinguishing between different types of classroom talk

Mercer and his colleagues suggested that the extract in Focus box 5.2 exemplifies a type of group exchange which they called **disputational talk** and that the one in Focus box 5.3 could be described as **exploratory talk**. The second of these extracts was recorded in a school where they had introduced a training programme to help the children learn 'Thinking Together'. You will not be surprised that they considered the second extract educationally more valuable than the first and that they thought it showed higher-order communication skills.

1. Can you identify what specific differences there are in the use of language between the two groups?
2. The extracts that are given here show only the language the children used and not their non-verbal communication. If a video had been available, what characteristics would you expect to find in the non-verbal behaviour and pragmatic skills displayed in each group?
3. When you have arrived at an answer to the first question, you may like to examine Mercer's own account of differences between 'disputational talk' and 'exploratory talk', which is summarized in the Focus box 5.4. How far has your analysis of these extracts identified the points he highlighted?

The programmes of study for English in the National Curriculum stipulate that children should be taught to:

- Speak clearly and to develop and sustain ideas in talk.

- Develop active listening strategies and critical skills of analysis.

- Take different roles in groups, making a range of contributions and working collaboratively. (DfES, 2003: 6)

The research programme undertaken by Mercer's team suggests one way in which educational psychology can help teachers to achieve these objectives. He has argued that it is because some children do not gain access to the use of language for sustained, shared reasoning at home that an explicit and structured intervention is required to enable all pupils to benefit from these approaches at school (Mercer, 2005).

Focus 5.4

Types of talk in classroom groups (adapted from Mercer, 2007: 62–63)

Mercer and his colleagues (Mercer et al, 2004; Mercer, 2005; Mercer and Littleton, 2007) differentiated between three types of talk in classroom groups, two of which are exemplified in Focus boxes 5.2 and 5.3.

Talk of a mainly 'disputational' type, they thought, has these features:

- It is not usually associated with processes of joint reasoning and knowledge construction.
- Although the children interact a good deal, they think on their own rather than developing ideas and reasoning jointly.
- They tend to be defensive and competitive.
- They show off with information and ideas or withhold them, but do not often share them.
- There are often what the research called 'tit-for-tat "yes it is", "no it isn't" patterns of assertion and counter-assertion'.
- They pass negative judgements on each other's contributions.
- They squabble and bicker rather than pursuing a reasoned argument.

This is to be differentiated from 'cumulative talk' which has these features:

- Ideas and information are shared and joint decisions are made.
- Participants rarely challenge each other's arguments or ask for evidence or offer constructive criticism of what someone else has said.
- There appears to be solidarity and trust among group members, and they draw on each other's ideas, but typically only by repeating or confirming them rather than building on them and taking the argument further.

Note that cumulative talk is not illustrated with an extract here.

The features of 'exploratory talk' are:

- Group members work together and show 'a joint, coordinated form of co-reasoning in language with speakers sharing knowledge, challenging ideas, evaluating evidence and considering options in a reasoned and equitable way'.
- Ideas and reasoning are put before the rest of the group in an explicit form that others can understand and evaluate.
- Peers compare possible explanations and seek to agree on the best reasoning possible with the information they have available.
- There is conflict, but it is constructive. It is clear that the group's aim is to achieve a consensus.
- Everyone is free to express their views and . . . the most reasonable views gain acceptance.

Summary

- The chapter began by outlining some key features of early language development – infants' early sensitivity to the speech sounds they hear, their experimentation with producing their own sounds and the stimulation provided by caregivers.

- The ideas about language development associated with the socio-cultural theory of Lev Vygotsky may be helpful in trying to understand how these early developments lay the foundation for effective communication in school.

- Non-verbal communication skills and pragmatic skills are crucial aspects of the overall communicative competence that children must develop. Their importance to effective communication has sometimes been underestimated in the past.

- For many children the move from home to nursery or school is made more challenging because the pragmatic rules they have learned at home lead them to misinterpret communications from others in the new setting or to communicate a meaning themselves that they do not intend.

- When children leave the domestic environments of early child care for the larger-scale, more institutional settings of nursery or school, new language demands are made of them. They bring multi-faceted communication skills to these new challenges, but many still benefit less than they could initially because of a mismatch between their language skills and the demands made of them.

- This mismatch is blamed by many teachers on poor preparation at home during the pre-school years. At the same time research in nurseries and schools has suggested that the environment they provide is not always as stimulating for children's language development as it could be.

- Whatever the limitations of either environment, however, there are continuing impressive advances in language development during the middle years of childhood – in vocabulary and range, syntactical complexity and pragmatic competence.

- Specific interventions have been designed to counteract the effects on language development of background deprivation, both through intensive short-term work with targeted groups and through changing the strategies employed for involving all children in classroom talk.

- The last part of the chapter examined how psychology has been applied to improving the strategies that are used to plan and manage discussion in the classroom. The aim was to draw on principles derived from Vygotsky's socio-cultural theory in order to help children move from 'disputational talk' to 'exploratory talk' when working in groups.

> **Key concepts and terms**
>
> Classroom talk
> Communication skills
> Culture
> Deprivation
> Disputational talk
> Exploratory talk
> Language environment
>
> Matthew Effect
> Non-verbal communication
> Pragmatic skills
> Socio-cultural theory
> Socio-economic status
> Vocabulary
> Vygotsky

Sample essay titles

- Many teachers think that their pupils lack the language skills they require when they start school. How would you account for this?
- Is the Matthew Effect on children's language development irreversible?
- 'The quality of language used in children's classroom discussions can be improved through the application of Vygotskean principles.' Discuss.

Further reading

Books

Jaswal, V.K., and Fernald A. (2002). 'Learning to communicate.' In: A. Slater and M. Lewis (Eds), *Introduction to Infant Development*. Oxford: Oxford University Press, 244–265.

Menyuk, P., and Brisk, M.E. (2005). *Language Development and Education: Children with Varying Language Experience*. New York: Palgrave Macmillan.

Mercer, N., and Littleton, K. (2007). *Dialogue and the Development of Children's Thinking*. London: Routledge.

Journal articles

Bickford-Smith, A., Wijayatilake, L., and Woods, G. (2005). Evaluating the effectiveness of an early years language intervention. *Educational Psychology in Practice*, 21, 161–173.

Calfee, R. (1997). Language and literacy, home and school. *Early Child Development and Care*, 127/8, 75–90.

Mercer, N., Dawes, L., Wegerif, R., and Sams, C. (2004). Reasoning as a scientist: ways of helping children to use language to learn science. *British Educational Research Journal*, 30, 359–377.

6 Do modern methods of teaching reading cause dyslexia?

Norah Frederickson

McGuinness (1997: 122) describes **dyslexia** as 'a label applied to children who are so confused by their poor reading instruction that they can't overcome it without special help', adding 'nor do so-called dyslexic children have any more trouble learning to read than other children if they are taught with an appropriate method'. By contrast, Vellutino et al (2004: 25) conclude that 'results obtained in genetic, neuroanatomical and psycho-physiological studies' support the view that dyslexia involves 'basic cognitive deficits of biological origin'. In this chapter we will examine controversies both in the definition of dyslexia and in methods of teaching reading. We will then review the evidence on different theories about the causes of dyslexia and evaluate the extent to which dyslexia can be attributed to inappropriate teaching.

Learning outcomes

When you have completed this chapter you should be able to:

1. Evaluate the advantages and disadvantages of different approaches to the definition of dyslexia.
2. Describe the principal approaches to the teaching of reading and their underpinnings in psychological theory and research.
3. Identify similarities and differences between different theories of dyslexia and evaluate their utility both in explaining findings from group studies and in describing the problems faced by particular individuals.

What is dyslexia?

Dyslexia is derived from Greek and translates as 'difficulty with words'. It is a term that has wide public recognition and lacks the stigma associated with many learning difficulties, as is illustrated by the lengthy list of 'celebrity dyslexics' on the British Dyslexia Association's website (www.bdadyslexia.org.uk/links.html). Stanovich (1991: 10) notes that 'the typical "media dyslexic" is almost always a bright child who is deeply troubled in school because of a "glitch that prevents him or her from reading". The subtext of such a portrayal is that the tragedy of the situation is proportionately greater because the child's great potential remains unlocked'. This popular conceptualization represents a somewhat oversimplified and outdated understanding of dyslexia. However, it does reflect key elements of the main controversy surrounding the definition of dyslexia: to define by exclusion or by inclusion. Activity box 6.1 presents three definitions of dyslexia.

Activity 6.1

Defining dyslexia

1. Read the following definitions of dyslexia and identify what they have in common.
2. Decide to what extent they use exclusionary criteria (say what dyslexia is not) or inclusionary criteria (say what dyslexia is).
3. What would be the implications of these different approaches for teachers and educational psychologists in identifying and assessing children with dyslexia?

Definition A: 'A disorder manifested by difficulty in learning to read despite conventional instruction, adequate intelligence and sociocultural opportunity. It depends on fundamental cognitive disabilities which are frequently of constitutional origin.' (World Federation of Neurology 1968, in Critchley and Critchley 1978)

Definition B: 'Dyslexia is one of several distinct learning disabilities. It is a specific language-based disorder of constitutional origin characterised by difficulties in single word decoding.' (International Dyslexia Association, in Lyon, 1995: 7)

Definition C: 'Dyslexia is evident when accurate and fluent word reading and/or spelling is learnt very incompletely or with great difficulty. This focuses on literacy learning at the "word level" and implies that the problem is severe and persistent despite appropriate learning opportunities. It provides the basis for a staged process of assessment through teaching.' (British Psychological Society, 1999: 18).

Definition C differs from the other two in that it is descriptive, with no explanatory elements. This accords with arguments made by some (e.g. Tonnessen, 1997) that identifying characteristics should be differentiated from causal factors and the latter excluded from definitions of dyslexia. This is considered desirable in order to provide a common basis for identifying a population on which various scientific explanatory models can be tested. However, definitions of dyslexia are not only used to select participants for psychological research. A major reason for the controversy surrounding definitions of dyslexia has been their use in conferring eligibility for non-stigmatizing special educational resources.

Until very recently variants of definition A have been either explicitly or implicitly incorporated in special education assessment policy and practice both in the UK (Frederickson and Reason, 1995) and the USA (Gresham, 2002). In line with characterization of the 'media dyslexic' presented at the start of this section, identification has in effect come to depend on the demonstration of a sufficiently large discrepancy between the child's scores on an intelligence test and a reading test. This 'IQ–achievement' discrepancy approach to defining dyslexia, apparently based on the assumption that intelligence defines potential for reading attainment, has attracted increasing criticism. It has been a hotly debated issue by educational psychologists in the UK (Frederickson and Reason, 1995; Ashton, 1996; Solity, 1996).

It has been demonstrated that children with low IQs can have good word reading skills, so undermining the assumption on which the **IQ–achievement discrepancy** approach is based (Siegel, 1992). Stuebing et al (2002) conducted a meta-analysis of 46 studies to assess the validity of classifying poor readers into those who demonstrated an IQ–achievement discrepancy (and qualified for special help) and those who did not. They concluded that large overlaps between the two groups and negligible to small differences found on variables closely related to the reading process seriously questioned the validity of the approach. In addition, the utility, and indeed equity, of the approach has been challenged by findings that poor readers with and without a discrepancy do not differ in their response to intervention (Stage et al, 2003).

The equity issue can be illustrated by reference to Figure 6.1. On a discrepancy model poor reader A will not qualify for special help, whereas a poor reader B will. As the two children have equally severe reading problems and are likely to respond equally well to intervention, it is difficult to justify the use of child B's higher IQ to allocate special help. Furthermore if child A does not receive special help their reading relative to their classmates is likely to get worse over time – until their reading score falls to point A2 where it is significantly discrepant from their IQ and they qualify for special help. This 'wait to fail model' (Stuebing et al., 2002) has caused particular concern and led to calls for its replacement with an approach which instead encourages early intervention.

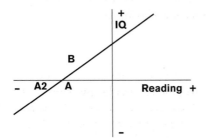

Figure 6.1 An illustration of the IQ–achievement discrepancy model of dyslexia.

Response to intervention

Response to intervention has been advocated, in place of an IQ–achievement discrepancy, as a qualification criterion for special educational provision (Gresham, 2002; Vaughn and Fuchs, 2003). Although conventional instruction and adequate socio-cultural opportunity are also listed in definition A, alongside adequate intelligence, little attention was previously paid to their systematic assessment. Clay (1987) convincingly argued that virtually all studies of reading difficulties failed to control for the potentially confounding effects of inadequate instruction or pre-reading experience, which could mimic the effects of organically based **learning disabilities**. This has continued to be a problem with the literature on dyslexia until very recently when emphasis has been placed on study selection criteria that include failure to respond adequately to interventions validated as effective for most children of comparable age/stage of reading development (see Vellutino et al, 2004). Such studies, which will be discussed in more detail later in the chapter, have indicated that the ease with which children's reading difficulties can be remediated is unrelated to IQ and that the use of IQ scores is contraindicated as a selection criterion in scientific studies of the biologically based cognitive deficits in dyslexia.

There are far reaching implications for research and practice of these developments in the field. Compared with administering tests of intelligence and reading to calculate a discrepancy, considerably greater time and cost will be involved in obtaining a dyslexic sample for a research study by first running an intervention programme to select non-responders. For practitioners also there are pressures for change. The US Department of Education, Office of Special Education Programs (2002) has recommended the elimination of discrepancy criteria from identification of learning disabilities and the use instead of **response-to-intervention** approaches using interventions that are supported by research.

Vellutino, Scanlon and Tanzman (1998) suggest that educational psychologists should shift the focus of their professional activities so as to place much greater emphasis on intervention and instruction, and much less emphasis on psychometric assessment. This will require that the educational psychologist 'broaden and/or update her or his knowledge base so as to learn more about the reading process and reading development vis a vis the cognitive, experiential and instructional factors that might influence such development, both positively and negatively' (Vellutino, et al, 1998: 392). Accordingly, the next section of this chapter presents a brief overview of key issues in reading instruction and development for normally developing readers and for children who experience difficulties in learning to read.

How is reading taught?

Over the last two centuries the issue of how best to teach children to read English has been a matter for considerable debate. This debate has sometimes become heated as can be seen from the magazine article in Focus box 6.1.

The balanced literacy approach illustrated in Focus box 6.1 represents a 'whole language' approach, where the emphasis is placed on contextual knowledge, using syntactic or semantic cues to identify a word, rather than features of the printed word. Popularized by Goodman (1967) and Smith (1978), reading was conceived of as a 'psycholinguistic guessing game' where features of a printed word were not seen as a primary source of hypotheses about its identity but were used to test

Focus 6.1

Extracts from: *Report on the Reading Wars, New York Magazine* http://nymag.com/news/features/16775/

A Is for Apple, B Is for Brawl

Why New York's Reading Wars are so contentious.

By Robert Kolker

Every morning, about twenty minutes or so before lunch, the eighteen children in Lauren Kolbeck's second-grade classroom are left to read quietly to themselves.

In a far corner of the room, a girl named Enami sits cross-legged on a moss-green rug, a floppy paperback in her hands. Her selection is from the *Henry and Mudge* series, about a boy and his dog. Tall and shy – she just turned 8 – Enami says she picked this book because, well, she likes dogs. With Kolbeck peering over her shoulder, Enami opens the book and starts reading aloud.

"On a sun day . . ."

It says *sunny day* in the book. But Enami's a little tentative. She hasn't read this one before.

"A man with a collar . . ."

The teacher has a suggestion. "Sometimes we look at the picture and figure out if it makes sense."

Enami eyes the drawing of a man walking a dog. She agrees *collar* doesn't seem right. After some discussion, it's decided that *collie* works better.

"A dog!" says Enami, satisfied.

She continues – and a page later she trips up on the word *disappeared*. She takes her best guess: "Stepped."

"Let's see if *that* makes sense," says Kolbeck.

Again, Enami checks the drawing: a man at the end of a street, turning a corner. Her eyes flash – "Disappeared!" And on she goes.

If throwing Enami into the deep end of the pool like this seems a little intense, that's pretty much the point. What's unusual about this lesson – and to its critics, flat wrong about it – is what's *not* happening. Enami and her seventeen classmates are not sitting in a row, repeating letter and pronunciation drills. They almost never are. There's not a textbook in sight, or, for that matter, in the whole school. Instead, they're learning by immersion, reading books of their own choosing, and when they mess up, which is often, they're told to keep going.

Balanced Literacy is rooted in an education philosophy known as whole language. Unlike traditional so-called phonics-based programs, in which kids repeat and memorize basic spelling and pronunciation rules before tackling an actual book, whole language operates on the presumption that breaking down words distracts kids, even discourages them, from growing up to become devoted readers. Instead, students in a Balanced Literacy program get their pick of books almost right away – real books, not *Dick and Jane* readers, with narratives that are meant to speak to what kids relate to, whether it's dogs or baseball or friendship or baby sisters. Over time, the theory goes, kids learn the technical aspects of reading – like contractions, or tricky letter combinations painlessly – almost by osmosis.

The reading wars, of course, aren't only about reading. Yes, reading skills matter tremendously to New York parents, whether they aim to get their children into Harvard or just to their age-appropriate reading level. But the Reading Wars are also about race and class. Everyone stands to gain from phonics, advocates say, but no one figures to benefit more than children from low-income families. Parents of children with *learning disabilities* say their children benefit similarly from phonics.

To phonics advocates, whole language is rooted in the worst liberal traditions: It's a freewheeling approach that lacks rigor and standards. Whole-language proponents, in turn, say phonics perpetuates authoritarian, patronizing "drill and kill" strategies that insult the art of teaching and turn kids into fifties-style robots, putting them off learning for life.

The issue in New York is that at the exact moment Balanced Literacy was made the cornerstone of the curriculum here, phonics scored several major victories in the Reading Wars. A National Institutes of Health–created commission of Ph.D.'s came down squarely on the side of phonics in a 2000 report, influencing the Bush administration to crack down – some say improperly, perhaps even scandalously – on non-phonics programs. And where hard science once had little to say about how various reading methods affected kids, a series of MRI studies done at Yale starting in the late nineties appeared to show that as many as one in every four children, regardless of class, race, or other demographic factors, needs direct instruction in basic skills before he can read. When kids with learning difficulties read with phonics, their brains light up on MRI scans like a Christmas tree. The conclusion, phonics advocates say, is clear: Kids need technical instruction in the basics before being immersed in the world of literature.

hypotheses generated from the grammatical context and the meaning of the passage. Even as a model of skilled reading, the assumptions of the 'psycholinguistic guessing game' approach were quickly found to lack empirical support. Skilled adult readers were only able to predict 25 per cent of the words in connected prose and prediction took longer than just looking at the word (Gough et al, 1983). Reading for meaning proved to be dependent on good word decoding skills, rather than the other way round (see Adams and Bruck, 1993).

A further assumption of the approach was that children and adults employ the same processes when reading, processes that utilize the neurological mechanisms underpinning spoken language. It was argued that through exposure to print and the use of semantic and syntactic cues in the context of meaningful stories, children would develop the knowledge required to decode print with minimal explicit teaching of letter–sound correspondences. These assumptions have been questioned from a cognitive neuroscience perspective:

> *Language is a human instinct, but written language is not. Language is found in all societies, present and past . . . All healthy children master their own language without lessons or corrections. When children are thrown together without a usable language, they invent one of their own. Compare all this with writing. Writing systems have been invented a small number of times in history . . . Until recently, most children never learned to read or write; even with today's universal education, many children struggle and fail. A group of children is no more likely to invent an alphabet than it is to invent the internal combustion engine. Children are wired for sound, but print is an optional accessory that must be painstakingly bolted on. This basic fact about human nature should be the starting point for any discussion of how to teach our children to read and write. (Pinker, 1997)*

The set of problems facing children learning to read is summarized by Snow and Juel (2005: 501):'the problem of the alphabetic principle, which requires

Activity 6.2

Re-read the article in Focus box 6.1 and make a note of any specific claims that purport to be drawn from the research literature. As you read the chapter, make a judgement on the accuracy of each of the claims made and, where you consider it necessary, reword it to improve its accuracy. Here is an example to get you started.

Claim: When kids with learning difficulties read with phonics, their brains light up on MRI scans like a Christmas tree.

Rephrasing:

learning how to segment speech into sounds represented by graphemes; the problem of English orthography, which requires going beyond simple phoneme-grapheme links to represent the morphemic, historical and etymological information preserved in the writing system; and the problem of comprehension which requires building a representation of textual and situational information'.

All of the major theories of reading development represent the solution of the first two of these problems as key achievements needed to move between qualitatively different stages or phases in the acquisition of word recognition skill (see Table 6.1). **Logographic** strategies involve the use of distinctive visual or contextual features to recognize words, alphabetic strategies focus on sound-spelling rules, and **orthographic** strategies on larger spelling patterns, especially morphemic units (as in 'sign', 'signal', 'signify').

The focus on sub-lexical (e.g. letter, syllable) elements apparent in the theories of early reading development in Table 6.1 parallels the findings of all the recent reviews and meta-analyses of the effectiveness of different methods for teaching reading. These have highlighted a need for explicit and systematic teaching of letter–sound correspondences in reading alongside a focus on reading for meaning (Snow and Juel, 2005). This has been interpreted by some as permissive of a haphazard eclecticism in selecting methods of teaching reading, an interpretation specifically denounced in the preface to at least one US report which has stressed that an integrated, coherent approach to literacy development is needed (National Reading Council, 1998).

A similar approach was taken in the UK when a national curriculum was introduced in 1989. The reading process was conceptualized as involving four strategies – or 'searchlights', sources of knowledge readers use to 'illuminate'

Proponents	Chall (1983)	Frith (1985)	Ehri (1992, 2002)	Stuart and Coltheart (1988)	Seymour and Duncan (2001)
Number of developmental periods	5	3	4	2	4
1. Pre-reading	Stage 0: Letters/book exposure	Logographic	Pre-alphabetic	↑	Pre-literacy
2. Early reading	Memory and contextual guessing		Partial alphabetic	Partial orthographic	Dual foundation
3. Decoding	Stage 1: Decoding, attending to letters/sounds	Alphabetic	Full alphabetic	Complete orthographic	Alphabetic Logographic
4. Fluent reading	Stage 2: Fluency, consolidation	Orthographic	Consolidated alphabetic, automaticity	↓	Orthographic Morphographic

Table 6.1 A schematic summary of different stage/phase theories of learning to read (Adapted from Ehri, 2005)

their processing: phonic (sounds and spelling) knowledge; grammatical knowledge; word recognition and graphic knowledge; and knowledge of context. However, reports from inspectors indicated that the statutory phonic component of the programme, increasingly identified as foundational, was often a neglected or a weak feature of the teaching. As a result a **national literacy strategy** was introduced in the UK in 1998. This strategy went beyond specifying what to teach and provided detailed guidance on how to teach it. There is certainly support for the view that an evidence-based approach to the teaching of reading may be necessary but not sufficient, and that how it is actually implemented in the classroom may also be very important (Taylor et al, 2000; Pressley et al, 2001).

More recently (Rose, 2006), the content of the literacy curriculum has been revised away from the 'searchlights' model of reading in favour of the 'simple' view of reading (Gough and Tunmer, 1986) where reading is seen as the product of single word decoding and language comprehension. It is now recommended that high-quality, systematic phonic work should be taught as the prime approach to decoding (reading) and encoding (spelling) words. What is more, a particular approach to teaching phonics, **synthetic phonics**, is endorsed.

The synthetic phonics approach is defined by Torgersen, Brooks and Hall (2006) as focusing on the phonemes associated with particular graphemes which are pronounced in isolation and blended together (synthesized). For example, children are taught to take a single syllable word such as *cat* apart into its three letters, pronounce a phoneme for each letter in turn /k, æ, t/, and blend the phonemes together to form a word. Synthetic phonics is contrasted with analytic phonics in which children analyse whole words to identify the common phoneme in a set of words. For example, teacher and pupils discuss how the following words are alike: *pat, park, push* and *pen*.

The Rose report (2006) has been criticized for basing the recommendation of synthetic phonics on insufficient evidence, for example by Wyse and Styles (2007), who cite the findings of systematic reviews from the USA and the UK in support of their criticisms. In the USA the National Reading Panel (2000) did not find evidence that teaching programmes focused on small units in words (phonemes) were any more effective than those focusing on larger units (onset-rime, e.g. sh-op, st-op, dr-op), or that synthetic approaches focused on blending were more effective than analytic approaches focused on word families. In the UK, Torgersen et al (2006) concluded that the weight of evidence was weak (only three randomized controlled trials were located) and no statistically significant difference in effectiveness was found between synthetic and analytic phonics instruction.

Do the same conclusions apply to young children at risk for reading failure?

A study by Hatcher, Hulme and Snowling (2004) suggests that they may not. Reception-year children (aged 4–5 years) were divided into four matched groups and randomly assigned to one of three experimental teaching conditions (delivered to groups of 10–15 children for three 10-minute sessions per week.):

- Reading with rhyme.

- Reading with phoneme.

- Reading with rhyme and phoneme.

- Reading – control condition where children were taught as a class, in groups and as individuals).

In each experimental condition there was a strong phonic component and the same amount of time was devoted to reading instruction. For normally developing children no differential effects of the different teaching programmes were found. However, for children identified as being at risk of reading failure, training in phoneme skills resulted in greater gains in phoneme awareness and in reading skills. These findings suggest that any reading programme that contains a highly structured phonic component is sufficient for most 4–5-year-old children to learn to read effectively, but for young children at risk of reading delay, additional training in phoneme awareness and linking phonemes with letters is required.

What intervention strategies are effective for children with dyslexia?

Compared with children who learn to read with ease, children who experience difficulties learning to read appear to need instruction that is more explicit, more intensive and more supportive, in terms both of motivating encouragement and cognitive structuring or scaffolding (Torgesen, 2002, 2005). Supportive evidence from a study by Torgesen et al (2001) is summarized in Figure 6.2. In this study two interventions were implemented with 9–10-year old children who had been receiving special education services for dyslexia for at least 16 months and whose reading attainments were at a 5–6-year age equivalent level. The children were randomly allocated to one of the interventions which provided *supportive* and *explicit* teaching on phonemic awareness and phonemic-based decoding strategies. The interventions, Auditory Discrimination in Depth and Embedded Phonics, differed in the proportion of time spent focusing on activities using single words (85 per cent vs 20 per cent), on building fluency with high frequency words (10 per cent vs 30 per cent), and reading words in meaningful context with teacher support (5 per cent vs 50 per cent). The interventions were both *intensive*, providing 67.5 hours of individual teaching in two 50-minute sessions each day for around 8 weeks.

From Figure 6.2 it can be seen that the programmes had very similar effects, producing large and lasting gains in reading attainment. The scores shown are standard scores which have a mean of 100 and standard deviation of 15, and allow a child's performance to be compared with others of their age. At the start of the study the children were scoring below 80 on average, placing them in the bottom 7 per cent of the population. This was despite having received special education services for the previous 16 months, during which they had made some improvements in their reading performance so that they had not fallen any further behind, but neither had they 'caught up' at all. Following the 8-week intervention the children were scoring close to 90 on average, a score which placed them above

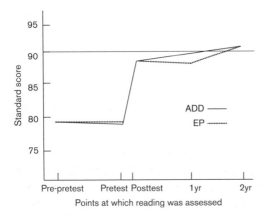

Figure 6.2 Standard reading scores before, during and after 67.5 hours of intensive intervention. ADD, auditory discrimination in depth; EP, embedded phonics.

Source: Torgesen et al, 2001.

30 per cent of children of their age, so they had caught up significantly with others of their age and were performing in the lower part of the average range (defined as within one standard deviation of the mean). An important caveat is that these are group averages; the interventions were not equally successful with all children. In addition, despite improvements in reading accuracy, reading fluency remained substantially below average, a common finding from intervention programmes for children with dyslexia (Torgesen, 2005).

What causes dyslexia?

Early researchers in the field characterized dyslexia as a visual processing problem: 'congenital word blindness' (Hinshelwood, 1900) or 'strephosymbolia' (twisted symbols) (Orton, 1925). Orton considered delayed establishment of hemispheric dominance responsible for failure to suppress mirror image alternatives, leading to confusions of 'b' and 'd', 'saw' and 'was', etc. These ideas held sway until the 1970–80s when careful experimental work showed that verbal mediation was implicated in the apparent visual difficulties, so that substituting a written for a verbal response could eliminate differences between normally developing readers and those with dyslexia (Vellutino, 1987). Instead it was suggested that dyslexia was a subtle language difficulty which appeared to involve difficulties with phonemic segmentation and **phonological** coding (representing and accessing the sound of a word as an aid to memory). It is argued that children with dyslexia form mental representations of the sounds of language that are poorly specified or 'fuzzy' which makes it difficult to develop an awareness of the internal sound structure of words and to learn letter–sound relationships (Snowling, 2000).

This understanding of dyslexia has since become established as pre-eminent. From a review of research on dyslexia over the past four decades, Vellutino et al (2004: 2) conclude:

The evidence suggests that inadequate facility in word identification due, in most cases, to more basic deficits in alphabetic coding is the basic cause of difficulties in learning to read. We next discuss hypothesized deficiencies in reading related cognitive abilities as underlying causes of deficiencies in component reading skills. The evidence in these areas suggests that, in most cases, phonological skills deficiencies associated with phonological coding deficits are the probable causes of the disorder rather than visual, semantic, or syntactic deficits, although reading difficulties in some children may be associated with general language deficits.

Almost identical conclusions are drawn by Ramus, White and Frith (2006: 27):

At the proximal level, almost everybody agrees that a phonological deficit is the direct underlying cause of most cases of dyslexia . . . At the distal level, the question is whether the phonological deficit is primary, or whether it is secondary to other cognitive, sensory or motor deficits. We argue that our results and the literature are consistent with the former, i.e. with the theory of a primary, specific phonological deficit.

The distinction between the **proximal** and **distal** levels is illustrated in Figure 6.3 which uses the **causal modelling framework** (Morton and Frith, 1995; Morton, 2004) to depict the primary phonological theory of dyslexia.

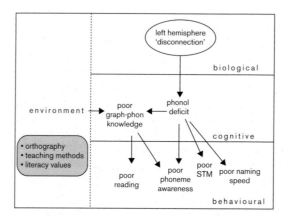

Figure 6.3 A causal model of dyslexia as the result of a phonological deficit

Source: Reproduced with permission, Frith, U. (1999). Paradoxes in the definition of dyslexia. Dyslexia, 5, 192–214. Copyright John Wiley & Sons Limited.

The causal modelling framework uses three levels of description to represent possible explanations of developmental problems: the biological, the cognitive and the behavioural. In addition, environmental factors can exert an influence at all three levels. Arrows are used to indicate hypothesized causal chains and in Figure 6.3 it can be seen that reading difficulties are hypothesized to be caused by a phonological deficit which disrupts the establishment of grapheme–phoneme (letter–sound) correspondences. However, in this case, at a more distant level of explanation, the hypothesized cognitive level difficulty links to an abnormality at the brain level in left perisylvian areas involved in phonology (Ramus, 2004). Other theories posit other distal causes. In the **cerebellar theory** of dyslexia (Nicolson and Fawcett, 1990), at a distal level the deficit in fluent automatic phonological skills is hypothesized to be caused by a timing/sequence deficit resulting from a cerebellar abnormality.

White et al (2006) tested the cerebellar and pure phonological hypotheses along with two further hypotheses:

- The **temporal processing** hypothesis (Tallal, 1980, 2004) which proposes a deficit in the processing of rapidly changing stimuli that impairs the ability to make fine discriminations between phonemes.

- The magnocellular hypothesis (Stein and Talcott, 1999) which proposes a deficit in the suppression of visual traces so that images of words persist for too long and exert partial masking effects.

Children with dyslexia and controls, aged 8–12 years, were compared on a range of measures and the clustering of difficulties examined for individual children. The article is followed by four commentaries, some from proponents of the theories challenged by the findings. Both methodology and interpretations are challenged in the commentaries which are subsequently responded to by the authors of the original paper. The sequence of papers relating to the White et al (2006) study offers an interesting demonstration of critical analysis and argument by leading researchers in the field.

White et al (2006) report multiple case study analysis as well as a between-group analysis. This is of particular interest given the challenges for educational psychologists of using findings from group studies to inform their work with individual children, which was highlighted as a theme in Chapter 1. Despite the weight of evidence supporting the phonological deficit approach, a sizeable minority of the children with dyslexia in the White et al (2006) study did not have a significant phonological deficit. Many of the children in that study had received specialist phonologically based intervention, which is likely to have improved their phonological skills. Phonological difficulties are usually found to be more prevalent (around 80 per cent) among children identified by educational psychologists as having specific reading difficulty/dyslexia but who have not received specialist intervention (Frederickson and Frith, 1998). Psychologists need to be aware of other possible causes of dyslexia if they are to be effective in working with the 20 per cent of children who do not show phonological impairments.

Other biological level information and hypotheses that can be recorded in the causal modelling framework include sensory or genetic factors. From their review of genetic research in dyslexia, Pennington and Olson (2005) note that there is a strong tendency for dyslexia to be inherited. Some progress has also been made in identifying the actual gene variants involved. However, the gene influences on dyslexia do not appear to be very specific as they are implicated in individual differences across the whole spectrum of reading skill and also influence disorders which often co-occur with dyslexia, such attention deficit hyperactivity disorder and speech sound disorder. Snowling, Muter and Carroll (2007) followed up at age 12–13 years 'at-risk' children born in families with a history of dyslexia, who had been studied longitudinally from age 3 years. Almost half the sample were classified as having significant reading and spelling problems (and emotional difficulties), while even those who did not meet the classification criteria did not read fluently. There was evidence of enduring literacy difficulties, with no evidence of catching up with normally achieving controls between ages 8 and 13. Although the at-risk children with and without significant literacy problems did not differ on measures of their family literacy environment, those who had significant problems read less themselves.

Can teaching methods cause dyslexia?

At the environmental level in Figure 6.3 'teaching methods' are shown as a possible influence. To what extent can it be said that methods of teaching reading cause dyslexia? Vellutino and Fletcher (2005) argue that because the acquisition of important reading sub-skills such as phonological awareness and letter–sound correspondences can be dependent on the type of teaching approach received (Foorman et al, 1998), it is important to establish that there has been adequate instruction before assuming that the cause of early reading difficulties is biological. Indeed, Vellutino et al (1996) reported findings which suggest that most early reading difficulties are related to deficiencies in early literacy experience and/or teaching and concluded that these are often a primary cause. They followed children longitudinally from 5 to 9 years of age. At age 6–7 years sub-samples of poor and normal readers were selected and randomly assigned to either a tutored group or a non-tutored 'contrast' group. Children in the tutored group were given daily tutoring (30 minutes per day) for between two and three school terms, depending on progress. Children in the non-tutored group received the normal special needs support available in their school.

At the start of the programme 9 per cent of 6–7-year-olds were found to have a reading test score below the 15th percentile and a significant IQ–achievement discrepancy. After a term and a half of individual tutoring for half an hour per day, only 1 per cent remained below the 15th centile (with a further 2 per cent below the 30th centile). Results on a battery of tests were interpreted as indicating that continuing reading difficulties were due primarily to basic deficits in phonological skills. IQ scores did not distinguish between poor readers who were easy and difficult to remediate whereas phonological skills (e.g. phoneme segmentation, rapid naming) did distinguish between and within these groups. Research Methods box 6.1 shows that there is now evidence of the impact of such interventions at the biological level.

The instruction received is one important environmental influence on dyslexia, the orthography of the language in which instruction occurs is another. Alphabetic writing systems demand high levels of phonological skills. Writing systems that do not use small speech sounds as the basis for written symbols, but instead use syllables, whole words or meanings, should present fewer difficulties for individuals with phonological problems. This is illustrated by the case study presented by Wydell and Butterworth (1999) of a dyslexic boy, bilingual in English and Japanese, who only showed reading and writing difficulties in English.

Research methods 6.1

Neuroscience and reading interventions – connecting brain and behaviour

Some recent studies with children have shown differences in measures of brain functioning between dyslexic and normally developing readers that ameliorate with improvements in word reading following intervention. For example, initial differences between normally developing readers and those with dyslexia were established by Simos et al (2000). They used **magnetic source imaging (MSI)**, which detects changes in magnetic fields surrounding neuronal electrical discharges, to describe the following sequence of activation when normally developing children read: occipital areas that support primary visual processing, followed by basal temporal areas in both hemispheres, followed by three areas in the left temporal and parietal areas of the left hemisphere (the superior temporal gyrus, Wernicke's area and the angular gyrus). By contrast, in children with dyslexia, in this final stage these areas are activated but in the right rather than the left hemisphere. It is unclear whether this different pattern reflects compensatory processing.

In a further study (Simos et al, 2002) when 8 children aged 7–17 years with severe dyslexia were given intensive (10 hours per week over 8 weeks) phonologically based instruction, reading accuracy scores rose into the average range and there was a significant increase in left hemisphere activation of those areas typically activated in normally developing readers. Consistent with the greater resistance to intervention of reading fluency, delays were apparent in these left hemisphere responses.

A further study provided evidence that normalizing changes in brain activity and adequate response to intervention were linked, but also that resistance to evidence-supported intervention was reflected in patterns of brain activity. Simos et al (2007) monitored spatiotemporal profiles of brain activity in 6–8-year-old children with dyslexia during a two-stage intensive intervention delivered to pairs of pupils. Stage 1 focused on phonological decoding skills for eight weeks (2 × 50 minute sessions/day) while stage 2 focused on rapid word recognition ability for a further 8 weeks (1 hour/day). The 15 children in this study had previously been identified as inadequate responders to reading instruction that was effective for most participants.

Clinically significant improvement in reading standard scores was noted in eight children who also showed 'normalizing' changes in their spatiotemporal profiles of regional brain activity (increased duration of activity in the left temporoparietal region and a shift in the relative timing of activity in temporoparietal and inferior frontal regions). Seven children who demonstrated 'compensatory' changes in brain activity (increased duration of activity in the right temporoparietal region and frontal areas, bilaterally) did not show an adequate response to intervention. A control group of normally developing readers did not show systematic changes in brain activity during the study which suggests that the changes observed were associated with the special programme and were not simply the result of developmental changes or of normal classroom teaching.

Alphabetic languages vary in the transparency of their orthographies (the consistency with which the written symbols map onto sounds). English is notoriously inconsistent and Seymour, Aro and Erskin (2003) found that the rate of literacy skills acquisition relates to the consistency of the orthography of the language. Correspondingly, Caravolas (2005) reviewed studies showing that children with dyslexia typically experience milder difficulties learning to read in more consistent languages, in particular with reading accuracy relative to reading fluency and spelling, and suggested that this reflected the lower levels of demand placed on phonological skills. Research study selection criteria for dyslexia in more **transparent orthographies** tend to centre on speed and fluency rather than error rate. Goswami (2005) has suggested that the failure of most studies to find differences between the efficacy of large versus small unit phonics instruction may reflect relative advantages of each instructional approach in dealing with the inconsistency of English and cautioned that generalization of research findings in English to other languages may not be valid.

Vellutino et al (2004: 18) describe dyslexia as a 'complex condition that depends on the dynamic interaction between certain innate susceptibilities as well as the home and school environments on the one hand, and the cultures in which children learn to read on the other'. They note that some transparent orthographies may aid learning to the point where the underlying difficulty is hidden, while others like English may aggravate the problem. There are clear parallels with reading instruction. It is possible to argue both that inadequate instruction or other experiential factors are responsible for the problems of many poor readers and that biological factors are important. This reflects developing understanding of the ways in which brain and environment interact in the process of learning to read.

Summary

- The definition of dyslexia is controversial. Central issues are the use of exclusionary or inclusionary criteria and the use of explanatory as well as descriptive elements.

- The IQ–achievement discrepancy approach to defining dyslexia, which was formerly influential in both research and practice, has been challenged on the grounds of validity, equity and utility. It is now recommended that response-to-intervention criteria are used instead in sample selection for research and decisions about eligibility for special provision.

- There has been hot debate over the best method for teaching reading. Psychological theory and research has supported explicit teaching of phonics for all children in the early stages of learning to read. For children at risk of reading failure and those with dyslexia, there is evidence that teaching needs to be more explicit, intensive and supportively structured.

- Intensive phonologically based intervention can produce significant improvements in the reading and related cognitive processes (notably phonological skills) of children with dyslexia. Findings from neuroscientific studies show that some differences between the brain function of children with dyslexia and normally developing readers can also be normalized by this kind of educational intervention.

- The overwhelming weight of evidence supports the phonological deficit theory of dyslexia. However, not all children with reading problems show phonological impairments, and other hypotheses for the difficulties experienced must be considered in these cases.

- Genetic influences on dyslexia and a strong familial incidence were identified.

- Environmental influences on the nature of the problems with reading that will be experienced include the language of instruction as well as the nature of the instruction received. It is concluded that dyslexia results from complex interactions between biologically based cognitive abilities and environmental demands and supports.

Key concepts and terms

Causal modelling framework
Cerebellar theory
Distal
Dyslexia
IQ–achievement discrepancy
Learning disabilities
Logographic
Magnetic source imaging

National literacy strategy
Orthographic
Phonological
Proximal
Response-to-intervention
Synthetic phonics
Temporal processing
Transparent orthographies

Sample essay titles

- Evaluate the strengths and weaknesses of two definitions of dyslexia.
- Produce a two-page leaflet for teachers entitled *Ensuring success and preventing failure in learning to read: Recommendations from psychological research*. Then write a critique of your leaflet evaluating the weight of evidence in support of each of your recommendations. (Alternatively, pair up with a partner and critique each other's leaflets).
- Poor reading instruction is the main cause of dyslexia and good reading instruction the most effective cure. Discuss.

Further reading

Books

Snow, C.E., and Juel, C. (2005). 'Teaching children to read: What we know about how to do it.' In: M.J. Snowling and C. Hulme (Eds), *The Science of Reading: a Handbook*. Oxford: Blackwell.

Torgesen, J.K. (2005). 'Recent discoveries on remedial interventions for children with dyslexia.' In: M.J. Snowling and C. Hulme (Eds), *The Science of Reading: A Handbook*. Oxford: Blackwell.

Journal articles

Frith, U. (1999). Paradoxes in the definition of dyslexia. *Dyslexia*, 5, 192–214.

Goswami, U. (2005). Synthetic phonics and learning to read: A cross-language perspective. *Educational Psychology in Practice*, 21, 273–282.

Ramus, F., White, S., and Frith, U. (2006). Weighing the evidence between competing theories of dyslexia. *Developmental Science*, 9, 265–269.

Simos, P.G., Fletcher, J.M., Sarkari, S., Billingsley, R.L., Denton, C., and Papanicolaou, A.C. (2007). Altering the brain circuits for reading through intervention: A magnetic source imaging study. *Neuropsychology*, 21, 485–496.

Stuebing, K.K., Fletcher, J.M., Le Doux, J.M., Lyon, G.R., Shaywitz, S.E., and Sheywitz, B.A. (2002). Validity of IQ-discrepancy classifications of reading disabilities: A meta-analysis. *American Educational Research Journal*, 39, 469–518.

Vellutino, F.R., Fletcher, J.M., Snowling, M.J., and Scanlon, D.M. (2004). Specific reading disability (dyslexia): what have we learned in the past four decades. *Journal of Child Psychology and Psychiatry*, 45, 2–40.

White, S., Milne, E., Rosen, S., Hansen, P., Swettenham, J., Frith, U., and Ramus, F. (2006). The role of sensory motor impairments in dyslexia: a multiple case study of dyslexic children. *Developmental Science*, 9, 237–255 [commentaries 256–257, 257–259, 259–262, 262–264].

7 Why does mathematics make so many people fearful?

Tony Cline

In this chapter you will consider how mathematics as a subject differs from other subjects in the school curriculum and will reflect on why that makes it intimidating for many students. As well as examining the impact of **maths anxiety** on learning, the chapter will outline how mathematical thinking and mathematical practices develop through childhood and will also examine how they are affected by cultural and linguistic diversity.

Learning outcomes

When you have completed this chapter you should be able to:

1. Identify key features of mathematics that lead to many people experiencing it as challenging.
2. Evaluate different accounts of how maths anxiety is thought to develop and how it may be addressed.
3. Outline key features of the development of mathematical thinking and mathematical practices during childhood.
4. Explain the significance that children's cultural background may have for their learning of mathematics and the development of any anxiety they may feel about mathematics.

The challenges of mathematics

Examine the statements in Activity box 7.1 that are shown against the letters that are in the words 'mathematics' and 'number'. These have been identified by Trujillo and Hadfield (1999) and Bibby (2002) as characterizing many people's image of maths lessons at school. The statements that are linked to other letters of the alphabet indicate reactions that are less often associated with mathematics in the literature.

Mathematical knowledge and mathematical reasoning are key tools that we use when thinking about how the world around us is organized. A person who is confident in the use of mathematics can deal with questions about quantity, about spatial and structural relationships, and about measurement and time. So

Activity 7.1

Which of the sentences below best describe school mathematics as you experienced it when you were at school and as you think of it now?

a) You need to learn a set of rules and procedures based on rules.
b) There is a fixed body of knowledge that cannot be questioned.
c) You learn through a variety of lively activities.
d) You sometimes get messy.
e) You are often asked a closed question and need to find the correct answer.
f) You have time to speculate and time to discuss important ideas.
g) It makes you more creative.
h) The teacher often works at a fast pace.
i) It makes you feel that you are being tested and judged.
j) It exercises your imagination.
k) It develops your empathy for other people who are different from yourself.
l) It makes you look around you with fresh eyes.
m) It makes you think logically.
n) There are lots of tricks you have to learn for how to do things.
o) Everyone in the class has an opinion, and every opinion counts.
p) You learn how to ask questions.
q) You learn to look at a situation from different perspectives.
r) It is efficient and requires you to be efficient.
s) You have to be neat in the way that you work, or you will make mistakes.

mathematical thinking is fundamental to other subjects both in the sciences and the humanities. As a school subject mathematics is important, a 'core' subject in the curriculum. At the same time it relies on the use of abstract concepts and rigorous logical reasoning. Its language is precise and has no redundancy. Each element in mathematical knowledge is related to every other element, and many of those elements can only be understood by following the sequence of assumptions behind them. So mathematics is not only important; it is also difficult. Perhaps that is why many people find it intimidating and some become anxious about mathematics tasks that they associate with school.

Early research showed that maths anxiety has a narrow focus: participants who had high scores on **general (trait) anxiety** questionnaires or on questionnaires about their general level of anxiety at school did not do markedly less well on mathematics achievement tests than controls, while people with high scores on a specific measure of maths anxiety did (Sepie and Keeling, 1978). Similarly Gierl and Bisanz (1995) analysed two kinds of feelings associated with maths anxiety:

■ *Mathematics test anxiety* – 'feelings of nervousness associated with past, present and future mathematical testing situations'.

- *Mathematics problem-solving anxiety* – 'feelings of nervousness associated with situations both in and out of school that require students to solve maths problems and use the solutions in some way'.

They found that, as children progressed through school between the ages of 9 and 12, maths test anxiety increasingly came to have a relatively greater impact on overall maths anxiety than anxiety about the task of tackling maths problems in itself. That suggests that, at least in the Canadian school system where that study took place, the regime of assessment at school may play a part in the evolution of maths anxiety.

But what are the initial causes of the problem? There has been a considerable research effort to identify the 'roots' of maths anxiety. It is salutary to bear in mind that the people studied by Trujillo and Hadfield (1999) and Bibby (2002), whose attributions were paraphrased in Activity box 7.1, were primary school teachers or trainee teachers. What kind of messages about mathematics as a school subject will they have communicated to their pupils? It has been suggested that teachers who have negative beliefs about mathematics may lay the foundation for a response of learned helplessness from their pupils. For example, Uusimaki and Nason (2004) interviewed a sample of 18 pre-service trainee primary school teachers in Eastern Australia who had expressed anxiety about maths in a large-scale survey questionnaire. Two-thirds of this group traced their negative beliefs about the subject back to their experience of it as children in primary school.

Most research on the causes and development of maths anxiety relies, as that study did, on retrospective questioning of older children and adults who are invited to look back and recall the roots of their negative feelings. Hypotheses have focused on environmental factors (such as negative school experiences), cognitive factors (such as mismatched learning styles) and personality factors (such as general self-esteem). This largely speculative theorizing about the causes of the anxiety has not contributed significantly to the development of strategies for overcoming the problem. Research on the *consequences* of maths anxiety has had much more influence. In order to understand the thinking that inspired much of that work it is necessary to review what is known about the development of mathematical thinking and mathematical practices through childhood. We will consider that topic before returning to the question of how people's anxieties and negative beliefs about mathematics can best be addressed.

The development of mathematical thinking and mathematical practices through childhood

Conceptual understanding and procedural knowledge

The language of mathematics involves symbols and diagrams that can be interpreted only by those who understand the conventions that govern them. When the symbols and conventions are fully understood together with the concepts that underpin them, information can be manipulated and communicated in a form that is concise, simple and transparent. All too often, however, pupils learn the symbols that are used in mathematics and the procedures for manipulating them but do not develop an understanding of what the symbols mean or why the procedures work. A child in this position might successfully use a carefully learned 'rule' to find the answer (198) to the sum:

$$792 \div 4 = ?$$

But they might complete the sum solely by knowing how to 'carry over' the remainder after dividing 7 in the hundreds column by 4 without understanding what transformation occurs when the remainder (3×100) is converted to a number (3) in the tens column. The effects of that lack of understanding may be seen in various ways: the child may make uncorrected errors that seem obviously mistaken to anyone who is following the logic of what is being done, and the child may be unable to apply the procedure for dividing large amounts to new numbers or to numbers in a different pattern or to numbers that are embedded in a word problem, such as:

If a team of four people won £792 in the Lottery and divided it equally amongst them, how much would be given to each person?

Figure 7.1 Conceptual understanding or procedural knowledge or both?
Source: Sally and Richard Greenhill/Alamy.

Procedural knowledge (knowing *how*) involves knowing the written language of mathematics (the system of symbols used to represent numbers such as '151' and mathematical operations such as '+' or '÷') and also the step-by-step prescriptions for manipulating numbers (such as rules and algorithms for addition and division). **Conceptual understanding** (knowing *why*) involves such processes as insight, discovery and the integration of different pieces of information (Baroody in Baroody and Dowker, 2003: Figure 1.2). This distinction between 'procedural knowledge' and 'conceptual understanding' has been very influential in mathematics education, and the terminology used to describe it has frequently changed. For example, Skemp (1976) outlined the differences he saw between 'relational understanding' ('knowing both what to do and why') and 'instrumental understanding' (which involves applying 'rules without reasons').

Skemp (1976: 25) illustrated his argument with a graphic example. 'When I went to stay in a certain town for the first time, I quickly learnt several particular routes. I learnt to get between where I was staying and the office of the colleague with whom I was working; between where I was staying and the university refectory where I ate; between my friend's office and the refectory; and two or three others. In brief, I learnt a limited number of fixed plans by which I could get from particular starting locations to particular goal locations.' Later, when he had some free time, he began to explore the town. At this stage he did not want to go anywhere specific, just to learn his way around. In the process he kept an eye open for whatever might be of interest. Now his goal was a different one – 'to construct in my mind a cognitive map of the town'. He pointed out that someone watching him might think he was engaged in more or less the same kind of activity at both stages. That was not the case. At one stage his goal was simply to get from one place to another, while later he was trying to build up his mental map of the town – a very different objective requiring a kind of thinking and a different kind of knowledge. Once he had a mental map of the area he could find his way anywhere. Before that he would get lost as soon as he left any of his familiar routes.

He argued that pupils who have an 'instrumental' understanding of mathematics will try to learn new plans so as to find their way 'from particular starting points (the data) to required finishing points (the answers to the questions)'. Each time they have to take a decision, they will have to hope that the plan will tell them where to go next. They will not be able to take a strategic decision about the route because they will not have an overview of the map of the town (the number system), and they will not be able to work it out for themselves. They will have to develop an ever-increasing number of fixed plans, each one of which will have a very limited range of application.

It has gradually become clear that this way of describing forms of mathematical knowledge does not offer a sound foundation for analysing what is known about children's learning processes. First, children often invent their own procedures, and a successful procedure needs at least some conceptual basis or underpinning. Second, some learning of new procedures is not driven by conceptual knowledge alone but instead draws directly on procedural instruction or procedural analogies. Baroody in Baroody and Dowker (2003: 26) described a framework comprising four aspects of proficiency in mathematics which is seen as providing a more adequate conceptualization of what children need to learn:

- *Conceptual understanding* . . . comprehension of maths concepts, operations, and relations

- *Computational fluency* . . . skill in computing efficiently (quickly and accurately), appropriately, and flexibly

- *Strategic mathematical thinking* . . . the ability to formulate, represent and solve mathematical problems ('strategic competence') and the capacity for logical thought, reflection, explanation and justification ('adaptive reasoning')

- *Productive disposition* . . . a habitual inclination to see mathematics as sensible, useful and worthwhile, coupled with a belief in diligence and one's efficacy.

Baroody argued that all of these elements are required for children to be effective in making use of their mathematical knowledge and to *want* to use it. He emphasized that the definition given here of **computational fluency** implies an expertise that is adaptive and is not just capable of being applied in a routine way to familiar problems. Those who study statistics as part of a course in psychology may like to reflect on how far their recent experience in this area of applied mathematics confirms or challenges Baroody's ideas.

The initial guidance for the National Curriculum in England and Wales adopted an approach to teaching that emphasized the broader goals of mathematics education of the kind envisaged by Baroody. However, Boaler (1998) showed that there were schools that continued to employ a much narrower, more tightly structured approach to mathematics teaching within the framework of that curriculum. If teachers value procedural knowledge above everything else (as they did, for example, in England in the nineteenth and early twentieth centuries), they tend to adopt repetitive drill methods based on behavioural principles such as associative learning. It is assumed that these methods will help students develop a confident grasp of the methods of calculation that they are required to learn. However, Boaler's evaluation demonstrated that pupils taught through a repetitive, 'drill' strategy disliked the subject more and were less able to apply their procedural knowledge to unfamiliar situations than pupils taught through what she described as a more open system.

What do these ideas and findings about the goals and outcomes of mathematics education have to do with maths anxiety? The connection is through the impact of the methods of teaching associated with different goals. Research into the impact of different methods of teaching is a difficult and controversial area of research in educational psychology. However, the study by Newstead (1998) that is featured in Research Methods box 7.1 illustrates the contribution that such research can make when the technical challenges that it presents are successfully overcome. Even so there are always limitations to the generalizability of such findings. Newstead acknowledged that larger samples than she had had would be needed in order to demonstrate clearer evidence of the relationship between teaching approach and types of anxiety needs. She also emphasized that her findings apply to young children and that the picture may be quite different with other age groups. For example, while a traditional approach appeared to exacerbate anxiety in children within the age group she studied, it may help to reduce maths anxiety in college students who have developed their negative feelings about maths when they were younger. Nonetheless, alongside Boaler's (1998) evidence, her work suggests that one element in a strategy to reduce the development of maths anxiety at school may be to review teaching methods and, in particular, to emphasize a broad range of learning goals in the subject along the lines of Baroody's (2003) framework.

Research methods 7.1

Newstead (1998) studied maths anxiety in a sample of 9–11-year-old pupils who were taught maths through 'traditional' or 'alternative' approaches in five mixed-sex primary schools in a 'relatively rural environment in the UK'. In a 'traditional' approach the pupils were taught standard, pencil-and-paper methods of computation through teacher demonstration followed by individual practice. The pupils had to practise and master the calculation methods first before they applied them to everyday situations in word sums. In Newstead's definition of an 'alternative' approach, on the other hand, 'pupils use and discuss their own strategies for solving word sums, which are used as the principal vehicle for learning. Solving non-routine problems and discussing strategies in small groups are of primary importance.' (p. 58) Careful checks were made to confirm whether or not each teacher was employing one of these approaches. The sample comprised 58 pupils learning mathematics through 'alternative' methods with two teachers and 113 pupils learning the subject from four teachers through 'traditional' methods.

Each pupil was given a questionnaire about maths anxiety. To illustrate the content of the questionnaire, the items which elicited the most anxious responses involved the teacher asking the pupil questions and division with big numbers, while the items which elicited the least anxious responses involved everyday situations such as deciding which cool drink is cheaper in a shop and working out what time it would be 25 minutes from now.

A factor analysis of the scores on this questionnaire indicated that two meaningful factors could be extracted from the results – a factor that was mainly concerned with doing actual sums and working with numbers (e.g. adding 97 + 45 on paper, working out the change from £5 after spending £3.87) and a factor that covered more social or public aspects of doing mathematics (e.g. the teacher asking questions about how much one knows about maths, having a classmate finish first). There were no significant differences between age groups or between boys and girls on the overall anxiety score, but pupils taught through a traditional approach showed significantly higher anxiety overall than those taught through an alternative approach ($p < 0.05$). When the factor profile was examined, it was found that the traditionally taught group had significantly higher scores than the alternative group on the social anxiety factor but not on the general sum/number factor.

Cognitive processing and maths anxiety

Cognitive psychology offers a quite different approach to studying maths anxiety. Ashcraft, Kirk and Hopko (1998) showed that students with high scores for maths anxiety obtained lower scores on a maths achievement test. But when they analysed the results on the achievement test in greater detail, they found that there were no maths anxiety effects in the easier section of the test that comprised arithmetic problems with whole numbers. Anxiety effects were only found when the items became more difficult (e.g. with mixed fractions such as 'ten and a quarter plus seven and two thirds'). In other studies the team highlighted a particular difference between groups with high and low maths anxiety: those in the 'high' group took a much longer time to complete somewhat difficult arithmetic problems. 'Our interpretation was that carrying, or any procedural aspect of arithmetic, might place a heavy demand on **working memory**, the system for conscious, effortful mental processing' (Ashcraft, 2002: 183).

In further work Ashcraft and Kirk (2001) employed a **dual-task procedure**. This involved asking participants to do mental maths, the primary task, while simultaneously remembering random letters, a secondary task that taxes working memory. Before each addition problem they were presented with either two letters (the simpler level of interference) or six letters (the more challenging level of interference). After they gave the answer to the problem, they were asked to recall the letters in order. The research team anticipated that, as the secondary task became more difficult, performance on the primary task would deteriorate in either speed or accuracy. They found that, when the addition problem involved carrying, errors increased substantially more for participants with high maths anxiety than for those with low anxiety (Ashcraft and Kirk, 2001: Experiment 2). This effect was magnified when the secondary task involved six letters. These results were interpreted in terms of processing efficiency theory (Eysenck and Calvo, 1992). This states that anxiety disrupts the performance of a task because those who experience it give attention to their **intrusive thoughts** and feelings rather than to the task they are supposed to be completing. These intrusive thoughts impact on their effectiveness in maths to the degree that the maths task depends on working memory. They concluded that this might explain why participants with high anxiety do as well as less anxious individuals on simple maths tasks but show a marked decrement in performance with more difficult items.

Cognitive abilities associated with proficiency in mathematics

Above, proficiency in mathematics was defined by examining the outcomes of learning. This section focuses on an approach that derives from a quite different tradition of psychological research – the **psychometric analysis** of cognitive abilities. The key questions that are asked (Carroll, 1996) are:

■ What cognitive abilities are required for effective mathematical thinking?

■ How do these abilities support the performance of mathematical tasks?

In Activity box 7.2 consider which of the abilities listed in the top half of the box are likely to be involved when a person solves the problems that are listed in the bottom half.

Activity 7.2

Here is a list of some of the cognitive abilities that have been associated with proficiency in mathematics (Carroll, 1996; Hegarty and Kozhevnikov, 1999; Baroody in Baroody and Dowker, 2003):

a) Oral language comprehension – ability to understand short sentences in real-life contexts.
b) Phonological short-term memory – ability to manage immediate serial recall of lists of monosyllabic nonsense words (non-words).
c) Pictorial imagery – ability to construct vivid and detailed visual images.
d) Procedural knowledge relating to the manipulation of numbers.
e) Reading comprehension – ability to answer questions about the meaning and implications of short pieces of text.
f) Reading decoding – ability to read aloud short passages of text fluently and accurately.
g) Schematic imagery – ability to represent the spatial relationships between objects and imagine spatial transformations.
h) Long-term verbal memory – ability to retain linguistic information over time.

Examine the list of mathematics problems given below, which are all taken from the original framework for the National Numeracy Framework in England where they illustrate the outcomes expected of pupils aged 8–11 (DfEE, 1999a). Which of the abilities (a)–(h) do you think is likely to be involved when a person solves each of these problems?

1. The perimeter of a square is 274 cm. What is the length of each side?
2. Every day a machine makes 100,000 paper clips which go into boxes. A full box has 120 paper clips. How many full boxes can be made from 100,000 paper clips?
3. Calculate 24% of 525.
4. Find two consecutive numbers with a product of 182.
5. (i) Δ (ii) ΔΔΔ (iii) ΔΔΔΔΔ The triangles represent counters which make up a number sequence. Calculate how many counters there will be in the 6th number and in the 20th number, and write a formula for the number of counters in the nth number in the sequence.
6. Count all the rectangles in this diagram:

We expect that you will decide, as you examine the question carefully, that most of the skills and abilities that are listed in the top half of the box are required for all of the six tasks to a greater or lesser degree. But there are probably one (or perhaps two) items that you will have decided are not important for those tasks. The first item that is not needed is pictorial imagery – the ability to construct visual images. Hegarty and Kozhevnikov (1999) showed that this was used less than schematic imagery by 11–13-year-old boys solving maths problems – a result that was subsequently replicated with a sample of students of the same age in the USA, including a group with learning disabilities (van Garderen and Montague, 2003).

There is a second item that you may possibly have identified as relatively less important than the others for solving the mathematical problems in the box – phonological short-term memory. This is a key component of Baddeley's model of working memory – the limited capacity storage system that is assumed to be responsible for manipulating and storing information during the performance of cognitive tasks (Baddeley and Hitch, 1974). The phonological loop has often been implicated in mathematical tasks along with the other components of working memory, but some studies have suggested that it is not so important in the mathematics learning of young children and only comes to play a significant role after the age of 7–8 (D'Amico and Guarnera, 2005; Holmes and Adams, 2006). So, if you did identify phonological short-term memory as less important than the other abilities, you would have been correct for younger children but not for those of an age to tackle the National Curriculum tasks set out in Activity box 7.2.

Perhaps one reason why some people do less well in school mathematics and are more anxious about it is that their profile of cognitive abilities has strengths in areas that do not contribute significantly to maths performance and weaknesses in areas that are psychometrically crucial for it. This idea has been used to explain group differences such as those between males and females. It used to be claimed that males do consistently better than females in mathematics, but that is not the case (Gallagher and Kaufmann, 2005). However, there are aspects of the subject where they do have greater success. For example, boys and men obtain higher scores than girls and women on some spatial tests, such as a test of the ability to visualize shapes and motion in three dimensions – an ability that is crucial to some forms of mathematical problem solving (Gallagher and Kaufmann, 2005). In addition, there is evidence that girls and women report anxiety about maths more often than boys and men do (Pajares and Kranzler, 1995; Osborne, 2001). Are the two findings linked? Steele (1997) has argued that the 'underperformance' of girls and women in what is treated by society as a traditionally male domain is due to 'stereotype threat'. Where negative stereotypes about a group are widely held, members of the group can fear being reduced to that stereotype. 'For those who identify with the domain to which the stereotype is relevant, this predicament can be self-threatening' (Steele, 1997: 614). Thus, while most students will experience some anxiety when taking a maths test, those who belong to groups with a negative stereotype will feel that more acutely because they will anticipate the possibility of confirming the **negative group stereotype**. Steele argued that that could increase their anxiety with the effect of making them do less well than they might otherwise have done.

Other researchers have challenged the assertion that women are more anxious about mathematics than men. For example, Ashcraft (2002) suggested that an artefact may have influenced the survey findings: women are more willing to disclose personal attitudes generally so that men who are equally anxious about the subject may not so readily acknowledge it in a survey. Perhaps too any **gender differences** in reactions to mathematics reflect more general gender differences in interests in dealing with people and living things (believed to be stronger in women) and interests in dealing with abstractions and non-living things (believed to be stronger in men). Jacobs et al (2005) showed that parental beliefs and attitudes might be a factor in sex differences in interest in mathematics. But is this because the parents are reacting to different interests shown by girls and boys, or are they themselves behaving in a way that leads to these group differences? The data that they report do not make it possible to decide between these alternative possible explanations. It is clear that the overall picture is very complicated, and a psychometric analysis of group differences in mathematics abilities on its own offers only a partial account of these phenomena. If we are to fully understand maths anxiety, we need to appreciate how social expectations and conventions influence the way maths is perceived by different groups in society.

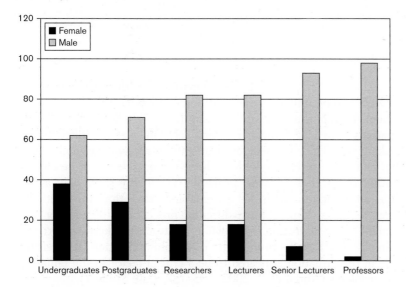

Figure 7.2 Gender of mathematics students and staff in UK universities (1997–98).

Source: Women in Mathematics Committee of the London Mathematical Society.

Mathematics in its cultural context

Mathematics is often seen as a universal language because it follows standard structural rules and refers to universal concepts in abstract terms. But, as we have seen, it is not possible to ignore the fact that mathematics is learned and practised in social settings. The ways in which people represent mathematical problems and the procedures that they use to tackle them will differ from one cultural context to another. For example, imagine that two baskets each contain three chickens. A primary school child in the UK would probably use their knowledge of the multiplication tables to calculate that there are six chickens altogether. In a classic study Gay and Cole (1967) asked a sample of members of the Kpelle, an indigenous group in Liberia, about this. They reported that the participants 'would either count 3 two times on their fingers or make two groups of three pebbles and count them' (Nunes, 2004: 13). A series of studies in different countries followed, demonstrating that young people could carry out complex mathematical tasks in an everyday context employing local methods that did not reflect what they were taught in school. Examples included children in Brazil calculating change in a street market (Nunes et al, 1993) and the size of an irregular sugar cane field (Abreu, 1995).

Home mathematics and school mathematics

In a multicultural society, children are likely to be exposed to different versions of mathematics as they move between home and school. How they negotiate the transition from one to another will be influenced by how their parents and teachers represent the value of each version. Thus Abreu and Cline (2003) reported that some immigrant parents taught their children multiplication tables by rote at home at a time when they were not being taught them in this way at school. The parents felt that otherwise their children would not be on the same wavelength as cousins and other members of the extended family 'back home'.

Children may become anxious about **school maths** when they perceive a large gap between what is represented as maths at home and what they are required to learn at school. Thus in the same study, Kashif (aged 7), who was born in this country to parents who had come here from Pakistan, was described by his teacher as lacking confidence in the subject in spite of receiving a good deal of help at home. During an interview with Kashif it became clear that he did not think his mother or sister did maths 'properly', i.e. in the same way as the teacher, while an interview with his parents indicated that they did not appreciate that requiring him to learn different procedures for addition and subtraction might cause confusion. Meanwhile his teacher acknowledged that she had not 'really met Kashif's mum'. The poor communication between the various people in this situation appeared to be a crucial factor in the failure to overcome the problems (Abreu et al, 2002: 135–138, Case Study 1).

Cross-cultural studies of mathematics learning

A series of international studies of attainment in mathematics have shown substantial differences between the standards achieved by children in different countries (e.g. OECD, 2003). One finding that has stimulated a great deal of discussion and exploratory research is that children in some Asian countries (specifically China, Japan and Korea) consistently outperform children from the USA, the UK and western Europe. Some have suggested that these national differences may arise because of differences in teaching methods (Naito and Miura, 2001), but a study that compared children in New York with children in Beijing within a month of their entering first grade showed that substantial group differences were already evident even before formal teaching had got under way (Zhou et al, 2005). It appears that the later differences between the groups cannot simply arise from differences in school teaching.

An alternative explanation focuses on differences in the way numbers are expressed in different languages (see Focus box 7.1). This idea has stimulated a great deal of research. Researchers suggested that many problems arise in some western languages because of the irregular way in which the decimal system is represented in words. They were able to show that children in countries where the language represented the number system transparently were particularly advantaged in tasks that involved judgements about place value (Miura, 1987).

Focus 7.1

Representation of numbers in various languages

	English	French	Chinese and Japanese
4	Four	Quatre	(Four)
9	Nine	Neuf	(Nine)
10	Ten	Dix	(One ten)
11	Eleven	Onze	(Ten one)
12	Twelve	Douze	(Ten two)
19	Nineteen	Dix-neuf	(Ten nine)
20	Twenty	Vingt	(Two ten)
21	Twenty-one	Vingt-et-un	(Two ten one)
22	Twenty-two	Vingt-deux	(Two ten two)
29	Twenty-nine	Vingt-neuf	(Two ten nine)
30	Thirty	Trente	(Three ten)
31	Thirty-one	Trente-et-un	(Three ten one)
89	Eighty-nine	Quatre-vingt-neuf	(Eight ten nine)
90	Ninety	Quatre-vingt-dix	(Nine ten)
91	Ninety-one	Quatre-vingt-onze	(Nine ten one)

However, it may be that too much emphasis has been placed on the language factor by some researchers. Cheng and Chan (2005) studied the detailed strategies that were used by a sample of 117 pre-school children in Hong Kong (aged 5.7–6.0) when tackling simple addition and subtraction problems. They found that this group of children very often relied on basic strategies such as finger counting and column counting, strategies that do not require an understanding of the base-10 system and place value. Their performance declined markedly when the sum involved that kind of understanding. This suggested that, if the Chinese number-naming system did give them some advantages, it just helped them with simple mechanistic counting of low numbers and did not benefit them in terms of an improved conceptual understanding of the number system and place value. In contrast to Zhou et al (2005) who were cited above, Cheng and Chan emphasized that many pre-schools in Hong Kong teach formal addition and subtraction the year before children enter primary school. Although they obtained more correct answers, this was not because they used more sophisticated or more mature strategies and 'may simply reflect Chinese students' more frequent and earlier practice with counting skills' (Cheng and Chan, 2005: 190).

Research methods 7.2

Cheng and Chan (2005) did not just examine the children's overall performance but also studied the detailed strategies that they employed to solve the problems and the errors they made. Valuable as this was, their research has a serious limitation: they considered only children who had been exposed to the number system in the Chinese language. Can you suggest how a study could be designed to overcome this limitation?

If children do learn more quickly when they use a language that represents the number system in a regular way, is it simply because mathematics is easier in such languages? It could be suggested that anxiety about the handling of an unpredictable vocabulary might be a mediating factor that makes learning maths even more difficult in these circumstances.

- Can you suggest a hypothesis that links language differences in the language used for the number system, the mathematics performance of school pupils and maths anxiety?
- Can you also suggest how your hypothesis could be investigated by a psychology researcher?

Conclusion: Addressing the problem of maths anxiety

If maths anxiety is thought of as a personal phobia, it is likely that the treatment will be a psychologically based intervention with the individual who is anxious, such as systematic desensitization. But if it is considered that anxieties develop because of the way the subject is taught, or the way in which language represents the number system, or if anxieties are associated with only some aspects of the subject and not others, it seems possible to address the problem not by pathologizing the individual learner and intervening with them personally but by adjusting how the subject is taught or presented to them. As in some other chapters in this book, this one has started with a problem that appears to be located at the individual level and has shown how the perspective of Educational Psychology now broadens out from that level and takes full account of the intellectual, social and cultural context in which the individual encounters mathematics. But a full account of the problem will not only adopt that broader perspective, it will also focus in on the level of cognitive processing. As we saw above, adjusting the burden that a mathematics task places on working memory can reduce the impact of maths anxiety on performance.

Summary

- Many people find mathematics intimidating at school, and some become anxious about it. There is some evidence that the regime of assessment at school may play a part in the evolution of maths anxiety.

- Research on the causes and development of maths anxiety that relied on retrospective questioning of older children and adults led to largely speculative theorizing about the causes of the anxiety and did not contribute significantly to the development of strategies for overcoming the problem.

- One element in a strategy to reduce the development of maths anxiety at school may be to review teaching methods and, in particular, to emphasize a broad range of learning goals in the subject.

- There is evidence that anxiety disrupts cognitive processing in more difficult maths tasks more than it does in easier tasks. This may be because intrusive thoughts impact on anxious participants' effectiveness in maths to the degree that the maths task depends on working memory.

- A psychometric analysis of group differences in mathematics abilities on its own offers only a partial account of these differences.

- As the complex relationship between gender and maths anxiety illustrates, a full account of maths anxiety must take account of the influence of social expectations and conventions on the ways in which maths is perceived by different groups in society.

- Mathematics is often seen as a universal language because it follows standard structural rules and refers to universal concepts in abstract terms. But it is not possible to ignore the fact that mathematics is learned and practised in social settings. The ways in which people represent mathematical problems and the procedures that they use to tackle them will differ from one cultural context to another.

- In a multicultural society, children may be exposed to different versions of mathematics as they move between home and school and may become anxious about school maths when they perceive a large gap between what is represented as maths at home and what they are required to learn at school.

- Research has not confirmed suggestions that international differences in standards of attainment in maths may be caused by differences in the way that the number system is represented in different languages.

- Thus the perspective of Educational Psychology on maths anxiety takes account not only of patterns of cognitive processing at the individual level but also of the intellectual, social and cultural contexts in which the individual encounters mathematics.

Key concepts and terms

Computational fluency
Conceptual understanding
Dual-task procedure
Gender differences
General (trait) anxiety
'Home mathematics'
Intrusive thoughts

Maths anxiety
Negative group stereotype
Procedural knowledge
Psychometric analysis
'School maths'
Working memory

Sample essay titles

- The Head of the Maths Department in a large secondary school has asked your advice as a psychologist on how to reduce the incidence of anxiety in maths lessons. Outline the advice you would give them and explain your reasons for it.
- What part does anxiety play in gender differences in mathematics attainment at school?
- What psychological processes appear to be involved when anxiety disrupts mathematics performance?
- What would you expect to be the implications for educational psychologists of cultural variation in mathematical language and practices?

Further reading

Books

Baroody, A.J., and Dowker, A. (Eds) (2003). *The Development of Arithmetic Concepts and Skills: Constructing Adaptive Expertise*. London: Lawrence Erlbaum Associates.

Gallagher, A.M., and Kaufman, J.C. (Eds) (2005). *Gender Differences in Mathematics: an Integrative Psychological Approach.* Cambridge, Cambridge University Press.

Journal article

Ashcraft, M.H. (2002). Math anxiety: personal, educational, and cognitive consequences. *Current Directions in Psychological Science*, 11, 181–185.

2 | Social, emotional and behavioural issues in school

8 Educating children with autism

What use is psychological theory and research?

Norah Frederickson

In this chapter you will learn about some of the challenges teachers face in educating children with **autism**. We begin by asking 'What is autism?', describing and illustrating key characteristics of autism and discussing associated difficulties and strengths. We then consider what is currently known about what causes autism, looking briefly at some controversies surrounding **prevalence** and diagnosis in particular. Recognizing the crucial role of cognitive level explanations in autism, three prominent cognitive theories of autism are reviewed: **theory of mind**, **executive dysfunction** and **central coherence**. Finally, we examine the significant role that psychological theory and research has played in developing approaches to the education of children who have autism. Two distinct strands of influence are identified, one that draws on behavioural psychology and takes no specific account of diagnostic features of autism, and one that draws directly on cognitive theories of autism. Examples of associated intervention programmes are described, together with ethical and methodological issues relating to their implementation and evaluation.

Learning outcomes

When you have completed this chapter you should be able to:

1. Describe the triad of impairments that characterizes autistic spectrum disorders.
2. Explain the principal cognitive theories of autism and the research designs that have been used to investigate them.
3. Evaluate the theoretical and research bases of educational approaches for children with autistic spectrum disorders.

What is autism?

Autism was first described by Kanner, an American psychiatrist in 1943, through the presentation of a number of case studies of children who shared certain characteristics: 'autistic aloneness' and 'desire for sameness'. In addition Kanner identified 'islets of ability' in some of these children, such as phenomenal memory for poems or names and precise recall of complex patterns. The difficulties experienced by children with autism were systematically investigated across a whole population of children by Wing and Gould (1979) and characterized as a 'triad of impairments': in reciprocal social interaction, verbal and non-verbal communication and imagination. The major international diagnostic classification systems, DSM-IV-TR (American Psychiatric Association, 2000) and ICD-10 (World Health Organization, 1995), identify the following diagnostic indicators for autism:

1. Qualitative abnormalities in reciprocal social interaction:
   Inadequate use of non-verbal behaviours to regulate social interaction
   Failure to develop age-appropriate peer relationships
   Lack of social or emotional reciprocity
   Little sharing of enjoyment, achievement or interests with others.
2. Qualitative abnormalities in communication:
   Delayed or absent development of language
   Difficulty initiating or sustaining conversation
   Repetitive, unusual or stereotyped use of language
   Lack of age-appropriate pretend or socially imitative play.
3. Restricted, repetitive behaviours, activities or interests:
   Interests that are extremely narrow, intense or unusual
   Unreasonable insistence on sameness and following specific routines or rituals
   Stereotyped and repetitive motor mannerisms
   Preoccupation with parts of objects.

Since the 1990s the classification systems have also applied these criteria in defining **Asperger's syndrome**, a disorder named after the Austrian paediatrician who first described it in 1944. As with autism, abnormalities in social interaction and restricted, repetitive behaviours are present. However, a diagnosis of Asperger's syndrome does not require that the child show early abnormalities in communication. In recent years the validity of drawing a categorical distinction between Asperger's syndrome and high-functioning autism has increasingly been questioned. As they grow older, children with these diagnoses become increasingly difficult to distinguish on the basis of their behaviour, their performance on neuropsychological assessments and the educational outcomes they achieve (Ozonoff and Griffith, 2000; Ozonoff et al, 2000). Accordingly, a dimensional approach involving a continuum of 'autistic propensity' (Rutter, 1999) has gained acceptance and the term **'autistic spectrum disorders'** (ASD) is increasingly used (Ozonoff and Rogers, 2003).

Autism: Other difficulties and strengths

Many studies that have been conducted with children attending clinics have reported that approximately 75 per cent of children with ASD also have moderate or severe learning difficulties (IQ scores below 70). However, more recent population-wide studies have reported lower percentages, for example 56 per cent for children with broadly defined autism and Asperger's syndrome, but 73 per cent for strictly defined autism (Baird et al, 2006). A consistent finding is

Activity 8.1

Interview with class teacher of Alex, aged 6 years 6 months (adapted from Dunsmuir and Frederickson, 2005)

Read the following description of Alex and identify which of the indicators of autistic spectrum disorder are present. Make a note of the evidence in support of each of your diagnostic decisions. Make a note also of any other behaviours the class teacher identifies as unusual that are not listed in the diagnostic indicators.

Alex has recently been diagnosed with Asperger Syndrome. He has a wide vocabulary. However his use of language tends to focus on factual information and areas of special interest, the grammar and syntax being reminiscent of stilted adult language rather than that of a young boy. He does not take turns well in conversation, tending to speak on his own terms about subjects of interest to him, usually dinosaurs or buses – he knows all the bus routes and route numbers in his area. He does not respond well to group directions, he does not understand in the same way as other children, he takes things more literally. For example, if you say 'sit down', he will sit down where he is. You need to say 'go to table 4 and sit down on a chair'.

His social interactions are on his own terms. Sometimes he's oblivious to the other children, and then at other times he wants to have some kind of interaction but the interaction is totally inappropriate, so if he's sitting on the floor he will grab another child and pull the child to him, so that that child is sitting near him because that's the way he sees having a friend sitting by him. He will also grab equipment he wants rather than ask for it. If he wants another child's attention he will grab them and physically try to get them to do as he wants, rather than talk to them. He can become distressed if others do not conform to his expectations or understand what he wants.

Alex finds PE difficult and can become particularly challenging in his behaviour, shrieking and screaming so that he has to be taken out of the hall. In the classroom he will only do a written task if he can do it on a whiteboard, he will not use a pencil and write on paper. He'll start the task and the first sentence will be one that he's been asked to do and then it will deteriorate and he'll just end up writing lists, such as the names of the children in his class, bus numbers or the names of countries. He likes all sorts of lists, particularly the names of people, so he can tell you the full name of every child in the class, and some of the children have got four or five names, and the spelling will be correct – this is really amazing!

that ASD is more common in males, with a ratio of 3 or 4:1 typically reported and proportionally more boys at higher IQ levels. While global IQ scores have been found to be predictive of progress, the profile of sub-test scores obtained by children with ASD is often uneven.

In reviewing findings obtained with the Wechsler Intelligence Scale for Children, Lincoln, Allen and Kilman (1995) report that attempts to identify relative strengths based on Performance or Verbal IQ scales have not produced consistent results. However, more consistent findings have been obtained from group studies at the level of individual subtests. Children with ASD often show relatively poorer performance on subtests requiring common sense social reasoning, such as the Comprehension sub-test which contains questions of the type 'What should you do if a friend lends you a toy and you accidentally break it?'. By contrast they can show as good or better performance than normally developing controls on the Block Design subtest, a test of spatial ability where cubes are arranged to match a pattern. Around 10 per cent of children with ASD also show some special talents, despite generally low intelligence. These 'savant' skills may be in a range of areas such as drawing, playing an instrument, calculating and being able to give the day of the week for any date in the calendar (Hermelin, 2001).

Unusual sensory responses have been frequently reported in children with ASD (Baranek, 2002). These may include hypo- or hyper-sensitivity, or unusual responses to sensory stimuli of various kinds, preoccupations with the sensory features of objects or perceptual processing problems. Although there are individual differences, auditory processing problems are often noted while visual-spatial processing tends to be identified as an area of relative strength. There are conflicting reports on the extent of motor skills difficulties in ASD and it is likely that considerable variability exists. It is suggested also that in some cases motor planning deficits, involving motivational aspects or slower movement preparation, may be mistaken for general clumsiness.

What causes autism?

It is now well established that autism is a neurodevelopmental disorder with a biological basis in which genetic factors are strongly implicated (Medical Research Council, 2001). Hereditability estimates greater than 0.90 have been obtained from twin studies where concordance rates of 60 per cent for monozygotic twins compared with 5 per cent for dizygotic pairs are reported. However, other factors must also be influential as there are substantial differences in the severity with which even monozygotic twins are affected, with as much as 50 point IQ differences between them being reported (Rutter, 1999). Evidence of structural and functional differences in the brains of individuals with autism comes from a range of studies (Baron-Cohen et al, 1999; see Frith, 2003, for a review).

One puzzle is the rapid increase in prevalence that has been reported, as this would not be expected in a biologically based disorder that is strongly genetically influenced. This does not appear to be explained solely by the introduction of broader classification criteria. For example, an occurrence rate of 4–5 per 10,000 was reported for strictly defined autism by Wing and Gould in 1979 while Baird et al in 2006 reported the prevalence of strictly defined autism as 39 per 10,000, with 116 per 10,000 for all autistic spectrum disorders. It has been argued that in addition to broader classification systems, increased awareness among practitioners, better identification and more sensitive assessment instruments could all have contributed to the increase (Wing and Potter, 2002). Suggestions that the measles, mumps and rubella (MMR) vaccination might be responsible have not been supported as no evidence has been found of changes in incidence of ASD following the introduction of the MMR vaccine or of increased incidence in vaccinated as opposed to unvaccinated children (Fombonne and Chakrabarti, 2001; Taylor et al, 2002).

It has been proposed that environmental risk factors may interact with genetic susceptibility involving several different genes to trigger ASD or affect the severity of its manifestation. However, both the specific genes and the environmental risk factors have yet to be identified. Although prevalence has increased overall, patterns across samples are consistent in indicating a biological and strongly genetic basis. For example, prevalence does not differ significantly between different geographical locations, ethnic groups or socio-economic status levels (Dyches et al, 2001).

Causation and cognition

So far we have considered the behaviours that lead to a diagnosis of autism and some possible biological causes in terms of changes to brain structure and function resulting from more fundamental biological (genetic) influences and from possible environmental influences. A small number of educational psychologists adhere to a strong behavioural position which holds that one need not go beyond the behaviour and environmental contingencies affecting it in understanding the functioning of children with autism and devising programmes to teach new behaviour. However, most would agree with Morton (2004) that cognitive variables have a crucial explanatory role in autism and other developmental disorders, mediating between the biological and behavioural levels of explanation. Currently, there are three prominent cognitive theories of autism, involving theory of mind, executive dysfunction and central coherence.

Theory of mind

Baron-Cohen, Leslie and Frith (1985) suggested that many of the characteristics of autism stem from an impairment in the ability to 'mind-read' or attribute mental states to other people in order to predict their behaviour. This **mentalizing** ability allows immediate implicit attribution of beliefs and motives to others. In order to test children's understanding of other's beliefs about a situation, as distinct from their understanding of the physical situation as such, Wimmer and Perner (1983) developed a method for inducing *false beliefs*. In their investigations of the development of theory of mind in young children, they found that from about 4 years of age children were able to understand that others could have a false belief, and to use that understanding to predict their behaviour. Baron-Cohen et al adapted Wimmer and Perner's method in the Sally–Anne experiment described in Research Methods box 8.1 which you should read now.

Research methods 8.1

The Sally-Anne false belief task (from Frith, 2003)

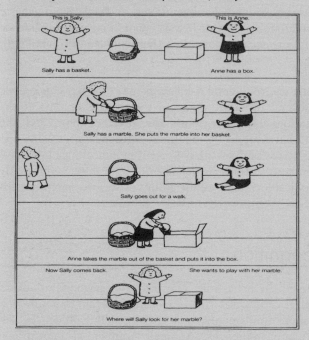

Figure 8.1 The Sally–Anne false belief task.
Source: Frith, 2003.

In the Sally–Anne experiment, two dolls are used to act out the story shown above. Children who are able to mentalize will say that when Sally comes back from her walk she will look in the basket for her marble because they will understand that she has not seen Anne move it and so will still believe that it is there. Children who are unable to understand that others have different beliefs from themselves will say that Sally will look in the box because that is where they know it is.

Three groups of children, all with a mental age above 3 years, took part in the Baron-Cohen et al (1985) experiment: children with autism, children with Down's syndrome and normally developing children. Most of the children with autism answered incorrectly while most of the children in the other two groups gave the right answer. The inclusion in the study of a group of children with Down's syndrome showed that the failure on this task of children with autism could not be attributed to their learning difficulties more generally. In addition all children correctly answered two control questions 'Where is the marble really?' and 'Where was the marble in the beginning?', demonstrating understanding of the change in the physical location of the marble during the story.

The interpretation of **false belief task** failure by children with ASD has been subjected to considerable investigation. If you look at the diagnostic criteria for autism at the start of the chapter you might wonder whether high-functioning children with autism who lack age-appropriate pretend play might fail the Sally–Anne task when asked to attribute mental states to two plastic dolls, but not if real people were involved. This possibility was tested by Leslie and Frith (1988) in a scenario that involved two adults. One hid a coin and then left the room while the other moved the coin in a conspiratorial manner and hid it elsewhere. In this experiment 70 per cent of the children with autism said that when the first adult returned he or she would look in the new location for the coin. When asked questions, the children with autism incorrectly answered that the first adult would think and know that the coin was in the new location, even though they correctly answered that the first adult had not seen the coin being moved.

Many subsequent studies have confirmed that children with autism experience disproportionate difficulties with mentalizing (see Frith, 2003). However, they can handle false representations of the physical world. When a scene is photographed (e.g. a bedroom where a cat is sitting on a chair) and then rearranged (the cat is moved from the chair to the bed), children with autism have no relative difficulty in correctly identifying where the cat will be in the photograph (Leslie and Thaiss, 1992). Deficits have also been identified in the first year of life in areas regarded as precursors to the abilities needed to pass false belief tasks and use language effectively for communication. These include imitation (Rogers and Pennington, 1991) and joint attention (Mundy et al, 1990) where a young child will follow their mother's eye gaze and 'read' her expression of pleasure or apprehension in deciding whether to approach an unfamiliar object or person. Young children may also engage others in joint attention when they point to 'show' objects to them. Children with autism tend not to engage in this proto-declarative pointing although they engage in instrumental pointing when they want an object.

However, not all children with autism fail theory of mind tests and their relative difficulties on tasks that involve mentalizing tend to diminish with age. Happé (1995) conducted a meta-analysis which showed that most normally developing children passed false belief tests such as the Sally–Anne task by the age of 5 years. The majority of children with learning difficulties were able to pass these tests when they had achieved a mental age of 5 years. By contrast, the majority of children with autism did not pass until a mental age of 10 years. Even for those children with autism who eventually succeed with simple mentalizing task such as the Sally–Anne task, more complex tasks can continue to present difficulties. Brain imaging studies conducted with adults who have high-functioning autism indicate differences from normal control adults in the pattern of brain activation elicited by tasks involving mentalizing (see Frith, 2003, Chapter 11). It appears plausible that individuals with autism can compensate to some extent for the lack of an inbuilt mentalizing mechanism by learning alternative strategies, e.g. applying explicit procedures and rules.

Executive dysfunctions

The absence of an inbuilt mentalizing mechanism, 'mind-blindness', can account for many of the impairments in reciprocal social interaction and communication that are characteristic of autism. However, restricted, repetitive behaviours, activities or interests cannot be explained by delayed or absent mentalizing abilities. It had been proposed that impairments in executive function underlie these characteristics of children with autism (Ozonoff, 1997). Executive functions refer to the abilities needed to prepare for and carry out complex behaviour. These include planning, prioritizing, monitoring several tasks and switching between them, inhibiting inappropriate impulsive actions, generating novel approaches to a situation and weighing consequences for alternative courses of action. A common feature of executive function behaviours is the ability to disengage from the immediate environment or external context and direct behaviour instead by mental/internal processes (Shallice, 1988).

Although executive dysfunctions are not unique to children with autism, they are very often present. Children with autism typically score well below age norms on tests of executive function such as the Wisconsin Card Sorting Test. On this test children are initially asked to sort cards and are given feedback on whether they are sorting correctly according to an undisclosed rule (e.g. number, shape, colour). Once the child has achieved 10 correct card sorts the sorting rule is suddenly changed without comment. The number of perseverative responses is noted, that is responses that use the old sorting rule despite feedback that it is wrong. The lack of higher-order executive control can feasibly account for the repetitive actions of many children with autism and their difficulty in behaving flexibly and generating novel approaches.

Central coherence

Neither executive dysfunctions nor mentalizing deficits can easily account for special abilities or 'savant' skills shown by some children with autism, and sometimes despite very low scores overall on tests of general intellectual functioning. Frith (1989) proposed that this can be explained by impaired central coherence. In normally developing individuals there is an inbuilt propensity to integrate information, form coherence over a wide a range of stimuli and generalize over as wide a range of contexts as possible. People will automatically seek to make 'sense' from perceiving connections and meaningful links from meaningless materials.

Frith (1989) suggested that in children with autism this capacity for coherence is diminished and that this is sometimes relatively advantageous. For example, Shah and Frith (1993) sought to explain why children with autism tend to show relatively better performance on the Block Design sub-test of the Weschler Intelligence Scale for Children. This involves assembling four or nine cubes so that the top surfaces match a printed pattern. It was found that segmenting the pattern into single cube components greatly helped both normally developing children and those with learning disabilities. However, the performance of children with autism did not improve, suggesting that they were already well able to overcome the strong drive to cohesion experienced by the other children.

Happé, Briskman and Frith (2001) suggest that while mean scores on tests of central coherence will be lower in people with than in those without autism, central coherence may be a cognitive style that varies in the normal population and among people with autism. Using laboratory tasks such as the embedded figures task (which involves detecting a hidden figure within a larger meaningful line drawing, see Figure 8.2) they found a higher rate of weak central coherence in parents of boys who have autism than in parents of normally developing boys or of boys with dyslexia. There were parallel differences in everyday life, for example involving special interests, attention to detail, insistence on routines and intolerance to change (Briskman et al, 2001). Baron-Cohen (2002) has reported similar patterns of findings although the labelling of the hypothesized cognitive styles involved is slightly different. Baron-Cohen distinguishes a *systematizing* from an *empathizing* information processing style and defines these in terms of orientation to and understanding of physical as opposed to psychological information about the world. As these styles are often held to be characteristic of males and females respectively this idea has been referred to as the extreme male brain theory of autism. While supporting data are limited (Volkmar et al, 2004), this theory has attracted considerable popular press coverage and is often misrepresented as holding that all men are autistic!

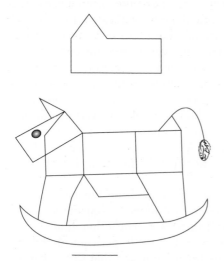

Figure 8.2 Sample item from the Children's Embedded Figures Test – 'house' embedded in 'rocking horse'.
Source: Witkins et al, 1971.

What can psychology offer teachers in educating children with autism?

Psychological theory and research have had a very significant impact on the education of children with ASD. Two distinct strands of influence can be identified. The first draws on behavioural psychology and takes no account either of diagnosis or characteristic features of autism. By contrast, the second draws directly on cognitive theories of autism.

Developed by Lovaas in the 1960s, the **applied behavioural analysis (ABA)** approach was successful in producing empirically validated improvements in language, learning and social behaviour of children with ASD, where previous approaches had failed. The approach involved highly structured operant learning techniques such as discrete trial training and task analysis. Task analysis was used on complex behaviour to develop a sequence of discrete responses that could be trained through a series of drills. A drill typically consisted of a trainer-provided antecedent (e.g. the instruction 'sit down'), a response from the child and a consequence rewarding a correct response (tangible reinforcers such as small bites of food or play with a favourite toy were often used initially, but paired with verbal praise so that the tangible reward could gradually be faded). Emphasis was placed on providing physical or verbal prompts to maximize successful performance and on shaping desired behaviour through rewarding successive approximations. An incorrect response might be ignored, or the child might be told 'no'.

Designed for children aged 2–4 years, ABA programmes are carried out at home on a one-to-one basis with the child by trained parents or other personnel. Because of their understanding of behavioural principles, psychology students are often encouraged to apply for training and part-time positions as ABA therapists. The programmes are intensive: initial studies indicated 40 hours per week as desirable, while later studies reported 27 hours per week over a period of 3 years together with planned integration experiences in a nursery school in the second and third year where taught skills could be generalized. Although criticized for placing unrealistic demands on parents, initial efficacy research highlighted the importance of programme intensity. Lovaas (1987) reported that children with ASD who received ABA for 40 hours a week achieved significantly better outcomes than either those who received 10 hours a week or those who received a different, non-specified treatment. A follow-up study suggested that there was good maintenance of treatment effects (McEachin et al, 1993).

However, a number of controversies have surrounded the Lovaas approach and its evaluation. One, relating to the use of **punishment** when the approach was first introduced, is considered in the Ethics box. The other that will be considered here is the strong claim by Lovaas that some 40 per cent of children achieve normal functioning as a result of the programme and that this 'recovery' from autism calls into question the existence of a neurological disorder. A number of methodological critiques of the evaluative research by Lovaas and his colleagues have been published (Schopler et al, 1989; Rutter, 1996; Gresham and MacMillan, 1997b). Gresham and MacMillan (1997a) challenged the criteria used to judge normal functioning (IQ and educational placement) on the basis that these are gross measures that do not necessarily reflect improvements in the characteristic areas of difficulty in autism. In addition they may reflect the operation of other, uncontrolled factors: for example, educational placement will be heavily influenced by the policy of individual school districts. Gresham and MacMillan (1997a) also raised concerns about participant selection and representativeness, substantial differences across groups in the time periods between assessments, the matching of the groups and the absence of random assignment. The issue of random assignment was addressed in two replication studies (Smith et al, 1997; Smith et al, 2000). The replications did not find gains in language and IQ of the same magnitude as in the original study. Also lower gains were found where children met the full criteria for autism, as opposed to occupying positions on the spectrum where fewer difficulties are experienced. However, available group data overall supported the conclusion that there is an overall enhancement of developmental rate where children receive an ABA programme for 27 hours or more per week from appropriately trained and supervised personnel (Mastergeorge et al, 2003).

Ethics

When first introduced, aversive consequences were employed in the ABA programmes pioneered by Lovaas with children who have ASD. These generally consisted of a shouted 'No!' or a slap on the leg. Lovaas and his colleagues did conduct one laboratory study which used electric cattle prods to shape the social behaviour of children with ASD (Lovaas et al, 1965), but there is no indication that such strategies were ever advocated to parents or nurseries! It appears that the aversives that were advocated were considered to have an important effect in achieving desired outcomes for the children. 'Introduction of contingent aversives resulted in a sudden and stable reduction in the inappropriate behaviors and a sudden and stable increase in appropriate behaviors' (Lovaas, 1987: 7).

Aversives are no longer used in ABA programmes because of changes in ethical and legal frameworks which are illustrated by the following extracts. Read these and consider whether the use of physical punishment could ever be justified. What arguments could be made, both for and against? Is there additional research evidence you would want to have in making your decision? Do you consider research evidence relevant in resolving ethical dilemmas?

UN Convention on the Rights of the Child
Article 37
States Parties shall ensure that:
(a) No child shall be subjected to torture or other cruel, inhuman or degrading treatment or punishment.
United Nations (1989). Convention on the rights of the child. Office of the High Commissioner for human rights www.unhchr.ch./html/menu3/b/k2crc.htm

British Psychological Society Code of Ethics and Conduct
3.1 Standard of General Responsibility
Psychologists should:
(i) Avoid harming clients, but take into account that the interests of different clients may conflict. The psychologist will need to weigh these interests and the potential harm caused by alternative courses of action or inaction.
British Psychological Society (2006). Code of Ethics and Conduct. www.bps.org.uk/the-society/ethics-rules-charter-code-of-conduct/code-of-conduct/code-of-conduct_home.cfm

The second strand of psychological theory and research that has been influential in the education of children with ASD is that relating to cognitive theories of autism. Explanations of these theories and their implications for adapting classroom environments and teaching strategies now feature prominently in preparing teachers to work with children who have ASD (Jordan, 1999; Warwickshire County Council, 2005). While implications of problems with executive functions and central coherence receive discussion, these are often already to be found in educational approaches for children with ASD. For example, the **TEACCH** approach (Treatment and Education of Autistic and Communication handicapped CHildren; Schopler and Mesibov, 1995), which was originally developed in 1972, uses a highly structured, visually based approach in organizing the classroom environment and learning materials. Key features of the approach include explicit prompts, signals to initiate as well as to finish activities, reminder notes, a transparently structured environment, use of visual timetables setting out sequences of activities across a whole day or week and advance preparation for any changes in routine (see Figure 8.3). Although derived from a study of the behaviour of children with ASD in different types of environments, rather than from cognitive theories of autism, the key features of the approach are likely to be of great help to people with executive dysfunctions or weak central coherence (Tutt et al, 2006).

math class	break	art class
$\begin{pmatrix} 2 & 3 \\ +3 & -1 \\ \hline 5 & 2 \end{pmatrix}$		
lunch	reading class	bus

Figure 8.3 An example of a visual timetable.

Source: www.sdpsupport.org.uk/vistimetable.html.

By contrast, the research on a theory of mind deficit in autism has changed practitioners' perspectives on the social problems experienced by children with ASD and led to the development of new intervention approaches. A number of programmes have been developed to teach the perspective taking or 'mind-reading' skills involved, for example Howlin, Baron-Cohen and Hadwin (1999). While it is generally found that children with ASD can be trained to perform successfully in the teaching sessions, they do not generalize the learning to other contexts or apply the strategies in conversation and other social situations. Ozonoff and Miller (1995) used a control group design with small numbers of

11–16-year-olds with ASD and normal intelligence. They provided explicit and systematic instruction in the underlying social–cognitive principles necessary to infer the mental states of others and, in addition, taught specific interactional and conversational skills. They found significant improvement in false belief task performance by the treatment group, but not the control group. However, there was no generalization to naturalistic contexts and no change in teacher and parent reports of social behaviour. Hadwin et al (1996, 1997) focused on the teaching of important general principles, for example perception causes knowledge: a person will know x if they saw or heard about it – Little Red Riding Hood doesn't know the wolf is in her grandmother's house because she didn't see him go there. Thirty children with ASD aged 4–13 years received intensive training involving many examples and different approaches (e.g. picture stories, puppet stories, role play). The results showed that it was possible to teach children with ASD to pass tasks that assess mental state understanding. However, there was no evidence of positive effects on spontaneous pretend play or conversational skills, leading the authors to conclude that the children appeared to be passing tasks by learning specific rules to apply, rather than developing any genuine understanding of the concepts involved.

In contrast to attempts to teach theory of mind abilities, the **social stories**™ approach, developed by Carol Gray (Gray, 1998; Howley and Arnold, 2005), draws on psychological theory and research in theory of mind and central coherence in providing compensatory information to assist individuals with ASD make sense of specific social situations. Specially constructed short personalized stories, usually written by teachers, speech therapists and parents, are used to teach children with autism how to manage their own behaviour during a social situation that they may find challenging or confusing. The stories are designed to provide 'missing information' about the perspectives of others, relevant social cues and expected social behaviour in a clear description of where the activity will take place, when it will occur, who will be participating and what will happen.

Recent reviews of research on the effectiveness of social stories (Nichols et al, 2005; Ali and Frederickson, 2006; Reynhout and Carter, 2006; Rust and Smith, 2006) have concluded that the approach shows promise. However, a number of methodological issues have also been raised, including inadequate participant description in some reports, the relatively modest extent of some of the changes in targeted behaviours, the frequent use of other interventions alongside social stories, and the predominant use of **single case experimental designs**. Single case experimental designs have particular strengths, both in their use by scientist-practitioners to develop the evidence base for practice (Barker et al, 2002) and in research areas where there are small samples and substantial participant heterogeneity. However, they also have weaknesses in terms of the adequacy of controls available for threats to internal validity such as maturation, placebo effects or experimenter artefacts (Rosnow and Rosenthal, 2005). All these recent reviews recommend further research that incorporates more rigorous designs and investigates also aspects such as generalization and long-term maintenance of intervention effects and critical components of the implementation of the social stories approach.

Summary

- The key behavioural features of ASD can be conceptualized as a triad of impairments: in reciprocal social interaction, verbal and non-verbal communication and imagination.

- Many children with ASD also have severe learning difficulties and hyper- or hypo-sensitivity to sensory stimuli. However, relative strengths in visuospatial processing and reasoning skills are also apparent and around 10 per cent have special talents or 'savant' skills.

- Autism is a neurodevelopmental disorder with a biological basis in which genetic factors are strongly implicated. While other factors are also influential, research has failed to support any link with the MMR vaccine and recent increases in prevalence rates appear primarily attributable to diagnostic practices.

- There are three dominant cognitive theories of autism.

  Theory of mind proposes a core deficit in the ability to 'mind-read' or attribute mental states to other people. False belief tasks have been an important source of supportive evidence. This theory can account for many of the impairments in reciprocal social interaction and communication in autism.

  Executive functions are needed to prepare for and carry out complex behaviours such as planning, prioritizing, switching between tasks, inhibiting inappropriate impulsive actions and generating novel approaches. Impairments in executive functions could account for the restricted, repetitive behaviours, activities or interests found in autism.

  Weak central coherence – a reduced drive to make meaning and an increased focus on parts rather than wholes – is seen as one end of a dimension. The theory helps to explain some areas of relative strength in ASD such as performance on visuospatial analysis tasks.

- Psychological theory and research have had a significant impact on the education of children with ASD in two ways:

  Through the application of applied behavioural analysis in programmes such as that developed by Lovaas.

  Through the application of cognitive theories of autism, programmes have been devised to teach 'mind-reading' skills and to develop compensatory strategies, such as social stories.

Key concepts and terms

Applied behavioural analysis
Asperger's syndrome
Autism
Autistic spectrum disorders
  (ASD)
Central coherence
Executive dysfunction
False belief task

Mentalizing
Prevalence
Punishment
Single case experimental
  designs
Social stories
TEACCH
Theory of mind

Sample essay titles

- To what extent can a 'theory of mind' deficit account for the triad of impairments in autism?
- Design an evidence-based intervention programme for Alex (Activity box 8.1), justifying the approaches you decide to include with reference to relevant literature.
- Evaluate the strengths and weaknesses of research evidence on the use of social stories with children who have ASD.
- You have been asked to give a talk to sixth form volunteers on 'Supporting children with ASD in school: Key insights from psychology'. Explain what you will include in your talk and why.

Further reading

Books

Frith, U. (2003). *Autism: Explaining the Enigma*, (2nd Ed.) Oxford: Blackwell.

Jordan, R., Jones, G., and Murray, D. (1998). *Educational Interventions for Children with Autism: A Literature Review of Recent and Current Research*. DfEE Research Report 77. London: Department for Education and Employment.

National Research Council (2001). *Educating Children with Autism*. Washington, DC: National Academy Press.

Journal articles

Howlin, P. (1998). Practitioner review: Psychological and educational treatments for autism. *Journal of Child Psychology and Psychiatry*, 39, 307–322.

Reynhout, G., and Carter, M. (2006). Social stories™ for children with disabilities. *Journal of Autism and Developmental Disorders*, 36, 445–469.

Rutter, M. (1999). Autism: two-way interplay between research and clinical work. *Journal of Child Psychology and Psychiatry*, 40, 169–188.

Tutt, R., Powell, S., and Thornton, M. (2006). Educational approaches in autism: What we know about what we do. *Educational Psychology in Practice*, 22, 69–81.

Volkmar, F.R., Lord, C., Bailey, A., Schultz, R.T., and Klin, A. (2004). Autism and pervasive developmental disorders. *Journal of Child Psychology and Psychiatry*, 45, 135–170.

Wing, L., and Potter, D. (2002). The epidemiology of autism: Is the prevalence rising? *Mental Retardation and Developmental Disabilities Research Reviews*, 8, 151–161.

9 Challenging behaviour in schools

Who is to blame?

Andy Miller

In this chapter we will consider attributions of responsibility for the difficult and unmanageable behaviour of some pupils in schools. We begin by showing that parties have differing and sometimes directly contradictory beliefs about causative factors and demonstrate the resulting challenges that this presents to the professional educational psychologist. Research evidence showing that teachers and parents working together can bring about significant improvements in children's behaviour is introduced following accounts from practitioners that illustrate just how hard it can be to bring together these three parties in such collaborative ventures. Attention is then focused on causal attributions, in particular the pioneering work of Bernard Weiner. The relationship between attribution, blame and sympathy will be outlined with implications drawn for educational psychologists working with challenging behaviour. We will then examine, in some depth, studies of the causal attributions for challenging behaviour made by teachers, students and parents and conclude by considering the positive potential of attribution retraining and ecosystemic consultation for the work of educational psychologists.

Learning outcomes

When you have completed this chapter you should be able to:

1. Critically analyse the suggested relationship between causal attribution, blaming, sympathy and willingness to help.
2. Demonstrate the similarities and clashes between students, teachers and parents in terms of the ways that they make sense of the causes of challenging behaviour in schools and classrooms.
3. Categorize causal attributions by means of their properties and outline the contexts within which this has influenced the practice of a range of applied psychologists.
4. Evaluate the evidence for the effectiveness of home-based reinforcement and attribution retraining programmes.

Conflicting views over responsibility for challenging behaviour in schools

Consider the statements in Focus box 9.1.

Focus 9.1

Teacher union hits out at parents

A second teaching union has hit out at bad behaviour by pupils in schools. The NASUWT (National Association of Schoolmasters Union of Women Teachers) called on parents to be responsible for children's behaviour in school. (BBC News Scotland Wednesday, 18 May, 2005)

They keep telling us about his behaviour. About how he's a risk in science and with woodwork tools and all that. But what can we do? You're not allowed to hit them any more and we've certainly tried threatening him. But they keep sending these messages home. What *else* can we do? In the end, it's the teachers who are actually there when all these things are supposed to be going off. (Father of a 12-year-old boy to the author)

These quotes typify a widespread dilemma – some might term it a 'stand-off' – when it comes to making sense of **challenging behaviour in schools**. It seems that at the very outset, there can be a fundamental disagreement between some teachers and parents as to who is responsible for this challenging behaviour.

The influential Elton Report, *Discipline in Schools*, commented on this as long ago as 1989:

> *Our evidence suggests that teachers' picture of parents is generally very negative. Many teachers feel that parents are to blame for much misbehaviour in schools. We consider that, while this picture contains an element of truth, it is distorted. (DES, 1989: 133)*

Tensions between teachers and parents over challenging behaviour

Perhaps it is not surprising, then, given this seemingly widespread and intractable set of beliefs, that professionals such as educational and clinical psychologists who have tried to bring together teachers and parents to develop joint approaches have sometimes experienced such spectacular failures. The following extract illustrates graphically the confrontational atmosphere that may be unleashed by professionals attempting to arrange such collaborative encounters:

> *. . . the project was made dramatically aware of the extreme sensitivities that can surround attempts to bring together school and home when a pupil is displaying difficult behaviour. Attempts were made to lessen mutual distrust and prejudice and ways sought to increase parental interest in the child's education and progress or, more generally, in school activities. Initially, the work consisted of carrying the teachers' ideas to the parents. Occasionally, it was necessary to reassure teachers that parents were concerned and interested . . . There was also the far more difficult operation of helping certain teachers to appreciate their personal impact on parents. This was perhaps the most sensitive area the school social workers had to deal with; when it constituted an important issue, it had to be broached with great diplomacy and caution . . . Sometimes, before meeting, parents or teachers proposed angry confrontations with each other . . . Sometimes the teacher thought the school social worker was siding with the parents, while the parents thought the opposite. (Kolvin et al, 1981: 194).*

Similarly, Dowling and Taylor (1989), offering an advisory service to parents within a London primary school, concluded that '. . . the seemingly humble goal of reopening communication between parents and teachers must not be underestimated'.

Many more examples such as these can be found in the published literature and the informal accounts of those professionals who work between homes and schools. Even where such relationships are of the highest quality, they can be severely tested by difficult pupil behaviour, again demonstrating that creating the conditions in which it is possible to launch home–school strategies is a potentially delicate and complex undertaking.

But it is certainly possible. The extracts in this section run the danger of exceeding their purpose, which is to highlight this delicacy and complexity, and of turning over instead into a mood of pessimistic helplessness. It is time, then, to turn to studies of successful outcomes.

Studies of teachers, parents and students working successfully together in cases of challenging behaviour

One approach with a strong confirmatory evidence base has been termed 'home-based reinforcement (H-BR)' and is an extension of applied behavioural analysis as described in other chapters in this book. Classroom-based ABA strategies were usually expensive in terms of the time and effort required from teachers. Often they necessitated changes in teaching style and required the use of tangible rewards that were limited or alien within classrooms. However, early practitioners realized that, at home, parents often had access to a wide variety of privileges, rewards and treats. In home-based reinforcement (H-BR) approaches, the teacher is responsible for specifying classroom rules, determining rule violations and communicating these to the parent. At home the parent is responsible for consistently dispensing rewards and sanctions to the child, based on the teacher's report.

In the USA, Atkeson and Forehand (1979) reviewed 21 papers that contained the results of 29 experiments or case studies using H-BR to influence the conduct or academic behaviour of pupils across the statutory school range. This review also scrutinized the methodology of these studies in order to evaluate the validity of the results and concluded that 63 per cent had 'adequate designs'. The general conclusion from the paper was that H-BR was consistently effective in improving both academic achievement and disruptive classroom behaviour across a wide range of ages, in both ordinary and special classrooms. In the same year Barth (1979) also reviewed this subject and concluded that 'the wide-scale application of this system need wait no longer'.

Despite such reviews and recommendations, however, the approach has not generated widespread discussion in the British research literature, although we may be seeing a less technical legacy in the form of government-recommended approaches (DfEE 1999b, 2000b). In the USA, Chafouleas, Riley-Tillman and McDougal (2002) have pointed out that a daily behaviour report card – built on basic ABA principles – may be viewed not only as a monitoring device but as an intervention approach in itself, and have called for more extensive investigations of the accuracy with which these are used in educational settings, their inter-rater reliability, and their social validity, particularly for teachers.

Various studies have demonstrated that students do indeed value positive information being sent home about their behaviour in schools (Merrett and Tang, 1994; Infantino and Little, 2005), and that parents also judge this to be an effective method for encouraging good behaviour (Miller et al, 1998). Similar studies with teachers, though, suggest that, whereas information about misbehaviour being sent home is regarded as an effective punishment, reports of good behaviour are not construed as positively motivating for students (Caffyn, 1989; Harrop and Williams, 1992). These differing perspectives may provide the beginnings of an explanation for the animosity to be found between teachers and parents in cases of challenging behaviour and this theme will now be more centrally developed in relation to one of the cognitive underpinnings of blame – the process of **causal attribution**.

Attribution and attributional theory

Within psychology, attribution and attributional theory are concerned with how individuals invoke causes and explanations for various phenomena and the effects of these 'cognitions' on their subsequent behaviour. Forsterling (2001) draws attention to the two sub-fields of research into the attribution of causation: *attribution theories* which are concerned with the different antecedent conditions to causal attributions, and *attributional theories* which focus upon the psychological consequences of such attributions. A major figure in the study of causal attribution within educational contexts, both in terms of the nature of such attributions in themselves and in their links to behaviour such as blaming and help-giving, has been Bernard Weiner (see Focus box 9.2)

Focus 9.2

The contribution of Bernard Weiner

Weiner's major contribution to the subject of this chapter has been to relate **attribution theory** to school learning. By means of a series of studies employing factor analytic methods, Weiner (1986, 2000) identified three dimensions along which most attributions for successes and failures were found to lie:

1. *Locus* (whether the cause was internal or external to the person).

2. *Stability* (whether the cause is fixed or can vary).

3. *Controllability* (whether the person is able to control the cause).

So, for example, if a student (or a teacher or parent) attributed some success or failure to luck this would be an external, unstable and uncontrollable cause. On the other hand, an attribution of effort could be categorized as internal, stable and controllable.

Weiner's framework has been enormously influential in areas other than educational psychology, including clinical, health and sports psychology (Graham and Folkes, 1990).

Weiner also investigated the relationship between causal attribution and **help giving**, finding that teachers were more likely to feel sympathy towards a student and be willing to help that student learn appropriate ways of behaving if they attributed the misbehaviour to causes outside the student's control (Reyna and Weiner, 2001).

Summarizing the contribution made by Weiner's research and other studies within the framework he developed, Woolfolk Hoy and Weinstein (2006: 203) state that:

> . . . when teachers assume that student failure is attributable to forces beyond the student's control, they tend to respond with sympathy and avoid giving punishments. If, however, the failures are attributed to a controllable factor, such as lack of effort, the teacher's response is more likely to be anger; retribution and punishments may follow.

Causal attribution and challenging behaviour

Weiner's classic studies make an understanding of causal attribution around challenging behaviour central to the search for effective interventions. In fact, instead of asking, as the title of this chapter does, 'who is to blame?', the real question becomes 'how might the act of blaming become an obstacle to effective home–school strategies?' And consequent upon that, and even more important for practitioners such as educational psychologists, 'how can we work productively in an emotionally-charged climate of mutual blaming between school and home?'.

In an attempt to answer these questions, we turn to various research studies into the causal attributions made by teachers, students and parents for the difficult behaviour of some young people in our schools.

Teachers' attributions for challenging behaviour

A range of studies employing a variety of designs have demonstrated that teachers view parents and home circumstances as most to blame for difficult pupil behaviour in schools. For example, Croll and Moses (1985) used a postal survey to elicit the views of 428 junior school teachers and found this group to attribute misbehaviour in schools to parents in 66 per cent of cases. A later survey (Croll and Moses, 1999) obtained similar results, with teachers attributing 'emotional and behavioural difficulties' to home factors in 52 per cent of cases. The Elton Report (DES, 1989), cited above, concluded that parents and home factors were judged in schools to be the major causes of difficult behaviour in schools.

Using intensive interviews with 24 teachers who, with educational psychologists, had devised and successfully implemented intervention strategies for specific pupils, Miller (1995) found that these teachers located the origins of pupils' difficulties with factors under the control of parents in 71 per cent of cases, thus fulfilling Weiner's pre-conditions for 'blame'. A similar finding also emerged from a vignette study carried out with 18 junior school teachers, which again showed home factors to be judged the biggest contributory factor to classroom misbehaviour (Miller and Black, 2001).

From the small number of British studies so far published, studies employing a range of investigative methods, there is a common finding that teachers attribute the responsibility for challenging behaviour in schools primarily to home and parent factors.

Students' attributions for challenging behaviour

The causal attributions made by students for the challenging behaviour of their contemporaries in schools have been examined by Miller, Ferguson and Byrne (2000) using an exploratory factor analytic approach outlined in Research Methods box 9.1. This study sought to go beyond questionnaire approaches asking respondents to allocate causation to a limited number of options such as 'home background' or 'peers' by examining the potentially greater complexity that might exist within various factor structures.

The first two of the factors listed in Research Methods box 9.1 were also seen as more significant contributors to pupil misbehaviour than the latter two – a finding in marked contrast to the results from studies of teachers' views of the causes of pupil misbehaviour (Croll and Moses, 1985, 2000; DES, 1989; Miller,

Research methods 9.1

Investigating students' causal attributions for difficult classroom behaviour by means of exploratory factor analysis (from Miller et al, 2000)

Constructing the questionnaire

Step 1. The questionnaire was developed using items supplied by small groups of students aged between 11 and 12 years and attending the first year of a secondary school in the north of England.

Step 2. The researcher worked with these students in groups by asking them to think back to their time in primary schools and to remember the types of misbehaviour they had witnessed, and perhaps engaged in. Discussion was then encouraged by means of a set of questions to encourage the pupils to think of all the possible reasons why there might be misbehaviour in schools.

Step 3. These discussions were tape-recorded and all the suggested reasons were written up on a flip chart, and further prompts were used in an attempt to make sure that all possible reasons had been elicited. In general, the discussion groups were able to list possible causes related to parents and families but were reluctant to elaborate upon them. Items concerning teachers and other pupils were, however, discussed and elaborated upon at length.

Step 4. The questionnaire was then constructed incorporating all the possible reasons provided by the groups using, wherever possible, the actual terminology of the pupils. The resulting questionnaire consisted of 27 items and pupils were asked how important they judged each to be as a cause of difficult behaviour in schools on a four-point rating scale.

Administering the questionnaire

Step 5. In the second part of this study the remaining students from the year group, 105 in total, completed the questionnaire.

Analysing the results from the questionnaire

Step 6. Initial screening of the data for kurtosis and sphericity was carried out and indicated that the data, with one item removed, were suitable for **exploratory factor analysis** (Ferguson and Cox, 1993). Factors were extracted using principal components analysis and rotated to simple structure using orthogonal (varimax) rotation (Gorsuch, 1983). A four-factor model was found to account for 37.8 per cent of the variance and to be more readily interpretable than three- and five-factor models.

Results

The four factors reflected 'fairness of teacher's actions', 'pupil vulnerability', 'adverse family circumstances' and 'strictness of classroom regime'. The items with the highest loadings are shown below.

The most important causes of misbehaviour deriving from a factor analytic study with pupils

Factor 1 named as: **'Fairness of teachers' actions**'

Teachers shouted all the time
Pupils were picked on by teachers
Teachers did not listen to pupils
Teachers had favourites

Factor 2 named as: **'Pupil vulnerability**'

Other pupils wanted pupil to be in gang
Other pupils told pupil to misbehave
Pupil was unable to see mum/dad
Pupils were worried about other things

Factor 3 named as: **'Strictness of classroom regime**'

Too much class work was given
Too much homework was given
Teachers were too strict

Factor 4 named as: **'Adverse family circumstances**'

There were fights and arguments at home
Alcohol/drug abuse by family members
Parents let pupils get away with too much
Families did not have enough money to eat or buy clothes

Further analysis of this data showed that these pupils rated 'teacher's unfairness' and 'pupil vulnerability' as statistically significantly more important causes of misbehaviour than either family problems or how strictly the classroom was managed. There were no significant differences between the results obtained from boys and girls.

1995; Miller and Black, 2001). In an almost comical reversal, Kelsey et al (2004) investigated students' explanations for when *college teachers* misbehave and found that these students applied an interpretive framework in which they view the teacher, not external factors or they the students themselves, as the primary cause of teacher misbehaviours.

A study by Tony (2003) of 384 Hong Kong students in the junior forms of secondary schools demonstrated the link between causal attributions and actual behaviour with the finding that an external orientation of **locus** of control and a passive pattern of attribution remained significant predictors of discipline problems when other factors were held constant. This contrasts somewhat with the finding from Elliott's (1996) study that there was very little relationship between behaviour and locus of control in 237 children specifically judged to have emotional and behavioural difficulties.

On a related theme, behaviour difficulties in the form of aggressive acts towards peers have been linked to '**hostile attribution of intent**'. de Castro et al (2002) conducted a meta-analysis of 41 studies with 6017 participants and found a robust significant association between children's hostile attribution of intent towards peers and their aggressive behaviour. They summarize the well-accepted hypothesis that

> *well-known risk factors for the development of aggressive behaviour problems, such as rejection by peers . . . and harsh parenting . . . predispose children to attribute hostile intent, particularly if their cognitive capacities to process these experiences are limited . . . Hostile attributions of intent, in turn, are believed to cause aggressive behaviour, instigate more problematic social interactions, and thereby limit non-aggressive interactions that could provide opportunities to learn prosocial behaviours . . . Thus, it is suggested that hostile attribution may be a key element in the development and persistence of behaviour problems over time. (de Castro et al, 2002: 916)*

In summary, students' attributions for challenging behaviour in schools tend to focus on causes external to themselves, such as teachers' unfairness and pupils' hostile intent, or to aspects of the perpetrators' vulnerability (an internal attribution but one beyond the actor's control). In addition, causal attributions which are external and beyond the control of the actor are significant predictors of discipline problems. A particular form of these, the attribution of hostile intent towards peers, is found to be strongly associated with aggressive behaviour.

Parents' attributions for challenging behaviour

The repeated finding that teachers view parents and home factors as the major cause of classroom misbehaviour is likely to present a major stumbling block in terms of being able to initiate successful home–school strategies such as H-BR. This attribution is also likely to be a major contributor to tensions found between teachers and parents in such circumstances. Government advice that home–school agreements will work best where they are 'a product of genuine discussion between all parties concerned' (DfEE, 1998) is unlikely to be received in the spirit intended when set against these widespread attributions towards parents. However, the extent to which parents might make 'genuine' contributions within such partnerships will similarly depend upon the nature of the attributions they implicitly make for the causes of classroom misbehaviour, hence the need to examine parental attributions which have been studied in terms of children's behaviour both outside and within the school context.

Generally, and not specifically in relation to behaviour within school, Johnston, Patenaude and Inman (1992) cite research linking parents' attributions for children's behaviour to their affective and behavioural responses to that behaviour (e.g. Dix et al, 1989). Using written vignettes of children's difficult behaviour, Dix and his colleagues found that the misbehaviour of older children was more likely to be attributed by mothers to personality factors and seen as intentional, than was that of younger children. In addition, if the child was judged to be responsible for, or in control of the behaviour, then parents were much more likely to choose 'power-assertive' methods of discipline. Cornah (2000) used a vignette and questionnaire study with mothers of children around 9 years of age to look explicitly at attributions made towards their own and other people's children. When mothers were explaining their own child's difficult-to-manage behaviour, they reported this as being caused by factors that were less stable and less global than when they explained similar behaviours in other children. Cornah argues that this may be an extension of the self-serving attributional bias by mothers into what she terms a 'child-serving bias'.

Turning to studies of behaviour specifically within a school context, Phares (1996) investigated the perceptions of parents for the development and treatment of pupils classed as having emotional/behavioural difficulties. Parents were shown one of four vignettes and were asked to rate the responsibility the mother, father, child and teacher had for the development of the child's problem and the responsibility to intervene. Overall parents and children were viewed as more responsible for the development and treatment of problems than were teachers. However, for younger children, parents and teachers were seen as more responsible. Snyder et al (2005) reported a longitudinal study of 268 children and their families during kindergarten and first grade. In this, parent discipline practices were ascertained from four hours of coding of parent–child interactions whereas maternal attributions about child behaviour were assessed by means of a structured interview. This study found that ineffective maternal discipline and the interaction of ineffective discipline and hostile attribution predicted growth in child conduct problems at home during kindergarten and first grade. Of particular interest to the central discussion of this section, changes in teacher-reported and observed child conduct problems at school during this period were predicted by growth in conduct problems at home and by the interaction of ineffective discipline and hostile attribution.

In an extension to their factor analytic study of students' attributions, Miller, Ferguson and Moore (2002) employed a similar method to examine the factor structure of parents' attributions for challenging behaviour in schools, and to make a subsequent direct comparison between students and teachers in this respect. Factor analysis of questionnaire replies from 144 parents for the same items as in the students' questionnaire (Miller et al 2000) indicated that parents' attributions for misbehaviour were best represented by three factors – 'fairness of teacher's actions', 'pupil vulnerability to peer influences and adverse family circumstances', and 'differentiation of classroom demands and expectations' – the first two factors being seen as more significant contributors to pupil misbehaviour than the third.

In summary, parents (usually mothers in the reported studies) appear to make different attributions for their own and for other people's children (at least at around 9 years of age). Parents tend to see the causes of their own children's misbehaviour as less stable (not occurring at all times) and less global (not appearing in a wide variety of contexts) than that of others' children. In the latter instance, parents attribute misbehaviour of older children as due to personality factors and judge it to be intentional in nature. The difficult behaviour of younger children (other people's) at school is seen as being caused by both teachers and parents, but teachers are not judged to contribute for older children.

Generalizability of attributional patterns

These studies of the attributions made by teachers, students and parents must be interpreted carefully in the light of other studies that demonstrate the likely influences of various cultural and social processes. For example, Ho (2004) examined the causal attributions for student behaviour made by 204 Australian and 269 Chinese teachers. Although both groups attributed misbehaviours most to student effort and least to teacher factors, the Chinese teachers emphasized family factors more while Australian teachers placed greater importance on ability. Ho interpreted these findings in cultural terms, attributing these differences to individualistic and collectivist values likely to be influencing the two different groups. Another potential cultural variation may be found in Poulou and Norwich's (2000) study in which 391 Greek elementary teachers perceived school and teacher factors as causal of students' emotional and behavioural difficulties.

Another study suggests that seemingly very minor alignments in terms of group membership can still exert an influence. Guimond, Begin and Palmer (1989) studied university students in the final year of a social sciences degree and found them to attribute more importance to situational factors and less to dispositional factors than did social science students at earlier levels of education and students in other areas at all levels, providing results consistent with a microcultural interpretation of attributional diversity. Gender too has been shown to exert 'subtle differences' in a study examining the attributions, emotions and attribution-emotion associations of a large group of primarily middle-class, European American college students (MacGeorge, 2004).

In summary, these various sets of studies demonstrate that causal attributions are heavily implicated in the approaches teachers, students and parents take towards each other around difficult behaviour. While there are general areas of agreement between these various parties, there are also some persisting clashes that are likely to exacerbate tensions and difficult relationships. The practising educational psychologist, while remaining aware that subtle developmental, cultural and group factors can lead to variations into attributional styles, will be alert to the causal attributions that various parties are likely to be making. In this way, she or he may be able to effect interventions that move beyond blaming and mutual scapegoating.

Attribution of responsibility for action and of ability to act effectively

Attributions of *causation* are, however, only one set of considerations for educational psychologists working with pupils deemed to be displaying challenging behaviour. Equally important may be the attributions that each party makes in terms of the *responsibility to take action*. A simple but very useful model proposed by Fiske and Taylor (1984) sets judgements about the responsibility for affecting a solution to a problem alongside judgements about responsibility for original causes, as in Figure 9.1.

		Responsibility for solution?	
		Yes	No
Responsibility for cause?	Yes	Moral model	Enlightenment model
	No	Compensatory model	Medical Model

Figure 9.1 Fiske and Taylor's model of combinations of attributions for the cause and solution of problems. (Adapted from Fiske and Taylor, 1984.)

Thus, for example, an agent may be perceived as having the responsibility for solving a particular problem whether they were responsible for causing it in the first place (moral model) or not causing it (compensatory model). Similarly, differing responsibilities for affecting a solution may also be attributed in instances where an agent is not perceived as implicated in the original cause of the problem. Activity box 9.1 gives an opportunity to test out judgements within Fiske and Taylor's model.

Activity 9.1

In each of the four examples, a teacher is making either a moral, medical, enlightenment or compensatory model attribution towards an actor – who may be a pupil, a parent or the teacher her- or himself. Decide with your fellow students which attributional model is being *applied to the actor* in each of the four examples.

Start by deciding whether the actor is being held responsible by the speaker for the cause and for the solution. Then map your decisions onto Fiske and Taylor's model in Figure 9.1.

1) Attribution made by teacher to the *pupil* for the *cause*:

Having my own daughter, who is two, I could draw so many parallels between their behaviour. It was incredible because you see he was six and she was two. But he was acting in a very toddlerish way . . . It was as if I'd got a big two-year-old in the room all the time . . .'

. . . and to the *pupil* for the *solution*:

Well, something worked . . . I think he matured obviously as he went on a little bit.

2) Attribution made by teacher to *herself* for the *cause*:

My hands were tied because of the fact that the problem was in the home.

. . . and to *herself* for the *solution*:

I think it was purely and simply because of the total pressure and rules that I kept him under.

3) Attribution made by teacher to *mother* for the *cause*:

The more you learn about his home background the more you realize how negative it is, and has been . . .

. . . and to the *mother* for the *solution*:

She (mother) needed help in that area of being consistent because she was so extreme. The first sign of anything and he was up to bed for the rest of the evening. It's no wonder he climbed out and wrecked his bedroom because this was tea-time.

4) Attribution made by teacher to *herself* for the *cause*:

There weren't enough records being kept, and there wasn't enough incentive for him to improve . . .

. . . and to *herself* for the *solution*:

I think it was (me) being positive (that led to the improvement) and I think it was the incentive of the rewards. I think it was the attention as well – him having the chance to speak to me.

How can educational psychologists use their knowledge of attribution theory in cases of challenging behaviour?

One approach advocated by some practitioners and researchers is **attribution retraining**, which involves working directly with the young person. Alternatively, and less directly, others promote working with all parties – teachers, parents, students and maybe others – in an attempt to arrive at mutually agreeable and effective plans, an approach sometimes subsumed under the generic description of '**ecosystemic consultation**'.

Attribution retraining

Attribution retraining, as the name implies, involves strategies that aim to help the young person make different types of causal attributions for their own behaviour, usually away from external and uncontrollable ones – such as the hostile intent of others or the unfairness of teachers – and towards some element of internal and controllable causation.

Hudley et al (1998), for example, employed the BrainPower Programme, a 12-lesson attribution retraining intervention, as part of a controlled study involving 384 third to sixth grade students in four elementary schools in Southern California.

This programme consisted of 12 one-hour sessions designed to:

■ Strengthen students' ability to accurately detect others' intentions.

■ Provide training in searching for, interpreting and properly categorizing the verbal, physical and behavioural cues exhibited by others.

■ Increase the likelihood of attributing negative outcomes to accidental causes.

■ Link appropriate non-aggressive behavioural responses to ambiguously caused negative social outcomes.

■ Generate decision rules about when to enact particular responses (e.g. 'When I can't really tell why he did that, I should act as if it were an accident').

Hudley et al's study was particularly aimed at students judged as aggressive on teacher and pupil ratings and was able to report moderate to strong effects for many students but none for some students and with treatment effects that generally diminished over time. So, the limited evidence so far suggests that, although bearing some signs of promise, attribution retraining has yet to establish a firm evidence base as an effective intervention with young people displaying unmanageable or aggressive behaviour in schools.

Ecosystemic consultation

In the accounts above, we have seen that teachers and parents tend to blame each other for the origins of the difficult behaviour of some, or many, students as a consequence of the causal attributions they make. When this blaming becomes intense, another form of causation can come into play – that of perpetuating 'the problem', whatever its original causes. In such cases, working only with the attributions of the student, even if the evaluation evidence can be taken as convincing, and even if ethically acceptable, will fail to address perpetuating factors within the student's 'ecosystem'.

Educational psychologists have addressed a number of these concerns by means of approaches such as ecosystemic consultation (Miller, 2003), ecobehavioural consultation (Gutkin, 1993) or joint systems consultation (Dowling and Osborne, 1994), typically involving work not only with a student but also with the most important others in the home and school environments. Miller (2003) has, for example, provided an in-depth analysis of 24 successful strategies devised between an educational psychologist and a teacher, parent and student in instances where the latter's behaviour was considered difficult and challenging. These cases were often characterized by the teacher seeing the pupil in question as among the most difficult, or as the most difficult they had ever encountered. An additional feature for inclusion on the study was that the work with the educational psychologist had to be judged by the teacher as having brought about considerable improvements.

These different strategies took various forms but most involved some aspects of home-based reinforcement (see above) including one or more meetings jointly with parent and teacher. Interviews with the teachers in this study highlight a number of interpersonal skills displayed by these psychologists (see Table 9.1), which have enabled a shift in unhelpful attributions on the part of teachers and parents.

We have seen earlier that bringing teachers and parents together over issues of challenging behaviour is no small accomplishment. The small sample of skills illustrated here contributes crucially to the formation and maintenance of a working alliance in which attributions of blame can gradually be replaced by respect for the positive contributions that each party is able to make in these most contentious and emotionally demanding of circumstances.

Skill displayed by educational psychologist	Example
Providing a model of emotional self-regulation	'She seemed calm and always positive . . . she would never get cross.'
Problem analysis	'The most valuable thing for us is for somebody to listen to our problems, like talking it through and trying to help us see one thing at a time.'

Table 9.1 Examples provided by teachers of skills displayed by educational psychologists during ecosystemic consultation (mostly from Miller 2003).

Skill displayed by educational psychologist	Example
Focused questioning	'I think the way she questioned me . . . I think I almost discovered something of what I was doing myself, and probably I didn't even know I was doing it.'
Displaying sensitivity to role boundaries	'I don't think she was trying to teach me my job or whatever.'
Helping to reframe causal attributions	'(Mother) had caused so many problems here. She's a very bristly lady, very much on the ball, but in her own way she really did care for Barry. Maybe not the way that you and I would care for our children but she did . . . she really was a caring mum.'
Reattribution with respect to *locus* of attribution	'He helped us see that it wasn't all in the home, that there were things we were doing in school that weren't helping as well.'
Reattribution with respect to *stability* of attribution	'One thing that stood out in my mind was when I said "we just can't communicate with this boy" and she said "well, maybe you haven't found a way *yet*".'
Reattribution with respect to *controllability* of attribution	'We had been feeling helpless really, but she helped us feel that there were things we were able to put in place that would move things forward.'

Table 9.1 (continued)

Summary

■ Many studies and practitioner accounts highlight strong animosity between teachers and parents when students display antisocial and challenging behaviour in schools.

■ Meta-analytic reviews demonstrate that home-based reinforcement approaches can bring about substantial improvements in student behaviour if teachers and parents can be encouraged to participate, and trained, in their use.

■ Attribution theories are concerned with the different antecedent conditions to causal attributions, and attributional theories focus upon the psychological consequences of such attributions.

- Weiner (1986, 2000) identified three dimensions along which causal attributions could be located – locus, stability, and controllability – and found that teachers felt sympathy towards, and were more willing to help, students whose misbehaviour they attributed as beyond the student's control.

- Factor analytic studies have demonstrated that teachers, students and parents may make different causal attributions for the causes of difficult behaviour in schools.

- Students appear to conflict with teachers by attributing difficult behaviour to teacher unfairness, with which parents concur. Teachers and students, however, are in agreement that 'pupil vulnerability' is a major cause. Teachers and parents meanwhile both identify 'adverse home circumstances' as a major cause whereas students do not.

- A robust significant association between children's 'hostile attribution of intent' towards peers and their aggressive behaviour has been demonstrated, implicating the process of attribution further in this additional form of challenging behaviour in schools.

- A variety of cultural and social processes appear to influence the types of attributions made by teachers, students and parents around challenging behaviour, thus questioning the widespread generalizability of such research findings

- Attribution retraining attempts to devise strategies that enable people to make different types of causal attributions for their own behaviour, usually away from external and uncontrollable ones towards some element of internal and controllable causation. As yet, there is not a strong evidence base for the efficacy of attribution retraining with pupils displaying challenging behaviour in schools.

- Ecosystemic consultation is a method adopted by some educational psychologists, involving joint working with the young person and also his or her teacher(s) and parent(s). Research attests to positive outcomes from this form of consultation.

Key concepts and terms

Adverse family circumstances
Attribution retraining
Attribution theory
Causal attribution
Challenging behaviour in
  schools
Ecosystemic consultation
Exploratory factor analysis

Help giving
Home-based reinforcement
Hostile attribution of intent
Locus
Pupil vulnerability
Strictness of classroom
  regime

Sample essay titles

- How might educational psychologists use attribution theory to help them in their work around challenging behaviour in schools?
- 'Many teachers feel that parents are to blame for much misbehaviour in school. We consider that, while this picture contains an element of truth, it is distorted.' (The Elton Report). How might educational psychologists understand and respond to this phenomenon?
- Is it possible to change attributions around antisocial behaviour in schools? And is it ethical to attempt to do so?
- What difficulties might an educational psychologist run into when attempting to determine the causes of a pupil's challenging behaviour in school?

Further reading

Books

Miller, A. (2003). *Teachers, Parents and Classroom Behaviour. A Psychosocial Approach.* Maidenhead: Open University Press.

Porter, L. (2007). *Behaviour in Schools. Theory and Practice for Teachers.* Maidenhead. Open University Press.

Woolfolk Hoy, A.M., and Weinstein, C.S. (2006). 'Student and teacher perspectives on classroom management.' In: C.M. Evertson and C.S. Weinstein (Eds), *Handbook of Classroom Management: Research, Practice and Contemporary Issues.* London: Lawrence Erlbaum Associates.

Journal articles

de Castro, B.O., Veerman, J.W., Koops, W., Bosch, J.D., and Monshouwer, H.J. (2002). Hostile attribution of intent and aggressive behaviour: a meta-analysis. *Child Development*, 73, 916–934.

Hudley, C., Britsch, B., Wakefield, W.D., Smith, T., Demorat, M., and Cho, S.-J. (1998). An attribution retraining program to reduce aggression in elementary school students. *Psychology in the Schools*, 35, 271–282.

Miller, A., Ferguson, E., and Moore, E. (2002). Parents' and pupils' causal attributions for difficult classroom behaviour. *British Journal of Educational Psychology*, 72, 27–40.

Snyder, J., Cramer, A., Afrank, J., and Patterson, G.R. (2005). The contributions of ineffective discipline and parental hostile attributions of child misbehaviour to the development of conduct problems at home and school. *Developmental Psychology*, 41, 30–41.

Weiner, B. (2000). Intrapersonal and interpersonal theories of motivation from an attributional perspective. *Educational Psychology Review*, 12, 1–14.

10 School bullies

Are they also victims?

Norah Frederickson

Recent surveys have consistently identified **bullying** as the issue of most concern to young people (House of Commons, Education and Skills Committee, 2007: 17). Although bullying can occur in a range of contexts, in this chapter we will focus on bullying at school. School bullies are typically portrayed as large, oafish thugs while the popular image of victims of bullying is of physically weak, sensitive and timid individuals. However, psychological research has shown that both these popular stereotypes are oversimplifications. Some school bullies are also victimized, and the incidence of negative circumstances and outcomes associated with bullying for all involved is very much higher than for pupils not involved. Theories of bullying range across explanations at the levels of the individual, family, peer group and school system. A wide range of interventions have been developed accordingly, although rigorous evaluation is lacking in most cases and some have aroused controversy. In particular, there is disagreement over intervention programme principles for children who bully, and it is here that the overlap between bullies and victims has particular implications.

Learning outcomes

When you have completed this chapter you should be able to:

1. Describe the principal theories of bullying and the research evidence relating to them.
2. Critically evaluate the main assessment and intervention approaches used in relation to bullying behaviour in schools.
3. Debate key theoretical and professional controversies in this research area, drawing on recent psychological literature.

What is bullying?

While there is no universally agreed definition of bullying, most authors agree on its key features, described as the 'double IR' (Orpinas and Horne, 2006):

Activity 10.1

Defining bullying

Think back to your school days. How would you define bullying? To what extent does the caricature shown in Figure 10.1 capture the key elements of your definition? In what ways is it inadequate?

Figure 10.1
Caricature of
bullying behaviour.
Source: ImageZoo/Getty Images.

I – Imbalance of power
I – Intentional
R – Repeated over time.

Can you identify each of these elements in the following definition of bullying? It is one of the most widely used in research studies with children and was adapted for use in the UK from the pioneering work of Olweus in Norway:

> . . . *we say a child or young person is being bullied, or picked on when another child or young person, or a group of children or young people, say nasty and unpleasant things to him or her. It is also bullying when a child or a young person is hit, kicked, threatened, locked inside a room, sent nasty notes, when no one ever talks to them and things like that. These things can happen frequently and it is difficult for the child or the young person being bullied to defend himself or herself. It is also bullying when a child or young person is teased repeatedly in a nasty way. But it is not bullying when two children or young people of about the same strength have the odd fight or quarrel. (Whitney and Smith, 1993: 7)*

Bullying is an area where research has had a significant influence on government policy in the UK and elsewhere. Hence the definition of bullying adopted by the UK government is also based on the 'double IR'.

The UK Government defines bullying as:

■ *Repetitive, wilful or persistent behaviour intended to cause harm, although one-off incidents can in some cases also be defined as bullying;*

■ *Intentionally harmful behaviour, carried out by an individual or a group; and*

■ *An imbalance of power leaving the person being bullied feeling defenceless.*

Bullying is emotionally or physically harmful behaviour and includes: name-calling; taunting; mocking; making offensive comments; kicking; hitting; pushing; taking belongings; inappropriate text messaging and emailing; sending offensive or degrading images by phone or via the internet; gossiping; excluding people from groups and spreading hurtful and untruthful rumours. (House of Commons, Education and Skills Committee, 2007: 7–8)

It can be seen from the first bullet point in the government definition that some questions are raised about the necessity of a repetitive element to the bullying. Questions have also been raised about the difficulty of establishing intentionality as perpetrators often claim that they 'didn't mean to hurt' and that it was 'just for fun'. As Juvonen and Graham (2004) conclude, the single most critical characteristic of a bullying relationship is the **power imbalance** whereby the victim is unable to prevent or stop the aversive behaviour. While this feature is represented in the caricature shown in Figure 10.1, power in children's groups is not only based on differences in physical size and strength, and associated access to resources, but may also be based on social attention-holding ability and success in forming affiliative relationships (Hawker and Boulton, 2001). Different types of bullying are distinguished, based on the type of power that is being abused:

■ Physical – hitting, kicking, taking belongings (resource-holding potential).

■ Verbal – name calling, insulting, making offensive remarks (social attention-holding power).

■ Relational – spreading nasty stories about someone, exclusion from social groups, being made the subject of malicious rumours (affiliative relationships/sense of belonging).

Clear distinctions are sometimes claimed – for example, relational bullying has been branded 'girls' bullying'. However, there appear to be complex interactions between pupil characteristics and prevalence of type of bullying. For example, from a meta-analysis Archer (2004) reported that girls were only found to be more involved in relational aggression in samples above 11 years, where peer ratings were used. Boys were more likely to engage in physical bullying than girls across all ages. Also, overall, males are more likely than females to be victims of bullying and **bully-victims** (Nansel et al, 2001; Solberg et al, 2007).

Who are the bullies?

Which pupils will be identified as bullies depends to some extent on the assessment method used. Four main methods can be identified, as shown in Research Methods box 10.1 (see Pellegrini, 2001; Cornell et al, 2006).

Research methods 10.1

Methods of identifying bullies
Self-reports

Children are typically presented with a definition of bullying and asked to rate the frequency with which they have been involved over a specified period in either bullying or being bullied. For example the *Peer Relations Questionnaire* (Rigby and Slee, 1998) contains a six-item bully scale and a five-item victim scale. Items such as 'I am part of a group that goes around teasing others' and 'I get picked on by others' are rated on a four-point scale ranging from 'never' to 'very often'.

These self-report questionnaires are usually anonymous to encourage honesty. Even then there may be effects of social desirability biases as pupils may resist endorsing responses that involve admitting to an unfavourable self-presentation. However, when the questionnaires are being used to identify bullies and victims for further study, assurances about confidentiality may not convince all pupils that it is safe to admit to school-prohibited behaviour.

Peer assessments

These methods generally involve surveying a classroom of pupils, asking each to identify classmates who meet behavioural descriptions characteristic of bullies and victims. Peer assessment methodologies are well established in the literature on **social competence** and in some cases existing instruments have been extended to collect data on bullying. For example, Nabuzoka and Smith (1993) extended the 'Guess Who' peer assessment method developed by Coie, Dodge and Coppotelli (1982), adding:

- A bully – someone who often picks on other children or hits them, or teases them or does other nasty things to them for no good reason.

- A bullying victim – someone who often gets picked on or hit or teased or has nasty things done to them by other children for no good reason.

Salmivalli (1999) has developed a set of scales (the Participant Role Scales) which collect information on the roles children may play in bullying incidents. These include, but are not limited to, the roles of bully and victim:

- Bully (5 items): active, initiative taking, leader-like behaviour.

- Assistant (2 items): active, but more follower than leader-like.

- Reinforcer (4 items): inciting the bully, providing an audience, etc.

- Defender (6 items): sticking up for or consoling the victim.

- Outsider (4 items): doing nothing in bullying situations, staying away.

- Victim (1 item): 'gets bullied', needs to be nominated by 30 per cent of same sex classmates to be classified as a victim.

Teacher questionnaires

Smith (2004) points out that these are generally considered less reliable than self- or peer-reports, as teachers are often unaware of much of the bullying that is occurring, for example in the playground. However, at younger ages, for example in nursery school, the balance of preference shifts in favour of teacher reports, both because child reports may be less reliable and because younger children are more closely supervised, so teachers are likely to be better informed.

Observation

This method is primarily used with pre-school children, although comparatively rarely even then as data collection and analysis are very time consuming. It is little used with older children for several reasons. Older children range over a much wider geographical area during their breaktimes at school when such observations are typically conducted, making data collection difficult. Much relational bullying will be very difficult to observe while, with physical and verbal bullying, reactivity between the method and the behaviour of interest is highly probable – the presence of an adult observer is very likely to greatly decrease the incidence of bullying.

Pellegrini and Bartini (2000) compared different methods of identifying bullies and victims and reported low to moderate correlations between them. Juvonen, Nishina and Graham (2001) found that compared to peer assessments, self-report measures of **victimization** better predicted psychological adjustment problems (depressive symptoms and low self-worth). However, peer assessments better predicted low social acceptance. They argue that the most appropriate assessment technique will depend on the goal of an investigation – 'to understand peer harassment as a social problem, as a personal predicament, or both' (Juvonen et al, 2001: 120).

Are some bullies also victims of bullying at school?

Of direct relevance to the question asked in the title of this chapter is the consistent finding that a proportion of the children identified as bullies are also identified as victims. Solberg et al (2007) reported data from over 18,000 Norwegian pupils aged 11–15 years who completed a self-report measure. They were given a definition of bullying very similar to that used by Whitney and

Smith (1993) (see earlier) and asked how often they had taken part in bullying in the previous two to three months in school. Response options were:

- Option 1 – I haven't.

- Option 2 – only once or twice.

- Option 3 – two to three times a month.

- Option 4 – once a week.

- Option 5 – several times a week.

Table 10.1 shows how cut-off scores on this measure were used to classify pupils. Across the whole sample 9.5 per cent were classified as victims, 4.6 per cent as bullies and 1.9 per cent as bully-victims. Hence close to 30 per cent of bullies were also victims.

		Had taken part in bullying	
		Options 3, 4 and 5	Options 1 and 2
Had been bullied	Options 3, 4 and 5	Bully-victim	Victim
	Options 1 and 2	Bully	Not involved

Table 10.1 Categories of bully, victim and bully-victim
Source: Solberg et al, 2007.

Similar results have been obtained in the USA where a nationally representative study of 15,686 students aged 11–16 years (Nansel et al, 2001) found that 29.9 per cent reported involvement in moderate or frequent bullying as a bully (13.0 per cent), a target of bullying (10.6 per cent), or both (6.3 per cent). The proportions identified are higher than in the Solberg et al (2007) study, but it should be noted that Nansel et al (2001) asked about the frequency of bullying and being bullied over the past term away from school as well as in school. In both studies about a third of self-reported bullies also reported that they were victims of bullying.

Nansel et al (2001) found that the bully-victim group experienced a range of problems common to both victims and bullies: social isolation, lack of success in school and involvement in problem behaviours. They have consistently been described as anxious, irritable, hot-tempered, prone to start fights and to exhibit retaliatory, or reactive, aggression (Olweus, 1978; Schwartz et al, 1997). There are contrasts between this pattern of behaviour and the behaviour both of 'pure bullies' and 'pure victims'. Non-victimized bullies are not characterized by overtly angry, dysregulated behaviour, but tend to exhibit organized and goal-directed, or proactive, aggression. Victims of bullying who are not also bullies are described as non-aggressive, shy, passive and submissive (Olweus 1978, 1991).

The suggestion that bully-victims may represent an especially high-risk group is supported by a number of findings. For example, they have been found to experience higher levels of depression than either bullies or victims (Swearer et al, 2001). A bully–victim cycle has been described, for example by Ma (2001), who investigated both pupil-level and school-level influences on it. The suggestion inherent in the cycle, that these pupils may first have been bullied and then imitated the bullying behaviour they experienced, has gained media attention following the finding from retrospective analyses of school shootings in the USA (Anderson et al, 2001; Vossekuil et al, 2004) that a considerable proportion (50–70 per cent) of the perpetrators had been bullied at school and 30 per cent had a record of violence prior to the attack. 'These bullied youth may represent the "provocative" or "aggressive" victims described in recent studies on bullying behaviour, who often retaliate in an aggressive manner in response to being bullied. This group represents a particularly high risk population' (Anderson et al, 2001: 2702). As Focus box 10.1 indicates, experience of being bullied and engagement in intimidating behaviour has continued to be linked to mass murder incidents.

Focus 10.1

www.thetimesnews.com/sections/contactus/

Former high school classmates say Va. Tech gunman was picked on in school

By MATT APUZZO / Associated Press Writer

April 19, 2007

BLACKSBURG, Va. (AP) – Long before he boiled over, Virginia Tech gunman Cho Seung-Hui was picked on, pushed around and laughed at over his shyness and the strange way he talked when he was a schoolboy in the Washington suburbs, former classmates say.

Cho shot 32 people to death and committed suicide Monday in the deadliest one-man shooting rampage in modern U.S. history.

"There were just some people who were really mean to him and they would push him down and laugh at him," said a former classmate. "He didn't speak English really well and they would really make fun of him."

Authorities on Wednesday disclosed that more than a year before the massacre, Cho had been accused of sending unwanted messages to two women and was taken to a psychiatric hospital on a magistrate's orders and was pronounced a danger to himself. But he was released with orders to undergo outpatient treatment.

Also, Cho's twisted, violence-filled writings and menacing, uncommunicative demeanor had disturbed professors and students so much that he was removed from one English class and was repeatedly urged to get counseling.

Why does bullying occur?

A wide variety of different theories have been advanced to explain bullying behaviour. In this section we will consider **socio-cognitive deficit** theories, theories of family influence, group process theories and ecological systems theories.

Socio-cognitive deficit theories

Socio-cognitive deficit theories have drawn on models used to account for aggressive behaviour more generally. The most influential of these is the **Social Information Processing (SIP) model** described by Crick and Dodge (1994) which is shown in Figure 10.2.

In *steps 1 and 2* children attend to and encode cues, drawing on social knowledge, schemata and scripts to interpret others' intentions and causal attributions. For example, a child is walking across the playground when something hits them hard in the back. They will first of all encode various cues about the situation (a nearby football, an interrupted game of football, the expressions on the players' faces) and draw inferences about why it happened (an accidental wayward shot or an opportunistic assault by an enemy).

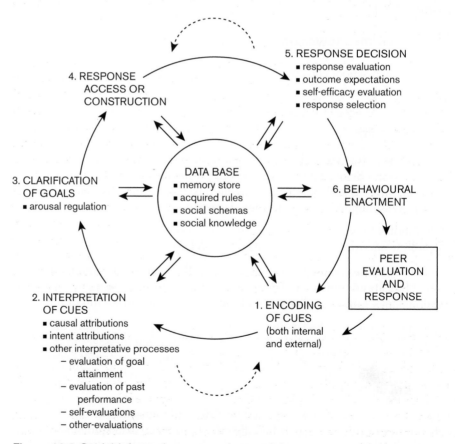

Figure 10.2 Social information processing model.
Source: Crick and Dodge, 1994: 76.

In *step 3*, children clarify their goals, the outcomes they want to achieve in a particular situation. In our example, the child who has decided that they have been hurt accidentally may consider maintaining friendly relations with their classmates the most important goal in the situation, even though they also want to signal their displeasure at the 'injury' done to them and warn off such invasions of their personal space.

In *steps 4 and 5* possible responses are generated and are evaluated in relation to their likely consequences, the child's goals and their self-efficacy for performing each response. Our child, shocked and smarting from the blow, may feel like throwing the football back hard to hurt the child who kicked it. However, they are likely to dismiss this possible response because it may lead to a fight, because it may be perceived as inappropriate by the other players and so be inconsistent with the child's main goal, or because they do not think they can throw the ball hard enough to hurt the kicker.

In *step 6*, they enact the behaviour chosen and the cycle starts again as they encode the responses of others in the situation. In our example the child picks up the ball and says in tones of moderate indignation 'hey you guys, watch it!'. The kicker steps forward and says 'sorry mate' – confirming the accidental nature of the event, acknowledging the injury and indicating a desire for an ongoing amicable relationship. The child says 'OK', throws back the ball in a relaxed manner and the game continues.

A wide range of evidence supports the view that skillful processing at each of these six stages is associated with **social competence**, while biased processing can lead to aggression and social problems (Crick and Dodge, 1996; Zelli et al, 1999). At *step 1* aggressive, as opposed to non-aggressive children, are found to encode fewer benign social cues, attending preferentially to hostile cues. At *step 2* there is a bias towards making more hostile attributions of intentions and at *step 3* to select instrumental goals (achieving desired outcomes for themselves) rather than relational goals (maintaining positive relationships with others). In the earlier example where a child was hit by a football in the playground, an aggressive child would be significantly more likely to conclude that the ball was kicked at them on purpose with the intention of hurting them, and to select the goal of hurting the kicker to teach them not to aggress in the future. Aggressive children generate fewer prosocial responses at *step 4*, and at *step 5* they evaluate aggressive responses more favourably, expecting that positive outcomes will result. They also feel more self-confident in their ability to enact the aggressive behaviour successfully at *step 6*.

It is disputed whether bullying, as distinct from other forms of aggression, is caused by socio-cognitive deficits in processes such as those depicted in the model. Instead Sutton et al (1999a: 118) have argued that 'many bullies may in fact be skilled manipulators, not social inadequates'. Drawing attention to the social nature of bullying, Pepler and Craig (1995) reported that peers are present in some 85 per cent of bullying episodes. They also argued that some bullying, such as more subtle relational bullying, seems to require a high level of socio-cognitive skill. They investigated one type of socio-cognitive skill in particular – theory of mind (TOM) abilities. Theory of mind (which was discussed in detail in Chapter 8) involves the ability to attribute mental states, such as beliefs, desires and intentions, to others and to predict behaviour accordingly.

Sutton et al (1999b) presented children with 11 stories, four assessing understanding of cognitive false beliefs and seven assessing false-belief-based emotion. Examples of the 'strange stories' used to assess cognitive false beliefs can be found in Chapter 8. Figure 10.3 shows an example of a false-belief-based emotion story. Bullies, victims, outsiders and other roles were identified using the peer-nominated Participant Role Scale described earlier and their scores on the false belief stories compared. Bullies scored significantly higher on both the cognitive and the emotion false belief stories than any other participant role (controlling for age and verbal ability) except the non-involved outsider role. By contrast, the victim role score was negatively correlated with social cognition. Sutton et al (1999b) therefore suggested that at least some socio-cognitive abilities may be superior in at least some of the bullies.

This article sparked considerable controversy (see Arsenio and Lemerise, 2001, and Sutton et al, 2001, for contrasting accounts of each side of the debate). The most hotly contested issue between different groups of researchers

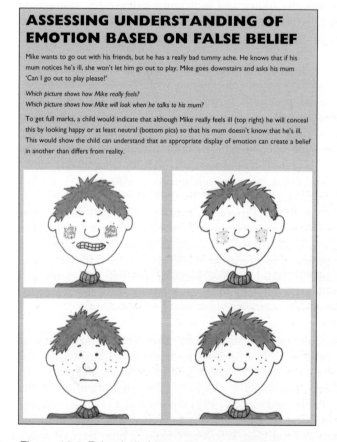

Figure 10.3 False-belief-based emotion story.

Source: © Jo Dearden (The Psychologist, Vol. 14, part 10, pgs 430–434).

has been whether bullying behaviour could be regarded as socially competent. This view has been advanced by Sutton et al (2001) on the basis that social competence equates to success in achieving one's own social goals 'it's easy, it works and it makes me feel good' (Sutton et al, 2001: 74). Crick and Dodge (1999), by contrast, have taken the position that the definition of socially competent behaviour needs to take account of the effects of the behaviour on others as well as self. They argue that 'hostile, harmful behavior' and 'engagement in highly aversive behaviors' should not be regarded as socially competent. Arsenio and Lemerise (2001) shifted the emphasis from behavioural effects on others to others' views of the behaviour, in particular in relation to 'shared standards about what is fair and right' (Arsenio and Lemerise, 2001: 62). As can be seen from Activity box 10.2, Sutton et al (2001) dismiss this view.

While these authors have disputed whether some bullies should be regarded as socially competent, there is substantial agreement on a variety of other issues such as the need to consider different groups of bullies and the potential explanatory value of the SIP model in relation to each. Sutton et al (1999a) acknowledge that further investigation of different types of children who bully others is indicated. Drawing on the finding that bullies have higher scores than victims and controls on the psychoticism scale of the Eysenck Personality Questionnaire (Slee and Rigby 1993), they suggest that 'It may be the aggressive, hot headed reactive bully-victims who fit the traditional picture of the social

Activity 10.2

Are bullies socially competent?

Consider the following arguments and identify their strengths and weaknesses.

Arsenio and Lemerise appear to be arguing that being socially competent involves maximizing shared standards concerning what is 'fair' or 'right'. This might be 'social conformity', socially acceptable behaviour' or even 'moral behaviour' but it is not social competence as we understand it. A 'socially conforming' behaviour might include shooting prisoners in Nazi concentration camps (conforming to Gestapo shared standards) or imprisoning suffragettes (conforming to society standards at the turn of the century). Such persons might or might not be 'socially competent' . . . Social competence should therefore not just be culturally defined in specific forms related to generally shared standards within that culture. We believe it is success at attaining individual goals, though the individual must take the social context they are in into account in order to do this.' (Sutton et al, 2001: 75–76)

Of the views put forward by Sutton et al (1999b), Crick and Dodge (1999), Arsenio and Lemerise (2001) and Sutton et al (2001), which do you find most convincing, and why?

skills deficient bully, while proactive aggressors may be more cold and calculating, actually possessing rather good social cognition' (Sutton et al, 1999a: 123). While bully-victims would have social information processing deficits in perceiving and interpreting social cues at the early stage of the model proposed by Crick and Dodge (1994) (see Figure 10.2), the proactive bullies may show skills in these areas, but have different goals and means of achieving them at the later stages of the model.

Arsenio and Lemerise (2001) agree that attention to goals is warranted and suggest that proactively aggressive bullies may be characterized by a focus on instrumental goals rather than relational goals. They also support the 'cold and calculating' characterization of proactive bullies, suggesting a lack of empathy to account for why they are undeterred by others' distress in their pursuit of instrumental goals. Parallels are drawn with research by Blair showing that children who are rated by their teachers as high on callous/unemotional behaviour (psychopathic traits) are less able than age mates to recognize specific emotions in others, namely sadness and fear, but not, for example, happiness. Sadness and fear are the very emotions, mediated by brain activity in the amygdala, whose recognition is thought to play a central role in inhibiting aggression (see Blair et al, 2006, for a review of work in this area). Hence deficient emotional, rather than cognitive, processing may be implicated in some bullying behaviour.

In conclusion, at the individual level there is considerable support for theories of bullying which give a large role to socio-cognitive processing problems, particularly in the case of reactively aggressive bullies. More recently the roles of goals and emotions in explaining bullying behaviour have also been highlighted.

Theories of family influence

These theories consider family relationships or processes that may cause or exacerbate bullying behaviour.

Social learning theory holds that bullying behaviour is acquired through modelling and reinforcement of behaviour and that early experience is particularly influential. A range of supportive evidence suggests higher levels of hostility and punitive responses by parents towards children who bully (Bowers et al, 1994). For example, Olweus (1994) reports high levels of physical aggression and emotional hostility in interactions between parents of bullies and their children. In addition, such parents tend not to set limits to their child's aggression so that it is often successful in achieving the child's goals. This contrasts with the parenting style of victim's mothers, which is described as overinvolved and overprotective (Bowers et al, 1994; Olweus, 1994).

Much of this research has been correlational and so open to alternative interpretations – maybe parents of bullies are reacting to their children's behaviour. However, the results of a longitudinal study by Schwartz et al (1997) suggest that parental behaviour is instrumental in the development of bullying in some children. They carried out assessments of boys and their home environments, first when the boys were pre-schoolers and again when they were

8–10 years of age. Bully or victim status was established by peer assessment in school on items such as 'gets picked on', 'says mean things'. Physical abuse, domestic violence, maternal hostility and harsh discipline in the early home environment were associated with later bully-victim status. The early home environments of bullies who were not also victims were not characterized by physical abuse or harsh treatment, although aggressive models and parental conflict were often present. In this study the home environments of victims who were not also bullies did not differ from those of children not involved in bullying. However, Schwartz et al (1997) point out that they did not assess overprotective parenting.

Attachment theory (Bowlby, 1969) posits that early caregiver–child interactions lead to the development of an 'internal working model' which is used to guide future relationships. A number of different types of caregiver–child interaction patterns, or attachment styles, have been described. They are typically identified through the Strange Situation Procedure (Ainsworth et al, 1978) in which a 10–24-month-old infant is briefly separated from their parent in an unfamiliar setting and then reunited with them. Three patterns of behaviour were originally identified, indicative of different attachment styles:

- *Secure* – these infants were happy to see the parent when reunited. If they had been distressed when the parent had left, they settled on the parent's reappearance and re-engaged in absorbed play or exploration.

- *Insecure–avoidant* – these infants typically showed little distress on separation and when the parent reappeared they moved or turned away, engaging in play and ignoring the parent.

- *Insecure–resistant/ambivalent* – these infants were very distressed on separation and, when the parent returned they tended both to seek contact and reject it when offered.

Compared to children with a history of secure attachment, those with a history of insecure–resistant/ambivalent attachment are more likely to be victims of bullying while those with a history of insecure–avoidant attachment are more likely to be perpetrators of bullying (Perry et al, 2001). More recently attention has focused on a fourth category, disorganized attachment, shown by 10 per cent of infants and comprising a variety of unusual and contradictory responses, which could not be classified as a consistent pattern of behaviour. Strong associations are reported between disorganized attachment, problems in regulating emotions, behaviour problems in school and psychopathology in adolescence (Green and Goldwyn, 2002). Future investigation of disorganized attachment, particularly in relation to bully-victim status, would appear to be indicated.

Group process theories

Rather than regarding bullying as the actions of deviant individuals, these theories seek to identify the functions that may be served by bullying in social groups. **Social dominance theory** will be considered as one example of this approach. Nishina (2004) suggests that bullying behaviour could serve particular social functions that may have been adaptive in evolutionary terms. It is argued that groups with clearly established dominance hierarchies are likely to be more successful both because within-group conflict will be minimized and because good organization will lead to higher levels of success in between-group conflicts. While it is possible to establish one's social dominance by pro-social as well as coercive means, Nishina suggests that 'bistrategic controllers' who use both strategies may be the most successful and admired by others.

Research with primates suggests that within stable group hierarchies there is little need for within-group aggression and the relative disadvantages of being low ranking (in terms, for example, of access to resources) are attenuated. On this analysis bully-victims are children who refuse to 'accept their place' in a group and challenge higher as well as lower status individuals. It is suggested that it is the group-destabilizing potential of this behaviour and the group discomfort generated as a result that leads to their dislike and rejection by peers. It is also suggested that involvement in bullying of someone outside a group can create feelings of belonging within the group and so represent a strong motivational force.

Nishina stresses that this kind of analysis should not be used to excuse bullying as a part of human nature. Rather, it may be helpful in explaining why the behaviour appears pervasive and difficult to eradicate. It may also suggest ways in which the school environment can impact on the incidence of bullying. For example, the ways in which adults in the school establish their dominance over the children might be expected to influence how dominance hierarchies among children are established, both directly through the systems of rules and sanctions in place and indirectly through modelling. It suggests that action against bullies is unlikely to be effective if it does not address the role others play in the bullying, or are perceived to play (Rigby, 2005), in particular in providing social reinforcement to the bully. Some theories go further in suggesting that the environment to which the child has been exposed can interact with individual and group factors in playing a causative as well as an ameliorative role in the incidence of bullying.

Ecological systems theories

A number of authors (Olweus, 1993; Sharp, 1999; Swearer and Espelage, 2004) argue that bullying can only be adequately understood by means of a multi-level analysis. 'In a nutshell, bullying does not occur in isolation. This phenomenon is encouraged or inhibited as the result of complex relationships between the individual, family, peer group, school, community, and culture' (Swearer and Espelage, 2004: 3). **Ecological systems theory** (Bronfenbrenner, 1979) conceptualizes an individual's social environment as four interrelated systems:

1. *A microsystem* is a pattern of activities, roles and interpersonal relationships experienced by a child in a particular setting where they are directly involved. The classroom, home and playground are three examples of settings where the child regularly interacts with others.
2. *A mesosystem* describes the relationships between two or more settings in which the child actively participates. The congruence between

attitudes towards bullying at home and at school would be an example at this level.

3. *An exosystem* is a setting where the child is not directly involved but which affects or is affected by what happens in settings that do involve the child. Local authority policy on bullying would be an influence on schools in the area and would be influenced by events in schools such as high-profile media reports on instances of bullying.

4. *The macrosystem* refers to the influence of cultural and subcultural mores and belief systems. Societal attitudes to bullying and common features of its representation in the media would be factors at this level.

Compared with the volume of research on individual-level factors in bullying, less work to date has been done on ecological factors that are associated with bullying. Useful reviews are provided by Doll, Song and Siemers (2004) and Payne and Gottfredson (2004). Doll et al (2004) reviewed the associations of two sets of classroom-level variables with lower levels of bullying:

■ The quality of social relationships (including pupil–pupil, pupil–teacher and teacher–parent).

■ Individual pupil responsibility in the classroom (including support for pupil self control, self-efficacy and self-determination).

Payne and Gottfredson (2004) summarized research on a range of school factors found to be related to bullying, in particular teacher interest and responsiveness, and pupil attitude, cooperativeness and alienation. Lower levels of bullying were found in schools where teachers were likely to discuss bullying with pupils, recognize bullying behaviour, show interest in stopping bullying and actually intervene in bullying incidents. More negative pupil attitudes to bullying were also associated with lower levels of the behaviour. Pupil cooperativeness was negatively correlated with bullying and victimization while pupil alienation and low levels of involvement in school increased the likelihood of involvement in bullying.

Which bullying interventions are effective?

Ecological systems theories have had a major impact on the design of interventions and it is typically recommended that bullying should be tackled through consistent implementation of strategies at organizational, group and individual levels (Sharp 1999: 5):

■ *Staff and students working together to develop a clear set of guidelines for everybody which specify what bullying is and what they should do when they know or suspect it is going on.*

■ *Long-term curriculum work about bullying and other forms of antisocial behaviour, including teaching students how to manage personal relationships assertively and constructively.*

- *Peer-led approaches, such as peer counselling and buddying, to offer support to pupils who are new to the school or who are feeling lonely, rejected or victimized.*

- *Direct intervention strategies when bullying has occurred or is suspected of occurring. Problem solving approaches which involve all students, including those who have been indirectly involved, are most effective. Early involvement of parents is recommended. Follow-up over time is always needed to check that the bullying has not resumed.*

International research indicates that this kind of multi-level intervention, modelled on the approach developed by Olweus (1993) in Norway, usually leads to reductions of around 5–20 per cent in victimization rates (Smith, 2004). This contrasts with the 50 per cent reduction in the original Olweus study. A number of factors have been identified that may limit the success of such programmes. For example 'tepid' support or lack of sustained effort from teachers overwhelmed by other demands is one important area (Stassen Berger, 2007). Another is failure to recognize the need to tackle peer culture and encourage bystanders to become defenders. The recommendation in the last bullet point above, that problem-solving approaches involving all affected pupils should be used in response to incidents of bullying, would appear relevant, and consistent with the literature on social information processing and group processes. Examples of such approaches that are commonly used by educational psychologists are the No Blame/Support Group Approach (see Young, 1998) and the Method of Shared Concern (Pikas, 2002; Rigby, 2005). However, this recommendation has proved controversial (Smith, 2001), as can be seen from Focus box 10.2.

Focus 10.2

To blame or not to blame ?

Guardian Unlimited *Wednesday January 4, 2006*

Council chiefs admitted today they were considering dropping a controversial policy of not blaming bullies in schools for their actions – following a scathing attack by the prime minister.

Teachers in Bristol had been advised not to "punish or humiliate" bullies in certain cases under the city council's **"no blame" approach** to the problem.

But the policy attracted fierce criticism from Tony Blair, who said it was an "extraordinary thing" for the Liberal Democrat-run council to advocate.

"I profoundly disagree with the decision that council has taken: bullying should be punished; children who bully must be made to understand the harm they have been doing," he told the Commons in November.

The existence of particularly vulnerable bully-victims can make a focus on punishing bullies rather problematic. This is especially so as reactively aggressive bully-victims are most likely to come to teachers' attention for **punishment**. Use of the imbalance of power that exists between teachers and pupils to punish bully-victims might be predicted to risk reinforcing counterproductive messages to this group. Even proactively aggressive bullies, who are not also victims, are already more alienated from school and have been more exposed to aggressive models at home. It is difficult to see how a punitive approach might be expected to have a positive effect and, indeed, RJR (not Tony) Blair et al (2006) review studies suggesting that children who show psychopathic tendencies, as proactively aggressive bullies appear to do, are more responsive to reward than to punishment.

By contrast, a social problem-solving approach that makes clear what behaviour is expected, puts in place a system of rewards and sanctions and works with the peer group to ensure that congruent consequences are operating at the group and organizational levels, may be more likely to succeed. In particular, despite exhortations to tell adults (e.g. 'Don't Suffer in Silence', DfES, 2002), children who are being bullied are often reluctant to seek help from school staff and more likely to do so where there is an anti-bullying whole school climate (Unnever and Cornell, 2004) when fears of inaction, ridicule or reprisal are likely to be minimized.

Juvonen and Graham (2004: 249) argue 'Unless an interventionist has a clear theory about what causes bullying, it is difficult to avoid what has come to be called a 'laundry list' approach . . . a little bit of everything and not much of anything specific to the targeted behavior'. Given the range of levels at which influences on bullying have been identified, multi-component programmes are likely to be needed. By drawing appropriately on theory at each level it is argued that a coherent set of proposals can be developed. Rigby (2004) offers an analysis of the implications for intervention in schools of key current theories of bullying which should assist educational psychologists working with schools on bullying prevention, or with children who bully. In their practice, educational psychologists will be collecting information on the type of bullying behaviour that is occurring and drawing on psychological theory and research to generate and test hypotheses about the causes of this bullying within the particular school situation. The results of this assessment will inform the selection of appropriate interventions and further collection of data in order that the interventions implemented can be evaluated. Bullying is a young area of psychological research and there are still many gaps in the knowledge base, particularly in relation to the effectiveness of interventions with different groups of children involved in bullying.

Summary

- The central characteristic in definitions of bullying is an imbalance of power which makes it very difficult for the target of aversive behaviour to prevent or stop it.

- Self and peer reports of bullying and victimization are the most frequently used methods of identification and assessment. The preferred method will depend on the purpose of the assessment.

- Findings from large national samples of school pupils indicate that approximately one-third of those who bully are also bullied. These 'bully-victims' may represent a population at particularly high risk of negative emotional and social outcomes.

- Among the theories advanced to explain bullying, the following have been most influential:

  Socio-cognitive deficit theories. Different types of bullies may be characterized by different types of problems with cognitive and/or emotional processing.

  Social learning theory and attachment theory are the leading theories of family influence on bullying.

  Social dominance theory is described as an important group process theory of bullying.

  Ecological systems theories consider a multi-level analysis of bullying to be essential where whole-school ethos interacts with individual-level variables to determine whether bullying will occur.

- Preventative programmes in schools draw largely on well-researched, moderately effective multi-level approaches. However, there is considerable controversy about the most effective direct intervention strategies to employ when bullying has occurred. Politicans 'talking tough' advocate punishment although psychological theory and research suggests that this may be unsuccessful or counterproductive with particular groups of pupils. A need for further research is highlighted on which bullying interventions work for whom under what circumstances.

Key concepts and terms

Attachment
Bullying
Bully-victim
Ecological systems theory
No blame approach
Power imbalance
Punishment

Social competence
Social dominance theory
Social information processing model
Social learning theory
Socio-cognitive deficit
Victimization

Sample essay titles

- Are bullies skilled manipulators or social inadequates?
- Compare and contrast the success of different theories in explaining bullying behaviour.
- Should bullies be punished? What can psychology contribute to this debate?

Further reading

Books and other publications

DfES (2000). *Bullying – Don't Suffer in Silence. An Anti-bullying Pack for Schools* London: DfES. http://publications.teachernet.gov.uk/eOrderingDownload/ DfES%200064%20200MIG479.pdf

Journal articles

Arsenio, W.F., and Lemerise, E.A. (2001). Varieties of childhood bullying: Values, emotion processes and social competence. *Social Development*, 10, 59–73.

Ma, X. (2001). Bullying and being bullied: To what extent are bullies also victims? *American Educational Research Journal*, 38, 351–370.

Rigby, K. (2004). Addressing bullying in schools. Theoretical perspectives and their implications. *School Psychology International*, 25, 287–300.

Rigby, K. (2005). Why do some children bully at school? The contribution of negative attitudes towards victims and the perceived expectations of friends, parents and teachers. *School Psychology International*, 26, 147–161.

Smith, P.K. (2001). Should we blame the bullies? *The Psychologist*, 14, 61.

Smith, P.K. (2004). Bullying: Recent Developments. *Child and Adolescent Mental Health*, 9, 98–103.

Stassen Berger, K. (2007). Update on bullying at school: Science forgotten? *Developmental Review*, 27, 90–126.

Sutton, J., Smith, P.K., and Swettenham, J. (2001). 'It's easy, it works, and it makes me feel good' – A response to Arsenio and Lemerise. *Social Development*, 10, 74–78.

11 How ethical are behavioural approaches to classroom management?

Andy Miller

In this chapter you will learn about the earliest studies by psychologists of **applied behavioural analysis** (ABA) in educational settings, particularly mainstream schools, as well as subsequent developments that illustrate the range of obstacles – practical, ethical and theoretical – experienced by educational psychologists and teachers attempting to work in this way. We will look in particular at controversies surrounding 'rewards' and 'punishments' as a prelude to addressing the central challenge raised in Winnet and Winkler's (1972) assertion that ABA was in danger of creating an educational climate in which children and young people were required to 'be still, be quiet, be docile'. Finally, we will consider the various ethical codes to which educational psychologists are subject and ask whether ABA can be accommodated within these.

Learning outcomes

When you have completed this chapter you should be able to:

1. Explain how the distinctive features of an ABA approach to challenging behaviour in school settings derive from the underlying theoretical rationale for such approaches.
2. Explain how various practical, ethical and theoretical considerations shaped the subsequent application of ABA approaches.
3. Evaluate the ethical implications of employing ABA in school settings.

Introduction

In 1968 in the USA, Madsen, Becker and Thomas published the first study demonstrating the positive benefits of ABA in a classroom context. As a result of their investigation, they felt able to claim that '. . . knowledge of differential social reinforcement procedures, as well as other behavioral principles, can greatly enhance teachers' enjoyment of the profession and their contribution to effective development of . . . students'. By 1971, the first British replication had been carried out by James Ward and some of his trainee educational psychologists at Manchester University, some of these students themselves going on to be enthusiastic proselytizers for the behavioural approach.

Practice spread rapidly and related publications increased. However, only four years after Madsen et al's pioneering study, Winnett and Winkler were warning that psychologists working with teachers in these ways were in effect subjecting youngsters in school to the injunction to 'be still, be quiet, be docile!' (Winnett and Winkler, 1972). Far worse was to come, with an official enquiry in 1991 into abusive practices by staff of a residential care establishment in Staffordshire being attributed to an 'ill-digested understanding of behavioural psychology' (Levy and Kahan, 1991). And yet, despite this chequered – some would argue, disastrous – history, it is possible to detect many of the central tenets of applied behavioural analysis in various recent and current British educational legislation and policy guidance.

How has this come about? And, what exactly is 'ABA'? Does it any longer inform the practice of educational psychologists? Or, on the other hand, has it seeped into the very fabric of educational policy making? Does it yield a wide range of practical approaches, some of which may be beneficial, or are all its manifestations of a distinctly unacceptable – an *unethical* – nature?

What is applied behavioural analysis?

Behavioural psychology assumed prominence during the first half of the twentieth century as a result of a huge number of laboratory studies carried out, in the main, with white rats and pigeons. These were supplemented by some studies using humans, usually drawn from a particular 'clinical' population. By the mid 1960s, however, *behaviourism* as a major theoretical standpoint within psychology was on the wane and Ulrich Neisser, for example, in the introduction to his classic *Cognitive Psychology*, was able to tease that

> *A generation ago, a book like this one would have needed at least a chapter of self defense against the behaviorist position. Today, happily, the climate of opinion has changed, and little or no defense is necessary. Indeed, stimulus-response theorists themselves are inventing hypothetical mechanisms with vigor and enthusiasm and only faint twinges of conscience. (Neisser, 1967: 5).*

And yet, despite the withering away of behavioural psychology's theoretical status in the face of 'the cognitive revolution', the latter half of the twentieth century, at least in the USA, was characterized, according to Landrum and Kauffman (2006), by the systematic application of behavioural procedures to socially relevant problems of children in clinical settings and ultimately classrooms. These authors saw ABA in particular as growing rapidly in popularity and influence in the 1960s and being characterized by

> *. . . systematic efforts to change socially important behaviours in positive ways through the application of behavioural principles, with strict reliance on the frequent, repeated assessment of observable and measurable behaviour (and with) the goal of establishing a functional relationship between independent and dependent variables. (Landrum and Kauffman, 2006: 53)*

This is perhaps best exemplified by taking a detailed look at the first major published study to employ ABA principles.

The origins of the use of ABA in mainstream classrooms

The first published study by Madsen et al (1968) was carried out in American schools and consisted of accounts of helping three pupils, two primary-aged and one kindergarten, improve their classroom behaviour. His teacher characterized the behaviour of this latter little boy when he entered the class as 'wild'. He would 'push and hit and grab at objects and at children. He had no respect for authority and apparently didn't even hear directions. He knew how to swear profusely. He would wander round the classroom and it was difficult to get him to engage in constructive work. He would frequently destroy any work he did rather than take it home.'

A set of categories of inappropriate behaviour was devised and confirmed with the class teachers concerned. Nine different categories of inappropriate and one of appropriate behaviour were described, the former consisting of gross motor, object noise, disturbance of other's property, contact, verbalization, turning around, other inappropriate behaviour, mouthing objects and isolate play. Two observers were trained over a two-week period to make precise records of the pupil's behaviour in the classroom (keeping a record of five 10-second intervals in every minute over a 20-minute period on three occasions each week). Figure 11.1 shows the proportion of inappropriate behaviour displayed by the kindergarten pupil during different intervention phases and a **baseline period** before the introduction of any of the experimental conditions.

The aim of the study was to investigate experimentally the effects on pupils' classroom behaviour of teachers varying their use of praise, ignoring and the explaining of **rules**. For the purposes of the experiment, in the first intervention phase the teachers were asked to aim for at least four to six repetitions of the rules each day at times other than when somebody had misbehaved, these rules being no more than five or six in number, short and to the point, and framed in a positive rather than a negative form (for example, 'sit quietly while working' rather than 'don't talk to your neighbours').

The second phase involved the teacher ignoring inappropriate behaviour unless this was leading to a pupil being hurt. The reason for this phase of the experiment was to test the possibility that inappropriate behaviour was being strengthened in some cases ('reinforced') by the attention paid to it by the teachers, even though this attention was intended to act as a punishment. Perhaps not surprisingly, the teachers in the study found this a particularly difficult strategy to implement and sustain as an intervention on its own.

The third phase, the praise condition, was framed as 'catching the child being good'. The teachers were asked to give praise, attention or smiles when the pupil was doing what was expected during the particular class in question. The teachers were also encouraged to 'shape by successive approximation', starting by giving praise and attention to the first signs of appropriate behaviour and building towards greater goals. Emphasis was to be placed on positive and helpful social behaviour and following group rules.

The results for the two pupils in the primary class were similar to those from the kindergarten setting shown in Figure 11.1. As this illustrates, the rules and the ignoring phases on their own produced little change from the baseline condition but the combination of **rules, praise and ignoring** proved highly effective in reducing inappropriate behaviour.

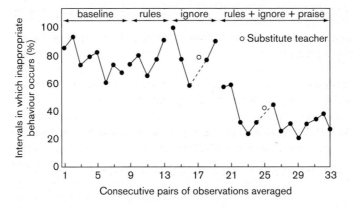

Figure 11.1 Inappropriate behaviour of one problem child as a function of experimental conditions.

Source: Madsen et al, 1968.

This pioneering study has been described in detail in order to illustrate the genesis of some of the fundamental features of the use of ABA approaches in classroom settings, namely:

- A concern with clearly defined and observable behaviour rather than assumed personality characteristics or motivations of pupils.

- The careful collection of and recording of data, often in graphical or tabular form.

- A focus on settings in which behaviour occurs and the signals or triggers that may act as **antecedents** to the behaviour as well as the **consequences** that follow the behaviour.

The single case experimental design

Figure 11.1 also illustrates many features of the **single case experimental design** (Kazdin, 1982; Barlow et al, 2008), which is a major methodological legacy from ABA. Robson (2002) contextualizes this contribution thus:

The work of Skinner arouses strong passions, and in consequence his approach to experimental designs tends to be either uncritically adopted or cursorily rejected. There is much of value here for the 'real world' investigator with a leaning to the experimental – mixed, as in Skinner's other work, with the unhelpfully polemical, the quirky and the rather silly. (Robson, 2002: 146)

Research methods 11.1

The graph from the work of Madsen et al (1968) shown in Figure 11.1 essentially takes the following form:

A A A A A A A A / B B B B B / C C C C C / D D D D D D D D D D D D D D

(where A = baseline measures, B = the rules condition, C = ignore, and D = rules + ignore + praise).

A more straightforward and quintessential single case experimental design, sometimes known as a **reversal design**, takes the form:

A A A A A A A A A A / B B B B B B B B / A A A A A A A A A A / B B B B B B B B

(where A is again the baseline measure and B the intervention under investigation).

In such a design, the experimenter is hoping to be able to infer a causal relationship between the intervention or treatment and the dependent variable(s). After the first intervention (B) phase, the experimenter removes the intervention and reverts to baseline conditions in the hope of demonstrating a return to baseline performance levels or behaviour. If this happens then there are grounds for inferring a causal relationship between the intervention (B) and the dependent variable(s).

However, in the work of educational and other applied psychologists there is considerable potential for the interests of the psychologist as *researcher* to act in conflict with those of the psychologist as *practitioner*. If, in the reversal design above, the work were to finish after the second baseline phase and if indeed the previously improved situation could be shown to revert to the original baseline, then the researcher's demonstration of a causal relationship would have been achieved by means of the ethically unacceptable practice of withdrawing and withholding an intervention shown to be beneficial.

A partial solution to this is to reinstate the intervention for a second time (as above) or, because this still involves the withdrawal of an intervention that seems to be successful, the more preferable **multiple baseline design** is instead employed.

The multiple baseline design

In this design, a behaviour might be observed in three different settings [for example, during formal teaching (1), less formal literacy activities (2) and less formal mathematics activities (3)]. A period of baseline observations (A) would be made in all settings before introducing the intervention (B) into the formal teaching condition (1) and continuing with baseline arrangements in the other conditions. After a subsequent period of observation across all three settings, the same intervention would also be introduced during the less structured literacy activities (2) with the intervention, after another period of recording, finally being used in the less formal mathematics activities condition (3). In this way, three graphs of data collected at the same time and across settings could be presented beneath each other, allowing visual inspection and the possibility of demonstrating the intervention's effects on the behaviour independent of setting.

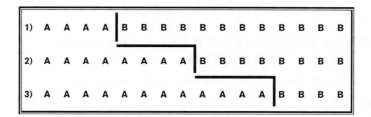

Figure 11.2 The multiple baseline design.

Activity 11.1

Multiple baseline recording

Figure 11.3 shows three graphs of the same pupil, recording the proportion of 10-second intervals in which 'off task' behaviour is observed in a number of five-minute sessions. During the 35-minute baseline period, the teacher is asked to use her usual teaching approach.

After 35 minutes of baseline observation, the teacher is trained in a 'rules, praise and ignore' (RPI) strategy and asked to employ this during formal teaching sessions only. Classroom observers record both pupil and teacher behaviour for a 35-minute formal teaching session. Next the RPI approach is extended to less formal literacy activities such as group and undirected work. And finally the RPI approach is extended to also include less formal mathematics learning activities.

The three sets of graphs display data collected on the same days and over the same time period.

Questions

- From visual inspection of the graphs, what *general conclusions* about the effectiveness of RPI for this pupil and teacher can be drawn with reasonable confidence?
- To what extent do the effects of RPI appear to be context dependent?
- What conclusions can be drawn about the generalization of any changed behaviour on the part of the pupil beyond the specific setting(s) of the intervention?
- Do the graphs yield any additional information that might be of interest to a teacher or educational psychologist?

1. During formal teaching sessions

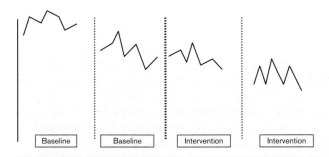

| Baseline | Intervention | Intervention | Intervention |

2. During less formal literacy activities

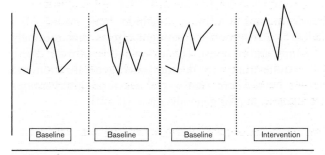

| Baseline | Baseline | Intervention | Intervention |

3. During less formal mathematics activities

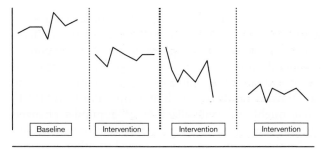

| Baseline | Baseline | Baseline | Intervention |

Figure 11.3 Graphs of a pupil's behaviour across three different settings.

Activity box 11.1 and Figure 11.3 present an example of a multiple baseline design *across settings*, but it is also possible to employ the same approach *across behaviours* and *across participants*. In the across behaviours version, the same intervention would be employed progressively in an attempt to influence three different behaviours exhibited by the same individual in the same setting. In the across participants variations, the same interventions would be directed at the same behaviour shown by three different participants in the same setting, the onset of the intervention being staggered across the participants. In each case, graphs of data obtained at the same time are displayed beneath each other to permit judgements to be made about the likely influence of the intervention on the dependent variable(s).

Generalization

Clearly, an intervention that demanded much in terms of the time of a teacher and psychologist would show relatively little return for this effort if its effects were to last only as long as the most intensive application of the intervention. Consequently, treatment **generalization**, or the extent to which improved behaviour is maintained and spreads after the ending of the intervention, became a topic of enduring interest. Drawing on the research literature, Presland (1981) outlined 24 suggestions that might aid generalization of a pupil's changed behaviour, including involving other children in providing reinforcement and explaining to the child how improvements can be transferred to other activities and contexts.

A little later, Gurney (1987) demonstrated, by means of a small-scale controlled study, that behavioural approaches could even be effectively employed in an area of interest traditionally seen as diametrically opposed in its focus – the area of humanistic psychology concerned with raising self-esteem. In this study pupils were taught, using contingent reinforcement, to make more positive statements about themselves and display more overt behaviours related to high self-esteem and, upon subsequent testing, were found to have internalized these and to be displaying a higher level of generalized self-esteem. In terms of the potential to aid generalization, proponents of humanistic approaches would predict that pupils with increased self-esteem would be likely to display less difficult behaviour in a range of settings.

In general though, Landrum and Kauffman conclude that classic ABA classroom studies have failed '. . . to produce treatment effects that routinely generalize to other settings, times and response' (Landrum and Kauffman, 2006: 60). They do, however, cite studies that have demonstrated generalization and call for further research that makes sure that '. . . behavioral interventions routinely include explicit programming for generalization' (p. 60).

Basic types of strategy

LaVigna (2000) reviewed three basic ABA strategies:

- **Differential reinforcement** of alternative response – most typically these strategies rewarded a student for 'being good', defined in some behavioural sense. This would be seen as a response that was a preferable alternative to whatever was causing the initial concern.

- *Differential reinforcement of the omission of a response* – in common parlance, rewarding a student for not committing some specified misbehaviour.

- *Differential reinforcement of lower rates of responding* – rewarding students for being 'naughty' less and less often.

In reviewing the evidence, LaVigna (2000) concludes that the *differential reinforcement of the omission of a response* is generally the most effective strategy for classroom settings. However, because of its negative formulation, in terms of the omission of something, it was recommended that such a strategy should always be accompanied by a direct teaching programme to teach the child positive alternatives to the problem behaviour in question.

A word about 'rewards'

Positive reinforcement in the form of praise from teachers was a distinctive feature of the Madsen et al study and rewards of various types have been incorporated into ABA studies and interventions ever since. However, Goodwin and Coates (1976) have provided a useful corrective to the uncritical application of rewards by pointing out that the goal of any intervention in an educational setting should be for the young person to experience the particular behaviours and accomplishments being encouraged as intrinsically motivating in themselves.

Social reinforcement such as teacher praise or peer encouragement is only necessary in circumstances where the student's skills level and accomplishment is not of a high enough standard for this to yet be a reinforcer in itself. Similarly, Goodwin and Coates argue that interventions should only employ **reinforcers** further to the left in Figure 11.4 if praise and encouragement are not powerful enough to increase a desired behaviour. In such circumstances, guiding principles

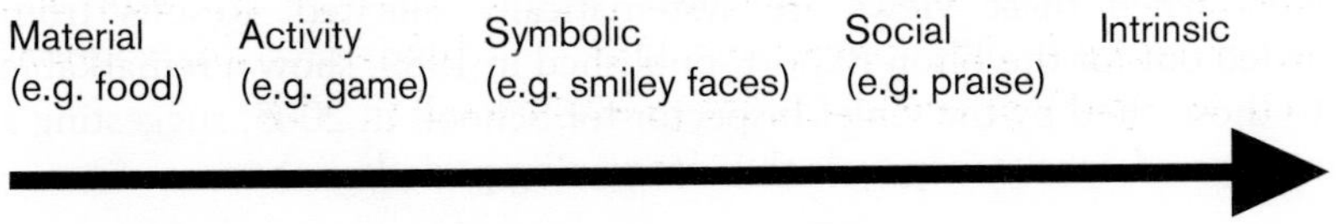

| Material | Activity | Symbolic | Social | Intrinsic |
| (e.g. food) | (e.g. game) | (e.g. smiley faces) | (e.g. praise) | |

Figure 11.4 The spectrum of classroom-based reinforcers.

Source: adapted from Goodwin and Coates, 1976.

would be to move only as far to the left as is necessary for increasing this behaviour, to always pair material, activity or symbolic reinforcement with praise and intrinsically motivating and interesting tasks, and to plan for progression to the right as it becomes possible to do so, phasing out these explicit and contrived reinforcers.

Following a comprehensive review of the psychological research literature, Henderlong and Lepper (2002) concluded that praise in itself may serve either to 'undermine, enhance or have no effect on children's motivation'. These authors identify the perception of the *sincerity* with which praise is used as being particularly beneficial to intrinsic motivation and also single out attribution to controllable causes (see Chapter 9), the promotion of autonomy and the avoidance of over-reliance on social comparisons, as other features strongly contributing to positive effects of praise upon outcomes for students.

A word about 'punishments'

Sanctions or punishments, *although not present in the original Madsen et al study*, soon became associated in the public mind with the practice of 'behaviour modification' and indeed were and are to be found as a staple feature of many ABA interventions.

Pitchford (2006), however, considers that a number of important ethical and professional implications follow from the research finding that ABA strategies can be successful without the use of punishment, or 'aversive approaches'. He points to the general trend of an apparently decreasing tolerance for the **punishment** of children and argues that, in an increasingly litigious society, where there is research evidence that non-aversive approaches can work then staff will become increasingly vulnerable if they advocate the use of punishments. Additionally, he argues that 'punishment-elicited aggression' may occur, with the anger of motorists towards traffic wardens cited as a particularly graphic example, resulting in 'counter-productive outcomes'.

A word about 'behaviour'

Considerations of difficult or challenging behaviour in schools often bring to mind images of extreme violence or threat. Although extremely serious when they do occur, these forms of behaviour do not feature as the major concerns of most teachers when these views are systematically solicited. Results from research carried out for the Elton Report, published in 1989, show a remarkable similarity to those cited by the Chief Inspector for Schools in 2005, suggesting a perhaps unexpected consistency over the intervening period:

Few teachers in our survey reported physical aggression towards themselves. Most of these did not rate it as the most difficult behaviour with which they had to deal. Teachers in our survey were most concerned about the cumulative effects of disruption to their lessons caused by relatively trivial but persistent misbehaviour. (DfES, 1989)

The most common forms of misbehaviour are incessant chatter, calling out, inattention and other forms of nuisance that irritate staff and interrupt learning. (Ofsted, The Annual Report of HM's Chief Inspector of Schools 2003/2004)

And it is, in fact, in helping to improve these very forms of misbehaviour that skillfully employed ABA approaches have been shown by the research to possess a convincing track record (Landrum and Kauffman, 2006).

UK developments in ABA

From consequences to antecedents

The emphasis in early studies on consequences – rewards and punishments – became most firmly associated with the term 'behaviour modification', a term that attracted many negative connotations. Kohn (1993), for example, challenged the popular propensity for employing rewards, his polemical title, *Punished by Rewards: The Trouble with Gold Stars, Incentive Plans, A's, Praise and Other Bribes*, hinting at the central thrust of his argument that, at best, rewards (and sanctions) produce a temporary compliance and, at worst, they prevent youngsters from ever becoming responsible decision makers in their own right.

Although early British developments seemed to represent a field of theory and practice distinctly separate from all other aspects of educational enquiry, subsequent work allied behavioural approaches more closely to wider educational concerns. For example, two of the original British proponents, Harrop and McNamara (1979), made the point that behavioural interventions had to ask whether the curriculum within the classroom where the difficult behaviour was being manifested should be altered to meet the pupil's interests and aptitudes before embarking upon a fuller behavioural intervention.

Considering the effects of classroom layout, Wheldall et al (1981) carried out an experiment with two classes of 10- and 11-year-olds in a junior school. The amount of 'on-task' behaviour was recorded over a two-week period while the children were seated around tables, the measurements then being repeated for a further two weeks while the children were seated in rows. Examination of the data revealed that the rows condition had the greatest effect on the children with low initial on-task behaviour, the very pupils for whom behavioural interventions might more usually have been devised. This strand of research interest still finds expression in publications such as that by Hastings and Wood (2002).

From 'on-task' behaviour to socially useful outcomes

In 1981, McNamara and Harrop concluded that until the early 1980s much practice had been 'somewhat naive' in focusing so much attention upon 'on-task' behaviour as opposed to 'academic work output', other academically and socially useful skills. These misgivings had been voiced most vividly by Winnet and Winkler (1972), who saw many early American approaches as encouraging pupils to 'be still, be quiet, be docile'.

In response, subsequent studies became far more driven by the recognition that pupils who succeeded at conventionally valued school activities were more likely, as a result, to identify more closely with the aims of the school and receive more naturally occurring praise and encouragement for their efforts. A creative and novel example was provided by Burland (1979) who described work in a school for pupils with emotional and behavioural difficulties in which behavioural principles were rigorously but creatively employed to teach pupils a range of social and leisure skills – everything from juggling to riding unicycles! In addition to introducing an element of fun and getting away from the image of behavioural approaches as being always aligned to control and conformity, this work had a serious intention of developing new talents as a source of satisfaction in themselves and as a probable aid to entry into a wider social acceptability for a group of children with underdeveloped social skills and restricted friendships.

From primary to secondary school age applications

Despite the accumulation of published accounts of successful work in primary and special school settings, similar outcomes in secondary schools proved far harder to achieve. McNamara and Harrop (1979), for example, found that, following a course for 100 probationary secondary teachers, there was only a limited response, compared with primary teachers, in terms of accounts of successful interventions supported by accompanying data. They concluded that these results, and the general paucity of studies in behavioural approaches in secondary schools, could mean that the complex nature of these schools did not easily lend themselves to such approaches.

From external control to self control

One means of overcoming the problem of trying to coordinate the responses of a large number of subject teachers in a secondary setting, and at the same time increasing a pupil's self regulation, came in the form of 'self-recording' studies, a clear account of which was initially provided by Merrett and Blundell in 1982. They reported on work involving a 13-year-old boy who displayed a very unsettled approach to many aspects of his work and also distracted other class members from theirs. Following a baseline period, an intervention was introduced which required the pupil to tally his on-task behaviour during the same periods that his teacher collected a similar record and it was explained that tally marks of his that agreed with his teacher's would be the only criteria leading to a reward. The boy's on-task behaviour rose from a mean level of approximately 30 per cent during the baseline period to a mean level of more than 60 per cent during this intervention period.

From a focus solely on behaviour to the inclusion of cognition and affect

Clinical applications of ABA with adults soon extended into considerations of the thoughts and feelings of clients, these developments being marked by the founding of the British Association for Behavioural Psychotherapy in 1972 and the theoretical formulations and practical techniques of cognitive behaviour therapy (CBT) as developed by Beck in 1976.

As its name indicates, CBT concerns itself with cognitive processes as well as overt behaviour, particularly those implicated in selective attention and in irrational beliefs in the form of 'negative automatic thoughts'. Treatment plans, often conceived of as experiments in doing and/or construing things differently, are drawn up to address such unhelpful thoughts and beliefs. Within this context, attribution re-training may be thought of as a specific type of cognitive behaviour therapy. The clear descriptions of antecedents, behaviour and consequences that are central to applied behaviour analysis are also often employed in CBT and research studies into effectiveness often employ single case experimental designs.

Recently, in 2005, with the British government priority of addressing mental health issues for children and young people in mind, the National Institute for Health and Clinical Excellence (NICE) published its review of the literature and concluded that cognitive behaviour therapy was one of the main treatments of choice for childhood depression (NHS, 2005). Since this time, Greig (2007) has provided a detailed analysis of the challenges involved in applying CBT to the particular range of difficulties often encountered in, and the specific contexts typical of, the work of educational psychologists.

From individual pupils to whole-class approaches

As research and practice developed, there was a recognition that the time commitment required from a psychologist promoting ABA was considerable, thus stimulating an interest in the most effective deployment of the scarce professional resource that is an educational psychologist. The first British experimental validation of the behavioural approach's positive contribution to *management of a whole class* was provided by Tsoi and Yule (1976), who used extra break time as a reinforcer. Two types of strategy were each shown to be effective: one where the behaviour of a single child formed the basis for reinforcement for all the class, and one in which changes in the behaviour of the whole class were required. Subsequently, Merrett and Wheldall (1978) rigorously evaluated the effective combination of a 'rules, ignore and praise' approach with a 'timer game' while Rennie (1980) demonstrated the positive outcomes achieved by other game strategies, all with whole classes.

From reactive strategies to preventative approaches

As well as approaches with whole-class groups as a means of capitalizing upon the potential of behavioural approaches, a parallel drive among psychologists and others was towards the prevention of classroom difficulties by means of various teacher training and school policy development initiatives. It was at this stage that a wider research base was drawn upon.

For example, a particularly innovatory set of training materials, titled *Preventative Approaches to Disruption* (Chisholm et al, 1986) and drawing upon Kounin's (1970) studies of **classroom management** as well as the ABA research literature, was devised by a group of educational psychologists in 1986. In another influential set of resource materials, *Building a Better Behaved School*, Galvin, Mercer and Costa (1990) combined a similar breadth of research studies with extensive professional experience of working in schools, drawing specific attention to the crucial importance of establishing clear and mutually agreed policies within schools for encouraging positive pupil behaviour.

A particularly popular approach to classroom management delivered as a package through accredited workshops is ***Assertive Discipline***, developed by Canter and Canter (1992). Although these materials originally concentrated heavily on systems of rewards and punishments allied to clear statements of classroom rules, subsequent revisions have placed a greater emphasis on students' self regulation and the underlying rationale for classroom rules although, as Brophy (2006) notes, the effectiveness of this package has not yet been determined by means of systematic research examination.

The 'Pindown' scandal

The apprehension that existed in some quarters concerning 'behavioural approaches' increased dramatically in the public mind with revelations in 1989 concerning the regime practised in a residential setting in Staffordshire and known as 'Pindown'. A briefing paper subsequently prepared for the Scottish Parliament (2004) observed that

> . . . *an adolescent girl was found to have been confined to a barely furnished room for long periods; required to wear night clothes during the day; deprived of contact, education and sensory stimulus; and prevented from communicating with other children or going out* . . . *It eventually emerged that 132 children aged from 9 to 17 had been subjected to Pindown between 1983 and 1989.* (Scottish Parliament Information Centre (SPICe), 2004: 9)

The architect of this regime was a social services area officer who claimed to be implementing a system of 'behaviour modification'. Commenting in the official enquiry on the origins of Pindown, Levy and Kahan (1991) concluded that the approach was '. . . likely to have stemmed initially from an ill-digested understanding of behavioural psychology. The regime had no theoretical framework and no safeguards'.

Two very different conclusions (at least) may be drawn from this episode: first, that ABA and behavioural approaches in general may sometimes acquire a negative reputation erroneously, but, second, that people engaged in such punitive and abusive behaviour might for whatever reason believe that they can find a rationale for their actions in such approaches. In this particular incident, however, as the enquiry noted, the root of the problem was judged to lie in the practice of placing vulnerable youngsters in closed institutional settings where external scrutiny and accountability is considerably reduced in scope.

Recent developments in educational policy and legislation

It is probably the case that very few, if any, individual interventions are now carried out by educational psychologists to the degree of detail exemplified by ABA approaches, and there is a tendency to favour other theoretical paradigms to a far greater extent. Paradoxically, however, over the same period of time, general practices in education appear to have changed from an initial wariness, if not outright hostility, towards ABA in early 1970s to a situation where nowadays some of the 'blunter' aspects of the approach, if not perhaps some of the finer and more crucial details, are to be found in an increasing range of educational policy and legislation. Talk of targets, rewards, sanctions, rules, strategies and plans pervades and can be found in, for example, pastoral support programmes (DfEE, 1999b), home–school agreements (DfEE, 2000b) and the Special Educational Needs Code of Practice (DfES, 2001). Recently, central government (DfES, 2007) has additionally cited the Elton Report (DfES, 1989) as the source for its claim that an effective classroom management policy is one that reflects a ratio of five rewards to every sanction.

ABA in classrooms – deciding between evidence and myth

Activity box 11.2 contains a range of statements that are sometimes made about ABA, either supporting or criticizing it. You are asked to evaluate these statements by referring to the material presented in this chapter and the accompanying references. The purpose of the exercise is to make an evidence-based assessment of the validity of these commonly expressed views.

Activity 11.2

Deciding on the evidence base for common claims about the use of ABA in educational settings

Statement	Arguments and evidence, if any, that support this statement?	Arguments and evidence if any, that refute this statement?
1. ABA essentially requires students to 'be still, be quiet, be docile'		

2. ABA encourages a temporary compliance among students at the expense of growth in their being able to exercise responsible decision-making		
3. ABA denies the complexity of young people's 'inner worlds' by focusing only on observable behaviour		
4. ABA provides a justification for aversive, punitive approaches		
5. ABA's use of rewards amounts to nothing more than bribery		
6. ABA concentrates on individual students and distracts attention from possible shortcomings in educational policy and practice		
7. ABA provides a more precise evaluation of its effects than most other approaches in education		

When you have filled as many of the columns as possible with evidence to support and/or refute each statement, make a judgement as to the overall weight of evidence for each statement and decide whether it indicates broad agreement or disagreement.

ABA in classrooms – passing the ethical challenge?

The previous activity required you to decide between what might be considered an evidence base for ABA and what unsubstantiated claims. In addition, the use of ABA needs to pass the test, as does all other educational psychology practice, of being ethically sound. Activity box 11.3 addresses this final challenge.

Activity 11.3

Deciding on the possible ethical challenges presented by the use of ABA in educational settings

This activity requires judgements to be made against the ethical code and professional guidelines set down for educational psychologists (BPS, 2002, 2006) for each of the statements in Activity box 11.2 you judged, on balance, to be supported by the evidence. So, consider the following extracts from the major relevant sections from these two documents:

Informed consent (BPS, 2006)

1.3 (i) . . . ensure that clients, particularly children and vulnerable adults, are given ample opportunity to understand the nature, purpose, and anticipated *consequences* of any professional services or research participation, so that they may give informed consent to the extent that their capabilities allow.

Ethical decision-making (BPS, 2006)

2.2 (iv) . . . analyse the advantages and disadvantages of various sources of action for those likely to be affected, allowing for different perspectives and cultures.

Recognizing limits of competence (BPS, 2006)

2.3 (iii) . . . remain abreast of scientific, ethical and legal innovations germane to their professional activities, with further sensitivity to ongoing developments in the broader social, political and organisational contexts in which they work.

Intervention (BPS, 2002)

4.4 . . . (EPs) should consider thoroughly the most reversible and least intrusive interventions before embarking on less easily reversible and more intrusive courses of action.

4.4 . . . (EPs) should encourage the young person to participate in processes and decision-making as far as possible. The informed agreement of the young person should be obtained before proceeding with an intervention (if it is possible to convey the information in terms she/he can understand). An exception to this would be those situations in which failure to intervene would result in harm or danger to the young person concerned.

4.4 . . . (EPs) should rigorously evaluate their involvement with young people, schools and families in order to review and modify intervention strategies.

Now, take each supported statement from Activity box 11.2 and decide whether it challenges or contravenes any of the sections from the Ethical Code and Guidelines. If you are unsure, make a note of what additional information in relation to the particular statement you would need to enable you to make a decision one way or the other.

Finally, make a note also of any other aspects of ABA you have become aware of that may also challenge or contravene these ethical principles.

Summary

- Studies have demonstrated that aspects of young children's classroom behaviour can be influenced by teachers employing a carefully developed system that combines the use of praise, ignoring and a clear statement of classroom rules.

- Studies of the use of applied behaviour analysis in educational settings have encouraged the development of single case experimental designs.

- Reversal designs attempt to show the effects of an intervention by withdrawing the intervention and judging whether the behaviour under observation reverts to its baseline level.

- The interests of researchers and practitioners can be brought into conflict within a reversal design and its use may in some circumstances be judged ethically unacceptable. Multiple baseline designs are an attempt to overcome these reservations.

- Generalization of behaviour change beyond the experimental setting and period has proved problematic.

- There are three main types of ABA strategy – differential reinforcement of alternative response, differential reinforcement of the omission of a response, and differential reinforcement of lower rates of responding. LaVigna (2000) concluded that differential reinforcement of the omission of a response is generally the most effective for classroom settings but needed to be accompanied by a programme that directly taught positive behaviours.

- A spectrum of possible classroom reinforcers has been posited and strategies should always aim towards children being able to find classroom and school experiences intrinsically motivating.

- Sanctions and punishments have become widely associated in the public mind with ABA although they were not present in the original published studies. Punishments raise a range of ethical and professional and possibly legal issues.

- Practice in ABA has seen an evolution from a focus upon 'on-task' behaviour encouraged by changed consequences to a concern with more socially and academically useful behaviour and a greater focus on environmental antecedents.

Key concepts and terms

Antecedents	Multiple baseline design
Applied behavioural analysis	Punishment
Assertive Discipline	Reinforcers
Baseline period	Reversal design
Classroom management	Rules, praise and ignoring
Consequences	Single case experimental design
Differential reinforcement	Social reinforcement
Generalization	

Sample essay titles

- 'Be still, be quiet, be docile' (Winnet and Winkler, 1972). Does this pretty much sum up the aims of 'applied behaviour analysis' in educational settings?
- Classic studies involving 'rules, praise and ignoring' in educational settings demonstrated positive outcomes. What subsequent problems and challenges did educational psychologists experience as they tried to widen the application of such approaches?
- A Director of Children's Services asks you, the educational psychologist, to brief her so that she can reply to a local politician anxious about the possible detrimental consequences of using 'applied behaviour analysis' in the Local Authority. Outline major considerations in terms of efficacy, application and ethics and offer your advice on future policy development.
- Applied behaviour analysis is, in essence, an elaborate system of 'carrots and sticks'. Discuss.

Further reading

Books

Barlow, D., Nock, M., and Hersen, M. (2008). *Single Case Experimental Designs*, (3rd revised edn). Needham Heights, MA: Allyn and Bacon.

Brophy, J. (2006). 'History of research on classroom management.' In: C.M. Evertson and C.S. Weinstein (Eds) (2006), *Handbook of Classroom Management*. London: Lawrence Erlbaum Associates.

Kohn, A. (1993). *Punished by Rewards. The Trouble with Gold Stars, Incentive Plans, A's, Praise and Other Bribes*. Boston: Houghton Mifflin Company.

Landrum, T.L., and Kauffman, J.M. (2006). 'Behavioural approaches to classroom management.' In: C.M. Evertson and C.S. Weinstein (Eds) (2006), *Handbook of Classroom Management*. London: Lawrence Erlbaum Associates.

Miller, A. (2003). *Teachers, Parents and Classroom Behaviour. A Psychosocial Approach*. Maidenhead: Open University Press.

Journal articles

Greig, A. (2007). A framework for the delivery of cognitive behaviour therapy in the educational psychology context. *Educational and Child Psychology*, 24, 19–35.

Henderling, J., and Lepper, M.R. (2002). The effects of praise on children's intrinsic motivation: a review and synthesis. *Psychological Bulletin*, 128, 774–795.

Useful websites

British Psychological Society. (2006). *Code of Ethics and Conduct*. Leicester: British Psychological Society. www.bps.org.uk/the-society/ethics-rules-charter-code-of-conduct/code-of-conduct/code-of-conduct_home.cfm

Department for Education and Science. (2007). *School Discipline and Pupil-Behaviour Policies: Guidance for Schools*. www.teachernet.gov.uk/wholeschool/behaviour/schooldisciplinepupilbehaviourpolicies/

Scottish Parliament Information Centre (SPICe). (2004). *Abuse of Children and Young People in Residential Care*. 04/85. Scottish Parliament Information Centre. www.scottish.parliament.uk/ business/research/briefings-04/sb04-85.pdf

12 School phobia and school refusal

Coping with life by coping with school?

Andy Miller

In this chapter we examine the puzzling phenomenon of **school phobia**, or **school refusal** as it is also known. We will consider the historical development of theoretical thinking around this topic and note that formulations within psychiatry and psychology have differed dramatically, leading to a wide range of recommended treatment and intervention strategies. Before that, however, we will look at the classic clinical features of school phobia and the debates around appropriate nomenclature – school phobia, school refusal, persistent and chronic **non-attendance** or **truancy**? – and consider the ways in which these debates centre on the question of whether school refusal, or whichever term we choose, may be considered a unitary phenomenon. We will examine research into the epidemiological features of school refusal before considering in detail two different intervention approaches developed by educational psychologists.

Learning outcomes

When you have completed this chapter you should be able to:

1. Describe the major theoretical formulations that have attempted to account for chronic non-school attendance.
2. Explain the link between major theoretical formulations and the intervention approaches that derive from them.
3. Identify those aspects of case presentations that have significant implications for assessment and intervention with school refusers.
4. Justify the selection of components of effective intervention plans for school refusers.

What is school phobia?

Consider the brief case study presented in Activity box 12.1. It is a real case, disguised to an extent to preserve confidentiality.

Activity 12.1

Case study – Part 1

The initial presentation

James Sharpe was 14 years old and in his third year in a secondary school that is widely regarded as providing a high-quality educational experience for its students along with a supportive pastoral system. Quite suddenly and unexpectedly he stopped attending.

By the time the school's Special Needs Coordinator (SENCO) brought James to the attention of the educational psychologist, school staff had visited James and his parents at home and had tried to ascertain the cause of this dramatic change in behaviour and to agree various plans for his return to school. The head of the year group and the SENCO had carefully pursued with James all his concerns about school. He seemed reasonably able and successful in most of his school subjects, except maths where his performance was only a little below that of the class average. His teachers were predicting that he had the ability to achieve reasonable GCSE passes. James did report some occasional teasing from some other students – he was somewhat overweight – but, on discrete investigation, his teachers felt that this was light-hearted in nature and not indicative of focused and persistent bullying. James could not cite many instances of teasing, the most hurtful being a taunt from some skate-boarding friends who said 'Don't you get on it, Sharpey, it'll break!'. His teachers did not underestimate the potential power of such remarks and promised to make every effort to prevent them recurring. They were also aware that other more serious or distressing events might be occurring to which, for some reason, James and other pupils were not allowing them access, but their instinct was that other more serious matters were not being hidden from them. When the educational psychologist first visited James and his family, he had been out of school for four weeks.

James said he would certainly attempt to complete any work that was sent home but when discussion turned towards a return to school he became quickly agitated and this built into a rage. His mother reported that he had complained of nausea and stomach pain in his first few days off school when it came to his normal time to leave for school but a visit to his GP had not revealed any medical cause for this. He had also been crying during the night and had begged her not to make him go.

His mother was very appreciative of the teachers' efforts and very much wished him to return. His father also recognized and supported the school's efforts but was also furious that his son had been made to feel uncomfortable about his size and weight and wished that the law and the school policy would allow more extreme punishments to be meted out to the perpetrators. He also felt it was a disgrace that no professional help had been available earlier and stated that he had personal knowledge of pupils in James' position who had committed suicide.

Activity

In groups, share your initial response to the following questions:

1. What hypotheses might plausibly explain James' behaviour?
2. Why might it be desirable for James to return to school?
3. Why might it be undesirable for James to return to school?
4. What might be the advantages and disadvantages of attempting to arrange a place at a different mainstream school for James?

Some aspects of James' case – the persistent and unexplained nature of his absences, the somatic complaints in the early morning, and his intense and fearful anger when the possibility of a return to school is discussed – figure

Focus 12.1

The 'clinical presentation' of school phobia

Historically, Broadwin (1932) was the first to describe a form of non-attendance at school that seemed to be typified by a consistent and long-standing absence from school, in which the young person stayed at home, seeming extremely fearful of going to school even though any reasons given usually seemed incomprehensible or disproportionate to parents and teachers.

The problem often starts with vague complaints of school or reluctance to attend progressing to total refusal to go to school or to remain in school in the face of persuasion, entreaty, recrimination, and punishment by parents and pressures from teachers, family doctors and education welfare officers. The behaviour may be accompanied by overt signs of anxiety or even panic when the time comes to go to school and most children cannot even leave home to set out for school. Many who do, return home half way there and some children, once at school rush home in a state of anxiety. Many children insist they want to go to school and are prepared to do so but cannot manage it when the time comes. (Hersov, 1977)

Anxiety symptoms often manifest themselves in a variety of somatic forms including headache, stomach pains, nausea, dizziness, fevers and so on. Sometimes the child protests with tears or temper tantrums leading to destructive or aggressive behaviour. Some children become lethargic and depressed and a few threaten suicide. Usually, once the pressure to attend school has been removed, the symptoms accompanying the school avoidance dissipate. (Blagg, 1987) centrally in the original description presented by Broadwin (1932) and in the classic 'clinical presentation' of school phobia put forward by Hersov (1977) and supplemented by Blagg (1987).

Making sense of school refusal/phobia

Pupils such as James who display the sort of behaviour above have long challenged educational and medical practitioners. School staff have been concerned about missed lessons, their inability to 'get to the bottom of the problem', disappointment sometimes when a student promises to begin attending again on a certain date and then fails to appear, and a suspicion on other occasions that the young person may be lying or manipulating them. The various other professionals who may become involved – such as educational psychologists, education welfare officers, child psychiatrists and general medical practitioners – sometimes struggle to arrive at a theoretical formulation and an effective intervention plan, particularly one that meets with the agreement of each of the involved parties.

So far in this chapter we have been using the terms 'school phobia' and 'school refusal' as if they are interchangeable. We will consider later whether the research evidence supports this assumption and whether school phobia and/or school refusal can be considered unitary concepts. For the time being, however, it will be helpful to adopt a basic set of distinctions put forward by Blagg (1987) when he came to investigate an intervention approach with young people who were persistently absent from school (Focus box 12.2).

Focus 12.2

Criteria used by Blagg (1987) for distinguishing between school phobia, truancy and other non-attendance

Criteria for defining *school phobia* (from Berg et al, 1969)

- Severe difficulty in attending school often resulting in prolonged absence.
- Severe emotional upset, which may involve such symptoms as excessive fearfulness, temper tantrums, misery, or complaints of feeling ill without obvious organic cause when faced with the prospect of going to school.
- Pupil remains at home with the knowledge of parents during school hours.
- Absence of significant antisocial disorders such as juvenile delinquency, disruptiveness and sexual activity.

Criteria for defining *truancy* (from Blagg and Yule, 1984)

- Absent from school without good reason on at least five occasions in one term.

- Pupil shows no evidence of a marked emotional upset accompanying the non-attendance at school.
- Pupil is absent without the parents' permission or approval, the majority of time off being spent away from home. Parents sometimes aware of the non-attendance but unable to exert any influence over their child.

Criteria for defining *other poor attenders* (from Blagg and Yule, 1984)

- Absent from school without good reason on at least five occasions in one term.
- Pupil shows no evidence of a marked emotional upset accompanying the non-attendance at school.
- Remaining at home with knowledge and permission of parents (possibly kept at home deliberately to help with an ill or 'needy' parent).

Epidemiological aspects of school refusal

Berg (1996) summarizes the research evidence for the epidemiological features of school refusal, using the term in the same way as Blagg (1987) does school phobia:

- Boys and girls are equally affected.

- There is no relationship to social class.

- There is no relationship with intellectual or academic ability.

- The youngest child in a family of several children is more likely to be affected.

- Parents of school refusers are often older than would otherwise be expected.

- It can affect a school child of any age but young teenagers at about the time of transition from primary to secondary school are more likely to develop school refusal.

- The onset tends to be gradual, but it may occur suddenly after time away from school because of illness or holidays or some upsetting event, or just come on without any obvious reason.

- There may be no associated social impairment but often there is, including staying home excessively and avoiding contact with other children.

Elliott (1999) cites studies that yield varying **incidence** rates, depending on the stringency with which school refusal is defined, and concludes that a proportion of 1–2 per cent of the school-aged population is now the widely accepted figure for school refusal defined in this way.

Activity 12.2

Case study – Part 2

Further assessment information and the initial formulation

The educational psychologist arranged for Mr and Mrs Sharpe to meet him with the SENCO in school after the end of lessons and to bring James with them if they could. James refused, and the first part of the meeting, which lasted in total two and three quarter hours, was spent listening sympathetically to Mr Sharpe's angry complaints about the quality of professional input. When a more collaborative tone to the meeting had been forged, the conversation yielded, among other things, the following information:

- James had been off school recovering from an operation on an in-growing toenail prior to this period of non-attendance, had returned briefly just before Christmas, and then not returned after the holiday.
- His attendance record for the previous academic year was 95 per cent and for the current year so far, 47 per cent.
- James' brother, who was 18 months older, had no problems with school attendance or work.
- James was completing school work sent home for him, and he and his parents wished for a home tutor to be appointed.
- James had had friends at school but now there was nobody. One person had rung but James said that he was 'only trying to save his own neck' because he had been involved in the teasing.
- School staff had investigated the incidents of teasing/bullying reported by James and had spoken with each of the other boys involved. They were of the view that this had not been persistent, was light hearted in tone and the boys did want James to return to school.
- When the SENCO had phoned home during the daytime about some of the set work, there had been loud music playing and James had put down the phone once he had realized it was her and had then set the answer-machine for when she dialled again.
- His parents described a typical day for James as getting up between 8 and 9am, having breakfast, then keeping busy on school work, his computer, walking the dog, or doing housework such as hoovering.
- Mr Sharpe did not think the teasing about James' weight was the trigger to the non-attendance and believed this was a 'more deep-rooted problem'. He reiterated that he feared James might kill himself.
- James had apparently said 'I hate school. I really, really, really hate school. I'm frightened. I really hate school'.
- The family lived in an owner-occupied house on a modern estate, Mr Sharpe was articulate and had a job in the professions and had relatives 'high up in education'. Mrs Sharpe did not currently work.
- Mr Sharpe had had major surgery on his back when James was 9 years old. At around the same time James had a more minor bout of non-attendance.

- Mrs Sharpe had been taking Prozac for the 6 months prior to this current episode but was now coming off this medication.
- School reports showed James to be hard working and well behaved.
- James had attended three different primary schools, Mr Sharpe being critical of all three for different reasons.
- Mr and Mrs Sharpe had separated briefly two years earlier but were now back together.

Activity

- Look again at Focus boxes 12.1 and 12.2 on the clinical presentation of school phobia and the criteria used by Blagg for distinguishing between school phobia, truancy and other non-attendance. Look also at the epidemiological aspects of school refusal provided by Berg (1996).
- In groups, decide on the extent to which James' case seems to be one of 'school phobia'. List all supporting and contraindicatory evidence.
- From the information given so far, generate a number of explanatory hypotheses for James' behaviour and give a percentage grade for each one in terms of your confidence in it as an explanation.

Early theoretical formulations

The earliest attempts at understanding and treatment were made by psychiatrists and other medical personnel, who drew on psychodynamic and other theories in their search for a conceptualization of these symptoms of school refusal. Three types of explanation were originally offered based on: 'separation anxiety', anxiety about aspects of schooling, and other social anxieties.

Explanations in terms of separation anxiety derive from psychoanalytic thinking and were first advanced by Johnson et al (1941). In this formulation, separation anxiety was seen as a product of an unresolved mother/child dependency relationship in which an excessively strong mother–child attachment resulted in a reluctance on the part of a child to leave the home. Later papers, such as that by Estes, Haylett and Johnson (1956), provided a more detailed account of the dynamic nature of the development of what was seen as a type of neurosis. In addition to the early dependency relationship, this process was also thought to be founded on an inadequate fulfilment of the mother's emotional needs within an intimate adult relationship. As a result of an interplay of hostility and dependency, and the subconscious mechanisms of displacement and projection, a level of anxiety about separation developed in the child to an acute degree.

An alternative psychoanalytic approach, suggested by Berry, Injejikian and Tidwell (1993), focused on the child's feelings of **omnipotence**. In this theory the child develops a grandiose attitude of himself or herself which, when challenged in school by realities that confront the child's limitations, leads to avoidance of school and staying at home, where parents further reinforce his or her distorted, omnipotent self-image.

A third view, deriving from a behavioural viewpoint, and more specifically from within **classical conditioning**, was that of **school-focused anxiety**, in which some particular features of school environments such as the size of buildings, the strictness of some teachers, the difficulty of some lessons and tasks, and the potential embarrassment associated with using the toilet or changing for physical education activities, become the source of fear and anxiety.

A fourth formulation was that of **social anxiety**, a more specific form of school-based anxiety centring specifically on interactions with others and incorporating fears of being rejected, isolated or bullied, and an inability to make friends.

Intervention approaches associated with these early conceptualizations

Blagg (1987) reviewed early treatment studies based on a traditional *psychodynamic approach*, beginning with a study published by Jung in 1911 and ranging through a number that reported the use of psychoanalysis either with children alone or mother and child together, with some courses of treatment lasting for up to three years. Also in this review, Blagg referred to a series of interventions, the first being published in 1948, in which children and young people were treated by means of admission to a hospital, usually psychiatric, as an inpatient.

More recent thinking within child and adolescent psychiatry has emphasized the need for a rapid return to school wherever possible (Goodman and Scott, 2002) with the possibility of individual psychotherapy to explore more persistent anxieties being offered once the child is back in school (Black and Cottrell, 1993). By 1993, Black and Cottrell were reporting that, in the British context, inpatient treatment of school refusal was most uncommon. Furthermore, in terms of efficacy of such approaches, King and Bernstein (2001) have pointed out that play therapy, psychodynamic psychotherapy or family therapy as treatments for school refusal have not been subjected to rigorous evaluation in randomized controlled clinical trials.

From a *behavioural psychology orientation*, **systematic desensitization** approaches were located within a classical conditioning framework and attempted to help the young person overcome the anxiety by reciprocal inhibition (Wolpe, 1954), by teaching any behaviours antagonistic to the anxiety, such as controlled breathing or imagining pleasant activities. Such treatments either took place entirely in imagination or *in vivo*, where some or all of the treatment would be carried out in the presence of the anxiety-producing stimuli, perhaps in the early morning before school departure or, if it were possible to arrange, at school itself.

Some behaviour therapists found the use of **emotive imagery** to be a powerful alternative to systematic desensitization approaches. Galloway and Miller (1978), two educational psychologists, reported on the case of an 11-year-old boy who regularly refused to go to school on certain mornings. Interviews with the boy and his mother revealed that he was fearful of showering after games and physical activities. A programme of systematic desensitization, using imagined shower scenes followed up by reciprocal inhibition training *in vivo*, enabled the boy to improve his attendance and take showers at school after a total of seven treatment sessions.

Flooding or **implosion** is a procedure for confronting the maximally feared situation, usually in imagination, directly rather than after graded exposure as in most desensitization approaches. Blagg (1987) cautioned that real-life confrontation of maximal fears – flooding – was a highly demanding and stressful treatment, not least as a result of the '**extinction** spike', a temporary accentuation of the fear, as an early phase of classical extinction. For this reason and others, Blagg suggested that, if used at all, flooding was likely to be used as one part of a more complex, composite approach.

From an **operant conditioning** stance, approaches have attempted to alter reinforcement contingencies either by attempting to maximize the reinforcement for being in school by building this into the school side of the intervention and/or minimizing as far as possible the incentives for remaining at home during the school day. Again, as with flooding, where operant approaches have been used in later applications, they have tended to be as part of multi-element interventions.

Intervention approaches employing cognitive behaviour therapy

A more recent focus of interest for practitioners lies in the use of **cognitive behaviour therapy** (CBT) interventions with school refusal. Heyne, King and Olendeck (2005) have set out a detailed CBT approach to school refusal that involves a coherent and comprehensive range of assessment and intervention components, drawing concurrently on child, parent and teacher perspectives and actions.

In terms of assessment, Heyne et al (2005) recommend assessment approaches and materials that enable a case formulation to be made on the basis of the following types of information:

■ Individual factors (e.g. learning history, cognitions, somatic symptoms, social skills, academic difficulties and co-morbid mood problems).

■ Family factors (e.g. parental anxiety/depression and response to non-attendance).

■ School factors (e.g. teacher support and isolation in the playground).

The detailed guidance given by Heyne et al (2005) incorporates many features developed within earlier interventions, such as the use of relaxation training procedures and the strong emphasis on securing a rapid return to school wherever possible (Blagg, 1987), but perhaps its most distinctive additional intervention component is the cognitive element of the therapy. This is deemed essential because events may be processed in a distorted manner by emotionally distressed school refusers. In essence, this aspect of CBT aims to modify '. . . maladaptive cognitions in order to effect change in the young person's emotions and behaviour, mobilising them towards school attendance' (Heyne et al, 2005: 331). These authors draw on their previous work in which the process of conducting cognitive therapy is aided by what they term the 'Seven Ds' (Heyne and Rollings, 2002):

- Describing the cognitive therapy model.

- Detecting cognitions (e.g. 'I know the teacher doesn't like me because she raises her voice').

- Determining which cognitions to address.

- Disputing maladaptive cognitions.

- Discovering adaptive cognitions or **coping** statements.

- Doing between-session practice tasks.

- Discussing the outcome of the tasks.

In addition to pointing out that, from the various psychosocial treatments employed with school refusal (see above), only CBT has been subject to rigorous evaluation using randomized controlled trials, Heyne et al (2005) summarize the outcomes of this research. Although the pragmatics and practicalities of conducting such research present considerable obstacles, these authors conclude that the evaluation research to date provides encouraging support for the efficacy of CBT with school refusers.

Is school refusal a unitary concept?

Do all cases of school refusal or school phobia share a number of basic common characteristics, making it in essence a unitary concept? Or are the broad distinctions adopted by Blagg (1987) – school phobia, truancy, and other instances of poor attending – justifiable as three distinct and disparate phenomena? Or, are there more valid distinctions that are either more complex and/or considerably less precise?

We have already seen that the 'clinical presentation' of school phobia (e.g. Hersov, 1977) differs considerably from the characteristics used by Blagg (1987) and others to delineate truants. Similarly, widely different theoretical formulations have arisen from within psychiatry and behavioural psychology to account for the type of school refusal characterized by high anxiety. However, these initially plausible distinctions are challenged by research which showed that approximately 10 per cent of a sample of chronic absentees demonstrated both the emotional characteristics usually associated with school phobics and the antisocial conduct disorders more typically found within definitions of truancy (Bools et al, 1990).

Chitiyo and Wheeler (2006) have promoted 'school refusal' as a term to denote emotionally based avoidance of school to differentiate it both from school phobia and truancy.

> *School phobia is the more restrictive condition, which involves fear of some specific aspect of the school situation. In contrast, school refusal refers to irrationality based chronic absenteeism that may involve a host of different causative factors including but not limited to school phobia. Viewed this way, school phobia is, therefore, a subset of school refusal. (Chitiyo and Wheeler, 2006)*

Pellegrini (2007), however, points out that a predominantly 'clinical' discourse permeates academic accounts of school refusal in British and American accounts, reflecting a focus on individuals and families. He contrasts this with the Japanese literature, which considers the meaning of school refusal/phobia within the society in which it happens, in the Japanese context, one where school serves a strongly 'socialising' function in which individuality is 'tamed'. Kearney (2003) argues that different sets of professionals are often 'not on the same page' when addressing students or clients, examining research samples, or classifying absentees, because of the considerable disparity that exists in terms of fundamental concepts such as definition, assessment and treatment.

In view of such considerations, Elliot and Place (2004) argue that it is now widely accepted that school refusal is not a unitary syndrome, even when the term is used only to denote 'emotionally-based' absenteeism, but rather is multi-causal and refers to a highly heterogeneous population. However, despite these reservations, practitioners still find it helpful to operate on the basis of there being a group of school refusers characterized by a very high degree of emotionality. Locally generated nomenclature among educational psychologists and local authorities in Britain seems to vary with, for example, 'emotionally-based school refusal' being used in West Sussex, 'anxiety-based school refusal' in North Somerset, and 'anxiety related school attendance difficulties' in Nottinghamshire.

The case for a functional analysis

This heterogeneity among young people who refuse to attend school led Kearney and Silverman (1990) to argue for an approach that examined the functions served by a pupil not attending school rather than a system based on categorization through symptoms. They suggested four main sets of reasons for non-attendance, which incorporate a number of previous formulations, some in novel rearrangements:

- *To avoid the experience of severe anxiety or fearfulness related to attending school.* One or more specific features of the school day may be feared or causing anxiety: for example, the toilets, the corridors, sitting examinations, or specific lessons (often physical education lessons).

- *To avoid social situations that are feared, or which cause anxiety.* This includes problems with peers, perhaps due to bullying or name calling, social isolation at school, and problems with individual teachers (e.g. being criticized or humiliated by a teacher in front of classmates).

- *To seek attention or to reduce the feeling of separation anxiety.* Kearney and Silverman (1990) combine these different concepts, arguing that functionally they are equivalent; the young person receives positive reinforcement for their non-attendance in the shape of special attention at home. This point is later presented by King et al (1994) as – 'the more fear and avoidance behaviour the child displays the more attention he or she receives'.

- *To enjoy rewarding experiences that non-attendance at school may bring.* For example, this could be watching television or playing computer games at home, or associating with friends. Depending on the company kept, this could lead to involvement in antisocial acts and/or criminal activities. This category therefore includes those children and young people usually referred to as truants.

In further research, Kearney (2007) has consolidated the usefulness of this four-function model as a way of organizing, assessing and treating this population by carrying out hierarchical regression analysis and structural equation modelling. Data on 222 young pupils aged between 5 and 17 years and displaying school refusal were provided by the young people and their parents. Kearney found that 'behaviour function' was a better determinant of degree of school absenteeism than 'behaviour form' (i.e. extent of depressive symptoms; school-based fear; negative affectivity consisting of worry, over-sensitivity, concentration problems and physiological symptoms of anxiety; social anxiety, and generalized anxiety). These different examples of behaviour form were all chosen for study because previous research studies had established their co-morbidity with school refusal. All measures, including those for behaviour function, were made using pre-existing and established psychometric instruments.

Intervention approaches developed by educational psychologists

The 'rapid response' approach

A major contribution to educational psychologists working with instances of school refusal was made by Blagg (1987) in which the author, a practising educational psychologist, put forward a detailed set of planning guidelines for attempting to ensure a rapid return to school. Blagg's work was distinctive for its time in a number of ways, in that it attempted to combine theoretical insights from both a psychodynamic and a behavioural perspective (including some rudiments of CBT), it set out very practical advice on information gathering, assessment and problem formulation, and it addressed the complex practical challenges of actually putting into practice multi-level plans that required a number of parties to work together, often under conditions of high emotional arousal and stress.

In addition, Blagg evaluated this **rapid response** approach by comparing its use with 30 young people against 20 who received home tuition and psychotherapy and 16 who were hospitalized (Blagg and Yule, 1984). These different treatment approaches were available to the researchers as a result of differing professional practices across geographical areas. Although therefore quasi-experimental in design (it was not possible to randomly assign the young people to treatments), the study was distinctive for its time in attempting to be scrupulous in its data collection and analysis, certainly compared to the prevailing trend in the literature of that time, which was dominated by descriptive case studies and clinicians' overviews and judgements. Blagg and Yule (1984) concluded that the rapid response approach achieved a better outcome, in terms of a maintained return to school, than the comparative treatment groups – and against any other reported study at that time dealing with young people in the 11–16 age range.

Interestingly, in view of the fact that some professionals, parents and pupils have advocated for home tuition, and still do, Blagg and Yule (1984) reported that they could find no other reported investigations in the literature of that time in which home tuition and psychotherapy were used in tandem. In their own study, these authors reported the progress of this group to be '. . . so uniformly poor . . . that one wonders whether home tuition with psychotherapy actually inhibited spontaneous remission' (Blagg, 1987: 104).

A 'school-focused' approach

Lauchlan (2003) has argued that, if a child is fearful of coming to school, then one may legitimately question whether the school should bear some responsibility for the problem and has focused on three levels of primarily school-focused intervention: the systemic, the individual and the group.

At the *systemic level*, Lauchlan notes various features of schools that may explain the onset and severity of chronic non-attendance, including:

- An environment in which there are high occurrences of bullying, truancy and disruption.

- A school setting or streaming policy that results in the pupil being grouped with a number of disaffected and troublesome peers.

- A school where teacher–pupil relationships are excessively formal, impersonal and/or generally hostile.

■ Where toilets and corridors and playground areas are not monitored carefully by staff, perhaps because such duties are not seen as their responsibility.

As with Blagg's (1987) rapid response approach, a careful examination of these and related environmental features should constitute part of the assessment of any individual case. Although it may sometimes prove difficult to persuade an organization to make policy and practice changes to benefit one single pupil, on other occasions such an occurrence may prove the perfect stimulus for systemic changes that can be seen to be of benefit to a considerable number of students (and staff).

At the *individual level*, Lauchlan (2003) refers to a number of interventions that have been considered earlier in this chapter: relaxation training or systematic desensitization, cognitive restructuring or self-statement training from CBT, exposure and flooding. *Group approaches* that are advocated include social skills training for students, and cognitive behaviour interventions that involve parents as well as their children.

By presenting a range of possible intervention approaches, including those with an explicit focus on the school system, Lauchlan (2003) is acknowledging the heterogeneity of school refusal and the probable need for a multi-element approach to intervention.

Activity 12.3

Case study – Part 3

The intervention

The educational psychologist made three home visits after the first meeting in school and the main elements of the intervention plan eventually developed could be seen as:

■ The legal position regarding school attendance was reiterated to James and his parents – namely, that it was the parents' responsibility to ensure school attendance but that it was very unlikely legal action would commence if a reintegration plan had been agreed upon. The Local Authority's policy on home tuition was outlined; basically that this could not be provided in instances of school refusal except as a component of a reintegration plan.
■ A series of solution-focused practice interviews (Ajmal and Rees, 2001) was undertaken with James and his parents. This approach focuses on identifying goals, analysing exceptions, sharing guiding assumptions and formulating prescriptions for action. At first, the intention was to work with all three together but, because Mr Sharpe seemed to dominate these proceedings, separate sessions for Mr Sharpe and for Mrs Sharpe were arranged after the first whole family meeting. A separate interview was held with James the following week. After these meetings,

James was still adamant that he would not attend school and on one occasion shouted this in front of the psychologist at the top of his voice. But he also acknowledged more calmly that his ideal – to have home tuition – was not the same as that of his parents', which was for him to return to school. Mr Sharpe reported feeling some relief, as if he was not walking on eggshells with James so much. And Mrs Sharpe said that she had become a bit more assertive with James and her husband. She also said that she had grown much more concerned about the long-term consequences of James not going back to school – in terms of his not getting any qualifications, becoming socially isolated, and learning that he was able to 'control' others.

- The educational psychologist wrote to the other professionals involved – school staff, the GP, school doctor and education welfare officer – stating the intention to work towards a reintegration plan and outlining the policy on home tuition.
- School staff again investigated the likelihood of bullying having occurred and satisfied themselves that there were no other undetected aspects to this.
- The psychologist and James rehearsed answers to hypothetical pupils (and teachers) who might tease or mock James for having been off school so long.
- A home tutor was employed to work with James with the express understanding that this was as part of the reintegration plan. The tutor would be able to accompany James on return to school if required, but would not continue if commitment to the plan were to falter.
- School staff arranged for James to join an after-school art club for five sessions. The home tutor went to the first meeting as did Mr Sharpe, who was persuaded to let James come alone after the second meeting. The home tutor acted as an additional helper to the teacher in charge and to all the pupils present.
- The educational psychologist wrote a letter to James, his parents and teachers outlining what he saw as the progress achieved, and the positive effort and qualities that had been displayed by each.

Activity

- Identify sources within the literature reviewed in this chapter for as many elements in the intervention plan as you can.
- Which aspects of the plan seem most 'theory-driven' and which might be more concerned with (probably very necessary) practical arrangements and the efficient use of resources?
- Decide also upon other aspects of interventions described in this chapter that might have been profitably incorporated into the plan.

Long-term outcomes for school refusers

Information about the **long-term outcomes** for young people with school refusal is inconsistent (McShane et al, 2004), depending on a range of factors such as whether treatment interventions have been offered and taken up, and their type, but also on characteristics of the young people involved such as the presence of co-morbid mental health difficulties or academic difficulties. So, for instance, in addition to possible educational outcomes such as low performance at public examinations and consequently reduced career options, Kearney, Eisen and Silverman (1995) aver that, if untreated, school refusal can result in long-term problems such as marital and occupational difficulties, anxiety, depression, alcoholism and antisocial behaviour. Somewhat in contrast, and in the shorter term, McShane et al (2004) found that, from a sample of 118 young people treated at a specialist adolescent unit in the Australian context, 70 per cent showed an improvement after 6 months and 76 per cent at 3 years. As a greater and more commonly agreed understanding of school refusal hopefully emerges, it should be possible to increase the quality and usefulness of data collected during longitudinal studies and hence eventually provide a more reliable prognosis for school refusal in relation to the range of pertinent person and environment variables.

Activity 12.4

Case study – Part 4

The outcome

After attending five after-school art club sessions, James told his parents that he was willing to attend school full-time after the impending summer holiday.

This he did, and in the subsequent year his attendance returned to the same high level of the year prior to the period of intense absenteeism. After completing this year of renewed high attendance he had made up for the missed lessons, and obtained gradings 'at the nationally expected standard for 14-year olds' in seven different subjects, including English, maths and science, and 'below average' gradings in only three subjects.

Coping with life by coping with school?

*Coping with adverse life events or pressures is a major requirement for maintaining reasonable functioning and has been recognised, together with the presence of **protective factors**, as the mechanism for reducing the risk of future mental health problems . . . Coping successfully with one situation strengthens an individual's ability to cope in the future. A failure to cope with a complex setting such as school can therefore have potentially serious long-term consequences as various outcome studies have shown. (Place et al, 2002).*

This chapter has examined a phenomenon that has challenged young people, their parents and teachers and associated professionals such as psychologists and psychiatrists, for more than 70 years. High degrees of distress and the lack of a common consensus among professionals all place a considerable strain on those attempting to help. Research and professional practice in educational psychology and elsewhere, however, are providing insights into, and exemplars of, successful interventions. For James, whose real-life case has provided illustrative comment through this chapter, it appears that his academic and career prospects and future ability to cope with life's challenges, pressures and obstacles may have been considerably enhanced by the application of this knowledge within the context of educational psychology practice.

Summary

- A set of symptoms that came to be taken as indicative of 'school phobia' was first reported in the literature over 70 years ago.

- Early conceptualizations divided school refusers into school phobics, truants and others, although later studies suggested that school refusal was a far more heterogeneous concept. This lack of a unitary conceptualization is further reflected in the very disparate approaches taken by different professional groups.

- For school refusal with strong emotional and somatic components, there are no differences in the incidence rates between boys and girls, different social classes and different levels of ability or academic attainment. There are, however, higher incidences reported for the youngest of several children in a family, for children of older parents, for those around the age for transferring from primary to secondary levels of schooling and for those with other social impairments.

- Incidence rates vary depending on the stringency of the definition adopted; using fairly strict criteria, the overall incidence within the child population is 1–2 per cent.

- Early theoretical formulations were developed within psychodynamic thinking and within behavioural psychology, the former utilizing the concepts of separation anxiety and omnipotence, and the latter school-focused and other more social anxieties formed through classical and operant conditioning.

- A range of discrete treatment approaches were developed from these formulations: psychotherapeutic child and family counselling and hospitalization from within psychodynamic and medical traditions; and systematic desensitization, emotive imagery, flooding or implosion and contingency management from within behavioural psychology.

- Currently, cognitive behaviour therapy is the most rigorously researched single intervention approach, and evaluation outcomes have been encouraging.

- A four-part functional analysis of school refusal has been provided by Kearney and Silverman (1990) and subsequent research has suggested that this may be the most useful way of organizing, assessing and treating this population.

- A range of approaches now emphasize that a rapid return to some form of school attendance where at all possible should be a treatment priority. Educational psychologists have developed such approaches, often incorporating multi-element interventions that pay due attention to school-based triggering and maintaining factors.

- The evidence for the long-term outcomes of school refusal is inconclusive and likely to be confounded by a number of factors. Some researchers have, however, suggested that untreated school refusal, especially if it is co-morbid with other mental health difficulties such as depression, has the potential to lead to serious mental health difficulties in adult life.

- The ability to cope with complex and sometimes challenging social situations such as school may serve to strengthen an individual's ability to cope with other testing life circumstances.

Key concepts and terms

Classical conditioning
Cognitive behaviour therapy
Coping
Emotive imagery
Flooding, implosion, extinction
Functional analysis
Incidence
Long-term outcomes of school
  refusal
Non-attendance
Omnipotence

Operant conditioning
Protective factors
Rapid response
School phobia
School refusal
School-focused anxiety
Separation anxiety
Social anxiety
Systematic desensitization
Truancy

Sample essay titles

- Is school refusal a unitary concept? If it is not, what are the implications for interventions?
- To what extent do various conceptualizations of school refusal lead to intervention approaches that educational psychologists might employ?
- A head teacher consults you, the educational psychologist, about an able pupil who has suddenly begun to refuse to attend school. The head teacher has been unable to persuade the pupil to return and has begun to feel very

frustrated and manipulated. Write a letter to the head, putting this behaviour into a psychological context.

- After at least three-quarters of a century of attention to school refusal, what major contributions have been made by psychology to understanding and intervening with this phenomenon?

Further reading

Books

Blagg, N. (1987). *School Phobia and its Treatment*. London: Croom Helm.

Elliot, J.G., and Place, M. (2004). *Children in Difficulty: A Guide to Understanding and Helping* (2nd Ed.). London: Routledge, Chapter 3.

Heyne, D., King, N., and Olendeck, T.H. (2005). 'School refusal.' In: P. Graham (Ed.), *Cognitive Behaviour Therapy for Children and Families* (2nd Ed.). Cambridge: Cambridge University Press.

Journal articles

Chitiyo, M., and Wheeler, J.J. (2006). School phobia: Understanding a complex behavioural response. *Journal of Research in Special Educational Needs*, 6, 87–91.

Elliot, J.G. (1999). Practitioner review: School refusal: issues of conceptualisation, assessment and treatment. *Journal of Child Psychology and Psychiatry*, 1001–1012.

Kearney, C.A. (2003). Bridging the gap among professionals who address youths with school absenteeism: overview and suggestions for consensus. *Professional Psychology: Research and Practice*, 34, 57–65.

Kearney, C.A. (2007). Forms and functions of school refusal behaviour in youth. *Journal of Child Psychology and Psychiatry*, 48, 53–61.

King, N., Tonge, B.J., Heyne, D., and Ollendick, T.H. (2000). Research on the cognitive-behavioral treatment of school refusal. A review and recommendations. *Clinical Psychology Review*, 20, 495–507.

Lauchlan, F. (2003). Responding to chronic non-attendance: a review of intervention approaches. *Educational Psychology in Practice*, 19, 132–146.

Place, M., Hulsmeier, J., Davis, S., and Taylor, E. (2002). The coping mechanisms of children with school refusal. *Journal of Research in Special Educational Needs*, 2, 1–10.

13 School ethos and student identity

When is wearing a uniform a badge of honour?

Tony Cline

In this chapter you will examine different ways of describing a school's ethos and culture and different ways of investigating them. We will reflect on how the ethos of a school is expressed in its day-to-day life. A school exists for its pupils. The chapter will also examine how an institution's ethos may impinge on the experiences of its students and the development of their identities as academic learners.

Learning outcomes

When you have completed this chapter you should be able to:

1. Explain and evaluate different strategies for investigating a school's ethos.
2. Analyse how a school's ethos may influence the development of its students' identities as academic learners.
3. Describe how educational psychologists can work to ameliorate the impact of **school ethos** on students in difficult situations.

Focus 13.1

Newspaper report

School uniform in Scotland

In February 2005, Scotland's First Minister, Jack McConnell, made an outspoken attack on what he saw as the damage caused by liberal values in education. Among other things, he said, a large number of Scottish schools had got rid of school uniform over the years. On 2 March 2005 the *Scotsman* newspaper invited two public figures to debate the issue.

John Wilson, education director in East Renfrewshire, 'Scotland's most successful education authority', wrote in support:

Uniform is important in East Renfrewshire and we encourage schools to promote it as part of our approach to an education based firmly on attainment, achievement and inclusion. Uniform helps promote the unity and ethos of a school and that, in turn, promotes the learning within. Security is boosted by making strangers not in uniform easier to spot. We've always said that we would meet private sector schools on their own ground. Part of the attraction they have for parents is their emphasis on uniform, so, as part of our strategy of encouraging our local children to go to their local schools at the heart of our communities, we do promote uniform.

Judith Gillespie, Convener of the Scottish Parent Teacher Council, opposed school uniforms:

School uniform "means what it says on the tin" – everyone looks the same. This denial of difference is nothing new. When I moved to a secondary school in the 50s, . . . it didn't take me long to identify their hypocrisy over school uniform. The adult argument that school uniform ended competition and meant you couldn't tell the rich from the poor was rubbish. Rich kids had uniform that looked smart and fitted, while those of us with less money made do with second-hand stuff or, worse, home-made gear that never fitted properly. As for competition, that just moved to areas that escaped adult attention . . . Where's the chance to express individualism that's so beloved of the new drive to create a more enterprising culture? Where's the chance to experiment with clothes and work out individual identity?

Defining school ethos

The tension between individuality and uniformity in schools is fundamental to their function in society: their task of preparing children for adulthood can only be achieved if they are successful simultaneously in managing large groups and responding to individual needs. In the 1960s and 70s the fashionable view among psychologists (reflected in the Plowden Report on primary education – Plowden Committee, 1967) was that schools made little difference. It was thought that home factors exerted much more influence on children's achievements at school than school factors did. In sociology too the influence of schools was played down. Sociologists tended to locate the causes of unequal educational outcomes in basic inequities in the structure of society. A research team led by Michael Rutter, who presented that outline of earlier thinking (Rutter et al, 1979: 1–2), sought to challenge it. They gave their book the title *Fifteen Thousand Hours* to reflect the fact that between the age of 5 and 16 young people spend that amount of time in school. Does it make a difference which school it is? Clearly John Wilson of East Renfrewshire thinks it does, and thinks that school uniform can help each school to impress its ethos on its students. Did the findings obtained by Rutter's team support him?

In what has become a classic study they collected performance data for 12 Inner London secondary schools and undertook extensive observations and interviews in each school. Mostly they concentrated on specific events and behaviours, although there were some interview questions on more general attitudes and values (see Research Methods box 13.1). They suggested that in many cases individual actions by members of staff may have been less important in their own right than 'in the part they play in contributing to a broader school ethos or climate of expectations and modes of behaving'. Their defence of the focus on specific actions was that they hoped to identify what sorts of actions teachers and pupils could take to establish an improved ethos if needed (Rutter et al, 1979: 55–56). Here are some of their findings:

- The schools differed markedly in the behaviour and attainments shown by their pupils.

- Although the schools differed in the proportion of children with difficult behaviour or low attainments whom they admitted, these differences did not wholly account for the variations between schools in their pupils' later behaviour and attainment.

- The variations between schools in different forms of outcome for their pupils were reasonably stable over periods of at least four or five years.

- In general, though with some exceptions, schools performed fairly similarly on all the various measures of outcome. That is, schools which did better than average in terms of the children's behaviour in school tended also to do better than average in terms of examination success and low rates of delinquency.

- These differences in outcome between schools were not due to such physical factors as the size of the school, the age of the buildings or the space available; nor were they due to broad differences in administrative status or organization. Some schools obtained good outcomes in spite of what seemed to be poor premises, and successful schools had a range of types of administrative arrangements.

- Some of the factors that had an influence on pupil outcomes were open to modification by the staff, rather than fixed by external constraints. Examples included the degree of academic emphasis, teacher actions in lessons, the availability of incentives and rewards, and the extent to which children were able to take responsibility within the classroom.

- Other factors that were shown to have an influence on pupil outcomes were outside teachers' immediate control. The most important factor of this kind was the academic balance of the schools' intakes.

- A crucial finding for the purposes of this chapter was that 'the association between the *combined* measure of overall process and each of the measures of outcome was much stronger than any of the associations with individual process variables. This suggests that the cumulative effect of these various social factors was considerably greater than the effect of any of the individual factors on their own. The implication is that the individual actions or measures combine to create a particular *ethos*, or set of values, attitudes and behaviours which will become characteristic of the school as a whole'. (Rutter et al, 1979: 177–179)

Controversially they argued that, although their data had been collected at one point in time, 'the total pattern of findings indicates the strong probability that the associations between school process and outcome reflect in part a causal process. In other words, to an appreciable extent children's behaviour and attitudes are shaped and influenced by their experiences at school and, in particular, by the qualities of the school as a social institution' (Rutter et al, 1979: 179). They concluded that a measure was required of how a school functions as a whole as a social organization. This process is discussed in Research Methods box 13.1.

Research methods 13.1

Treating behavioural process variables as a means of measuring school ethos

Rutter et al (1979) did not set out with a theoretical model of school ethos. Noting that they had not found a suitable instrument for their purposes in the earlier research literature, they developed a list of diverse school process variables that 'seemed potentially relevant to the pupils' progress'. They emphasized those variables that applied to the pupils as a whole rather than those that applied only to smaller groups with special needs or special problems. The following list shows a sample selected from every fifth item in the schedule of 46 process measures that they eventually used:

- *Work on walls.* Each room that was visited to administer pupil questionnaires and to observe third-year lessons was assessed on a five-point scale: 0 = nothing on walls, to 4 = all possible areas covered.
- *Subjects taught.* Each teacher who was interviewed was asked which subjects they taught. A school's score was the percentage of teachers who taught across subject areas rather than having a specific specialist subject.
- *Teachers' interventions in third-year classrooms.* Percentage of teacher observation periods when teachers were dealing with pupils' behaviour, e.g. curbing unacceptable behaviour.
- *Detentions.* Pupils' response to a questionnaire item asking how many times they had been kept in detention since the previous September.
- *Pupils caring for resources.* Observations during third-year lessons as to whether pupils brought and took away resources for learning such as books, folders and exercise books.
- *Staff's late arrival at school.* An item in the questionnaire for teachers asking whether anyone else was aware if staff arrive late for school.

As noted above, the research team argued that items of this kind did not affect pupil outcomes directly but through their combination in an overall impact through an institutional ethos. Their reasons were, first, that most of the individual process variables had only an indirect connection with the outcomes with which they were associated such as school attendance. Second, the same teacher actions had different effects in different schools.

For example, if a teacher left children on their own in one school, they might get on with their work, while in another school they would become involved in disruptive behaviour. Third, some of the variables did not bear on individual pupils directly but on the state of the buildings or the conditions of the staff group (pp. 182–183). They showed that the schools' overall scores for school process variables correlated highly with pupil behaviour scores ($r = 0.92$) and showed substantial, though slightly less strong, correlations with academic attainment ($r = 0.76$), overall attendance ($r = 65$) and recorded delinquency ($r = -0.68$) (Figures 7.27–7.30).

Activity

- Discuss what assumptions are made in the argument summarized in the last paragraph above.
- In the light of the information that is given here, can you suggest an operational definition of 'school ethos' that might have been employed by the research team? (Remember that an operational definition is a definition which describes as specifically as possible the precise elements and procedures involved in solving a research problem.)

The report by Rutter and his colleagues attracted a great deal of interest when it was published. There were critical reviews both of its statistical analyses (e.g. Goldstein, 1980) and of its 'managerial' focus (Burgess, 1980). For example, the team's conclusions about the management of pupils were described as being 'grounded in the worst traditions of behaviouristic experimental social psychology' (Pateman, 1980). Nonetheless, the study had a seminal influence on educational research. A major tradition of research on *school effectiveness* grew from the interest it generated (Teddlie and Reynolds, 2000) and a parallel tradition of professional work on *school improvement* (Macbeath and Mortimore, 2001). However, although it thus has classic status, the study was notably weak in its collation of unrelated variables to create a measure of 'school ethos'. The implicit assumption was made that there will be a consistent relationship in any organization between inputs and outputs and that this relationship can be discovered through correlating a wide range of input and output measures and identifying the most significant connections.

Critics argue that there are complex forces in play in the life of an organization such as a school that cannot be adequately captured by a 'reductionist' strategy of measuring factors like those listed in Research Methods box 13.1. In a complex human system what matters is not just what happens but how participants interpret what happens – what shared ideas they apply to the routines and events that characterize the institution, what 'culture' dominates it, and whether some of those who are involved resist the dominant culture. Classic – and more recent – quantitative research on school effectiveness is seen as failing to identify causal mechanisms and failing to take account of irregular and inconsistent processes within open systems (Wrigley, 2004). Later we will examine alternative approaches to investigating the culture or ethos of a school. But first we need to consider the other construct that appears in the title of the chapter.

The development of identity as a student

Infants in the first few months of life do not appear to be self-conscious, but by the age of 2 they develop a sense of themselves as a person, and in their third year they begin to be able to draw on the standards and rules that prevail in their society in order to evaluate their own behaviour. They may show embarrassment when they see a gap between what they are doing and what is expected of them, and they begin to experience further emotions such as pride, shame and guilt (Lewis, 2002). As they start to move more and more outside the immediate ambit of their home, they are exposed to a wider range of people and need to develop a sense of their own **social identity** as distinct from that of others. Questions such as 'Who am I?' are answered, in part, by categorizing themselves as members of groups with which they can identify.

Tajfel's (1978) theory of social identities has been influential in the development of psychological research on this process. The original aim of this theory was to explain the psychological basis of discrimination between groups. Tajfel assumed that a person does not have just one 'self' but rather several selves that are associated with the various groups to which they belong. The sort of groups we belong to define who we are. In experimental work with what were known as 'minimal groups' who never actually met, Tajfel and his colleagues showed that just being categorized as a member of the same group led to participants discriminating in favour of each other. Specifically, what matters in this process is how we evaluate the groups to which we belong. There is comfort and reassurance in seeing them in a positive light. For Tajfel this was the foundation of the development of prejudice and discrimination against people who were seen as belonging to other groups.

Later researchers have drawn on these ideas to show how children develop various social identities as they move into school and middle childhood, e.g. in relation to gender. However, they do not simply opt to be in one differentiated group or another (e.g. 'the boys' or 'the girls'). The process is more complex than that, as they learn about the various definitions of masculinity and femininity that are available and position themselves in relation to these possibilities within their groups. Lloyd and Duveen (1992) proposed that, as children encounter new social representations of gender after starting school, they reconstruct the social **gender identities** which they had developed during the pre-school years.

For our purposes an important finding in their study of four schools was that the way reception class teachers organized their classrooms constrained the ways in which gender identities were expressed there. It might be expected that traditionally minded teachers would encourage their pupils to adopt traditional sex roles in their play in the classroom, e.g. by giving boys 'male' toys to play with. This is not what happened. The process did not involve teachers imposing their vision of sex roles on the young pupils in their charge. It was rather that patterns of play and gender role affiliation were influenced by the way that the classrooms were run. Gender **differentiation** appeared to be most marked in those classrooms where the teacher allowed more time for peer-organized activities. For example, that allowed a small group of girls in one school to define their femininity through the exclusion of boys from their play. Classroom organization and ethos had a paradoxical impact: the regime imposed by the more 'progressive' teachers allowed more scope for the expression of traditional gender identities than the regime of the more 'conservative' teachers did. If we are looking for the effects of school ethos on student identity, we should not expect a simple imposition of the one on the other.

Internalized expectations

A key stage in this process, according to Duveen, is that children first learn how others see them and then gradually internalize these expectations and take a position in relation to them (Duveen, 2001). Thus a case study of a 7-year-old girl who thought of herself as good at maths suggested that she based this on what her teacher had written in a report, what her father had said about her and comparisons that had been made at home with one of her sisters (Abreu and Cline, 2003: 24–25). The key psychological construct in this process has sometimes been termed '**reflected appraisal**', children's beliefs about what their parents, teachers and peers think about them with respect to school achievement. Survey evidence, as well as case study evidence, has indicated that reflected appraisals predict what children themselves will see as their own level of academic ability in each subject area. The evidence also suggests that these mechanisms continue to operate into adolescence (Bouchey and Harter, 2005).

Abreu (1995) has used the concept of 'valorization' to describe the process by which some kinds of activity are given high status within the school curriculum while others are not. She studied farmers in a sugar-cane farming community in

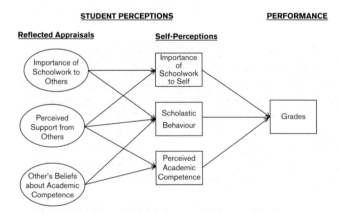

Figure 13.1 Model proposed by Bouchey and Harter (2005) to describe the processes underlying maths/science achievement. ('Others' includes mothers, fathers, teachers and classmates.)

Source: Bouchey and Harter (2005). Reflected appraisals, academic self-perceptions, and math/science performance during early adolescence. Journal of Educational Psychology, 97, 673–686, published by American Psychological Association reprinted with permission.

north-east Brazil and showed how they employed sophisticated traditional methods of calculation to work out acreage and crop yield in their irregularly shaped fields. However, neither they nor their children treated these calculations as 'real' mathematics, a term they reserved for the mathematics taught at school. In a process reminiscent of what happened in Tajfel's groups, the low occupational status of the peasant farmers in Brazilian society influenced their identification of the status of their mathematical practices. The internalization of reflected appraisals in school depends, in part, on the 'valorization' of the sources of these appraisals (Abreu and Cline, 2003).

There is evidence that pupils assimilate into themselves **academic identities** formed by school-related characteristics that are associated with their classes and their schools (Hallam et al, 2004). When a school groups its pupils by ability for some subjects, the children are clearer about what their estimated ability is and reflect the school's judgement in what they say about themselves. The questionnaire data from a structured sample of pupils in six primary schools challenged the assumption that many adults make that pupils are aware of the pecking order of ability within their class, whether that class is mixed ability or organized in separate sets by teacher-assessed ability. Their evidence suggested that children are '. . . perhaps not as aware as has been accepted. The children were asked to assess themselves academically and this revealed that the majority of pupils demonstrated a self-perception in accordance with that of their teachers. However, there were differences between the schools. The most accurate estimates (i.e. those most closely in accord with that of their teachers) were made in the school with the greatest degree of streaming and setting. The least accurate were made in the school which adopted mixed ability teaching in Key Stage 1 and streaming for the whole curriculum in Years 3 to 6' (Hallam et al, 2004: 526).

The survey of these pupils also made clear that, when a school gave signalled judgements about children's ability levels through its organization of pupil grouping, this led, in some cases, to low-ability (and also high-ability) pupils reporting more often that they had been teased or stigmatized by others.

Those processes arise from grouping *within* schools. Similar processes of group identity formation operate *between* schools. For example, Hamilton (2002) compared pupils at two independent schools and two comprehensive schools in Scotland. The independent schools selected their intake on the basis of '**ability**', and staff presented to parents and pupils an overt 'institutional ability identity'. In contrast, while the staff in the comprehensive schools also assessed their pupils regularly and emphasized aspirations towards achievement, they tended to talk about '**potential**' rather than a notion of fixed and unchanging 'ability'. In all the schools it appeared that the reflected appraisals of the teachers influenced the pupils' self-evaluations. An additional factor was the reflected appraisals of their parents. The process differed between the two types of school. In the comprehensive schools the parents were more likely to take on the evaluations of the staff while in the independent schools they were seen as playing a more active role in ability construction, especially at the point of choice when they identified their child as suitable for a selective school.

Hamilton argues that we should not assume that powerful external sources exert a uniformly decisive influence on individuals' self-definition. As in the case of classroom factors in gender identity formation that was described above, the process appears to be more complex than that. She suggests that it is helpful to think in terms of a tension at the boundary between the external and internal worlds of the individual. This tension might result in the individual accepting the assessment of, say, their abilities as defined by the institutional ethos of their school or by the results of formal examinations. But they may also deny or refute what is suggested to them by this external evidence. 'This is a dynamic relationship which allows individuals to represent and work with seemingly contradictory or conflicting constructions of ability and ability identity. This emphasises the individual as an active participant and negotiator.' At the same time Hamilton does not wish to discount power and control as important factors in the negotiation that takes place. Parents and schools remain crucial sources of messages to schoolchildren about their 'potential' or their 'ability' (Hamilton, 2002: 593).

Influence of school ethos

In the decades since the publication of *Fifteen Thousand Hours*, more evidence has accumulated showing that the ethos and culture of a school have a significant impact on a range of aspects of student identity and behaviour independently of such variables as the composition of the student population. Some of the research has focused on mainstream schools. For example, West, Sweeting and Leyland (2004) carried out a longitudinal study of 43 secondary schools in the West of Scotland and showed that, after adjusting for pupil and family characteristics, there remained a school effect on the likelihood of a child taking up excessive smoking or drinking. Some research has focused on the differences in ethos between mainstream schools and various types of independent establishment. For example, Rivers and Soutter (1996) found that children who had been the victims of bullying in mainstream schools left the status of victim behind after moving to a Rudolph Steiner school with a non-competitive, group-centred ethos. Creese et al (2006) found that Gujarati-speaking children had been enabled to negotiate new identities as learners in complementary schools run by the Gujarati community in their town. In these part-time schools, which the children attended once a week on a Tuesday evening or a Saturday morning, their linguistic repertoire as bilingual speakers was seen as important in a way that it was not in the mainstream schools that they attended full-time through the week.

Burden (2005) studied the learning careers of boys with dyslexia at a specialist boarding school and found that many who had had a sense of failure and embarrassment in their mainstream schools had developed what Burden called 'dyslexic pride' in that school. In part, the boys had been encouraged by the easy availability of help that was geared to meet their particular needs. But there appeared to be more to it than that. There was a sense of *belonging*, of feeling part of a group of people in the same situation. Keith (aged 12) said:

> *I liked that people listened to you and understand how you feel and everyone was the same. We looked at the usual comprehensive school but I didn't want to go there 'cos I'd be different and have to go out of class for extra help. (Burden 2005: 54)*

The impact of school ethos on the development of students' identities as learners is often indirect: it gives a message about the kind of person who is valued in this community and facilitates a process by which students come to think that they are that kind of person.

It is no accident that some of the most persuasive research on the impact of school ethos on student identity has focused on small schools with an unusual and well-defined purpose. In the most effective of the schools the teachers shared common goals and benefited from a strong consensus about the methods employed in the school to pursue those goals (Rivers and Soutter, 1996; Creese et al, 2006). In many large mainstream schools those conditions may not apply. The institution is a highly complex organization with diverse and sometimes competing subcultures. Groups of teachers and groups of pupils find themselves isolated from one another. Pupils develop their identities as learners across disparate departments and subcultures, finding those identities affirmed in some settings and challenged or undermined in others. Such schools are fragile organizations that lack the cohesion and strength to support their members – staff or pupils. In the next section we will examine how educational psychologists can contribute when a school's ethos has many negative features.

Can a school's educational psychologist influence its ethos?

It has long been argued that, in order to have greatest impact, educational psychologists should place more emphasis on work aimed at the organization, policy and structure of schools than on work with individual pupils (Gillham, 1978). One line of development has been to give attention to school ethos as a factor in some children's difficulties. For example, Cameron and Stratford (1987) and Stratford (1990) reported on the application of a 'problem-centred approach' to enable a school staff to work towards improvements at school level.

Briggs, MacKay and Miller (1995) described an intervention by two educational psychologists to help a Scottish primary school that had been making multiple referrals of children with serious behaviour problems. Greatest concern among staff focused on incidents of aggression in the playground. A class teacher ran small group sessions weekly, working with an experienced group worker with advice from educational psychologists. Pupils in some classes also participated in a bullying survey, the results of which were used as a basis for in-service training sessions with the entire staff. Workshops were also run for the parents of all pupils in these classes. The aim of the project was not only to improve the playground behaviour of a small group of difficult pupils but also to have a more general impact on all pupils.

There was a wide-ranging evaluation involving pupil questionnaires and interviews, behaviour ratings by class teachers, playground incident records and staff feedback reports and interviews. The results indicated that there had been many positive changes. Not only had the children in the target groups experienced the playground as a more favourable environment but class teachers reported improvements in classroom behaviour and in their own approach to disruptive behaviour. 'The wider effects on school ethos were seen as significant' (Briggs et al, 1995: 42). Thus what had initially been defined as a problem belonging to individual pupils had been transformed through the educational psychologists' intervention. The improvements that had been achieved generalized to the whole school community, and staff generally were able to take ownership of them.

In a more recent report Bettle, Frederickson and Sharp (2001) described the support provided to a school that was in great difficulties by a team from the local authority's Educational Psychology Service. The school, which was in a socially deprived area in Buckinghamshire, a relatively prosperous shire county, provided for children aged 7–11 years. After an official inspection it had been placed in 'special measures'. This is a category used by Ofsted inspectors when 'a school is failing or is likely to fail to give its pupils an acceptable standard of education'. After being placed in this category the school is required to produce an action plan setting out a proposed response to the inspection report (Department for Education, 1993). In addition, the Local Education Authority (LEA) has to produce a commentary on the school's plan and a statement of the action that it proposes to take to support the school. In this case the school's educational psychologist, as a member of the LEA staff, was asked by its new head teacher to give them extra time in order to process a higher number of formal assessments of special educational needs (50 per cent of the pupils in the school were on the Special Educational Needs register). 'The Chief Psychologist discussed this with the Headteacher and consequently they agreed that, given the key issues identified in the Action Plan, the Service should support specific initiatives relating to improving behaviour management or learning across the school. The time for this would best be accommodated . . . from time earmarked by the service for project work with schools, and a joint planning meeting was therefore held in order to discuss possible pieces of work.' (Bettle et al, 2001: 56) The schools' link educational psychologist also participated in a task force that gave attention to special educational needs in the school, but this account will focus on the project initiative.

In an initial discussion the head teacher highlighted what he called 'ethos in the school' as a key area for work, specifically a high level of conflict and hostility between pupils. It was agreed that this should be the focus of the educational psychologist and her colleagues, who would support the school to develop a more supportive and caring ethos among students. 'The Headteacher felt that many of the pupils needed to learn fundamental skills for getting along with others, valuing others as well as themselves, and feeling secure and cared for in their school environment' (Bettle et al, 2001: 57). The educational psychologists' contributions included investigating staff and pupil perceptions, feedback to staff, training and evaluation. The key point of interest here is the focus of their initial data collection. They did not attempt direct observations but focused instead on learning how the situation in the school was perceived by different groups of participants. Their approach was guided by **soft systems methodology**, an approach to the analysis of ill-structured problem situations of this kind that was developed on the basis of action research (Frederickson, 1993). This initial phase of the team's work is summarized in Research Methods box 13.2.

Research methods 13.2

Investigating stakeholders' perceptions as a means of measuring school ethos

Two educational psychologists spent half a day in the school, administering the questionnaires with classes of pupils and interviewing the staff. The staff interviews explored such questions as how they felt the children got along with each other in their individual classes and in the school. Staff were asked what had been tried before and what kinds of support they felt would be most useful in the future. Pupils in each year group completed two questionnaires – the *'My Class Inventory' short form* (which surveys perceptions of the classroom learning environment resulting in scores for constructs such as group cohesiveness and group friction) and the *Life in Schools Checklist* (which surveys perceptions of positive and negative events in school and results in scores such as a bullying index and a general aggression index). The educational psychology team aimed to assist the staff group to 'unfreeze', i.e. identify and accept the reasons for organizational change in the school. They kick-started the process by feeding back the data from this initial investigation at a staff meeting in the form of a '**rich picture**':

Figure 13.2 A 'rich picture' of the school situation that emerged from the educational psychologists' consultations there.

Source: Supporting a School in Special Measures: implications for the potential contribution of educational psychology. Bettle, S., Frederickson, N. & Sharp, S. *Educational Psychology in Practice*, 2001, 17, (1). Reprinted by permission of the publisher © 2008, Taylor & Francis Group.

Activity

- Discuss what assumptions are made in the portrayal of the school's 'behaviour ethos' that is conveyed in Figure 13.2.

- In the light of the limited information that is given here, can you suggest an operational definition of 'school ethos' that might have been employed by the educational psychology team?
- Compare the conclusions you have drawn from the data in this box with the conclusions you drew in Research Methods box 13.1. What do any differences between the two tell you about differences in the ways school ethos has been conceptualized in these two reports?

Conclusion

The concept of a school's 'ethos' refers to something vague and ill-defined – its 'feeling' or 'character' as an organization. It is possible to draw on analyses of **organizational culture** to clarify the concept (Solvason, 2005). The notion of school ethos can be viewed from three perspectives that have been developed within organizational psychology (Martin, 1992):

- *An **integration** perspective.* This approach stresses the value of a strong, cohesive organizational culture with clear leadership and a set of shared goals and values that are well understood and shared by all staff.

- *A **differentiation** perspective.* This view highlights the differing interests, tasks and expertise of members of staff and the existence of separate subcultures and groupings within an organization. Often (generally?) it is unrealistic to expect to be able to develop the features of a cohesive organizational culture. Rather, the aim is to ensure that the different parts of the organization co-exist with a degree of harmony and minimize internal tension and conflict.

- *A **fragmentation** perspective.* The integration and differentiation perspectives make organizations appear transparent and easy to understand. That overlooks the ambiguous quality of many of the signals and signs that are transmitted within an organization. These are the aspects highlighted in this third perspective. Different stakeholders interpret the same incidents (such as the announcement of exam results) as having different meanings. The interpretations that are placed on key symbols and routines are diverse and irreconcilable. There are uncontrollable uncertainties in an organization, and the proponents of this perspective would claim that their approach acknowledges that reality.

Which of those perspectives will be most useful in thinking about the ethos of a particular school will depend on the size and type of school and perhaps on its history and functions.

Within the framework of educational psychology, however, a school cannot be understood by focusing solely at a single level, whether that is the whole school or the communal context, group settings such as classrooms, the family or the individual. Schools exist for the sake of their pupils and to serve a community by preparing its youngest members for their roles in adult society.

There is a need to operate at multiple levels. The greatest challenge appears to lie in learning how factors at different levels interact. How do elements of a school's ethos and culture influence the personal development of its students? In his article for *The Scotsman* with which this chapter began, John Wilson saw the relationship as simple: symbols such as a uniform will help to 'promote the unity and ethos of a school and that, in turn, promotes the learning within'.

Once the complexity of the relationship between school ethos and student identities is fully understood, it becomes difficult to predict when wearing a uniform will be a badge of honour for students. In her article for *The Scotsman* Judith Gillespie recalled a school prize-giving she had recently attended. She had been 'impressed at the inventiveness of some youngsters in managing to turn an ordinary shirt and tie into a fashion statement'. Those individuals chose to flaunt an alternative identity on an occasion when their academic identity was supposed to be on show. No doubt their satisfaction in doing so will have been enhanced because they were able to transform the 'official' uniform for that purpose. This reinforces the interactive analysis which considers both the institutional ethos and the individual as an active participant in construing it. Students' identities are developed not by adopting their school's ethos as it is presented to them but by trying out various ways of positioning themselves in relation to it.

Summary

- Schools differ markedly in the outcomes they achieve with their pupils, even when variations in pupil intake are taken into account.

- These differences between schools have been attributed to their overall ethos or culture rather than to specific policies or individual staff actions.

- In the classic study which yielded those findings (Rutter et al, 1979) behavioural process variables were treated as a means of measuring school ethos.

- That approach has been criticized as reductionist on the grounds that the complex forces that are in play in the life of an organization such as a school cannot be adequately captured by such measures.

- The development of social identities is stimulated when children move more and more outside the immediate ambit of their home and are exposed to a wider range of people.

- Tajfel's (1978) theory of social identities has provided the foundation for recent developments in thinking about social identity development in school.

- The reflected appraisals of others such as teachers and parents influence children's own academic self-perceptions in the subject areas to which they relate, but that influence does not have a uniformly decisive impact on individuals' self-definition.

■ The evidence for a powerful impact of school ethos on the development of students' identities as learners is strongest in small schools that have a well-defined mission and values that are widely shared among members of the school community.

■ In a range of situations practising educational psychologists have given attention to school ethos as a factor in some children's difficulties.

■ Interventions in schools with serious problems have included projects based on 'soft systems methodology'. The analysis of school ethos in this strategy focuses on the perceptions of stakeholders and aims to influence their behaviour by changing the way that they view the situation.

■ The notion of school ethos can also be viewed from perspectives that have been developed within organizational psychology – an integration perspective, a differentiation perspective or a fragmentation perspective.

■ If research and professional practice in educational psychology are to be effective, a multi-level focus is required that gives attention not only to psychological processes at the communal, small group, family and individual levels but also to the ethos and culture of a school as a whole.

Key concepts and terms

'Ability'	'Potential'
Academic identities	Reductionist
Behavioural process variables	Reflected appraisal
Differentiation	Rich picture
Fragmentation	School ethos
Gender identities	Social identity
Integration	Soft systems methodology
Organizational culture	Special measures

Sample essay titles

■ Can school ethos be measured?
■ Assess the nature of the relationship between a school's ethos and its students' self-image.
■ You are the educational psychologist serving a large secondary school that has decided to liberalize its rules about school uniform. Drawing on what you know of psychological research in this area, design a research study to investigate the impact of this change on the development of student identities.

Further reading

Books

Duveen, G. (2001). 'Representations, identities, resistance.' In: K. Deaux and G. Philogène (Ed.), *Representations of the Social: Bridging theoretical traditions.* Oxford: Blackwell, 257–270.

Frederickson, N. (1990). 'Systems approaches in educational psychology practice.' In: N. Jones and N. Frederickson (Eds), *Refocusing Educational Psychology.* London: Falmer Press, 130–164.

Lloyd, B., and Duveen, G. (1992). *Gender Identities and Education: The Impact of Starting School.* Hemel Hempstead, Hertfordshire: Harvester Wheatsheaf.

Rutter, M., Maughan, B., Mortimore, P., Ouston, J., and Smith, A. (1979). *Fifteen Thousand Hours: Secondary Schools and their Effects on Children.* Somerset: Open Books.

Journal articles

Bettle, S., Frederickson, N., and Sharp, S. (2001). Supporting a school in special measures: implications for the potential contribution of educational psychology. *Educational Psychology in Practice*, 17, 53–68.

Hamilton, L. (2002). Constructing pupil identity: personhood and ability. *British Educational Research Journal*, 28, 591–602.

References

Abreu, G. de (1995). Understanding how children experience the relationship between home and school mathematics. *Mind, Culture and Activity: An International Journal*, 2, 119–142.

Abreu, G. de, and Cline, T. (2003). Schooled mathematics and cultural knowledge. *Pedagogy, Culture and Society*, 11, 11–30.

Abreu, G. de, Cline, T., and Shamsi, A. (2002). 'Exploring ways parents participate in their children's school mathematical learning: cases studies in multiethnic primary schools'. In: G. de Abreu, A.J. Bishop and N.C. Presmeg (Eds), *Transitions Between Contexts of Mathematical Practices*. Dordrecht, The Netherlands: Kluwer Academic Publishers, 123–148.

Adams, M.J., and Bruck, M. (1993). Word recognition: the interface of educational policies and scientific research. *Reading and Writing: An Interdisciplinary Journal*, 5, 113–139.

Adey, P., Csapo, B., Demetriou, A., Hautamäki, J., and Shayer, M. (2007). Can we be intelligent about intelligence? Why education needs the concept of plastic general ability. *Educational Research Review*. 2, 75–97.

Ainscow, M. (1995) Education for all: making it happen. *Support for Learning*, 10, 147–154.

Ainscow, M., and Tweddle, D.A. (1979). *Preventing Classroom Failure. An Objectives Approach*. Chichester: John Wiley.

Ainsworth, M.S., Blehar, M.C., Waters, E., and Wall, S. (1978). *Patterns of Attachment: A Psychological Study of the Strange Situation*. Oxford: Lawrence Erlbaum.

Ajmal, Y., and Rees, I. (2001). *Solutions in Schools: Creative Applications of Solution Focused Brief Thinking with Young People and Adults*. London: BT Press.

Ajzen, I. (1991). The theory of planned behavior. *Organizational Behavior and Human Decision Processes*, 50, 179–211.

Ali, S., and Frederickson, N. (2006). Investigating the evidence base of social stories. Educational Psychology in Practice, *22*, 355–377.

Alloway, T.P., Gathercole, S.E., Adams, A.M., and Willis, C. (2005a). Working memory and other cognitive skills as predictors of progress towards early learning goals at school entry. *British Journal of Developmental Psychology*, 23, 417–426.

Alloway, T.P., Gathercole, S.E., Adams, A.M., and Willis, C. (2005b). Working memory abilities in children with special educational needs. *Educational and Child Psychology*, 22, 56–67.

Allport, G.W. (1954). *The Nature of Prejudice*. Oxford: Addison-Wesley.

American Psychiatric Association (2000). *Diagnostic and Statistical Manual of Mental Disorder (4th Ed., Text Revision) (DSM-IV-TR)*. Washington: American Psychiatric Publishing.

Anderson, M. (1992). *Intelligence and Development: A Cognitive Theory*. Oxford: Blackwell.

Anderson, M., Kaufman, J., Simon, T.R., et al. (2001). School-associated violent deaths in the United States, 1994–1999. *Journal of the American Medical Association*, 286, 2695–2702.

Archer, J. (2004). Sex differences in aggression in real-world settings: a meta-analytic review. *Review of General Psychology*, 8, 291–322.

Arsenio, W.F., and Lemerise, E.A. (2001). Varieties of childhood bullying: values, emotion-processing and social competence. *Social Development*, 10, 59–73.

Ashcraft, M.H. (2002). Math anxiety: personal, educational, and cognitive consequences. *Current Directions in Psychological Science*, 11, 181–185.

Ashcraft, M.H., and Kirk, E.P. (2001). The relationships among working memory, math anxiety, and performance. *Journal of Experimental Psychology: General*, 130, 224–237.

Ashcraft, M.H., Kirk, E.P., and Hopko, D. (1998). 'On the cognitive consequences of mathematics anxiety'. In: C. Donlan (Ed.), *The Development of Mathematical Skills*. Hove: Psychology Press, 175–196.

Ashton, C. (1996). In defence of discrepancy definitions of specific learning difficulties. *Educational Psychology in Practice*, 12, 131–140.

Atkeson, B.M., and Forehand, R. (1979). Home-based reinforcement programs designed to modify classroom behaviour: a review and methodological evaluation. *Psychological Bulletin*, 86, 1298–1308.

Baddeley, A.D. and Hitch, G.J. (1974). 'Working memory'. In: G.H. Bower (Ed.), *The Psychology of Learning and Motivation*. New York: Academic Press, Volume 8, 47–89.

Baird, G., Simonoff, E., Pickles, A., Chandler, S., Loucas, T., Meldrum, D., and Charman, T. (2006). Prevalence of disorders of the autistic spectrum in a population cohort of children in South Thames: the Special Needs and Autism Project (SNAP). *Lancet*, 368, 210–215.

Bak, J.J., and Siperstein, G.N. (1986). Protective effects of the label 'mentally retarded' on children's attitudes toward mentally retarded peers. *American Journal of Mental Deficiency*, 91, 95–97.

Baker, C. (2001). *Foundations of Bilingual Education and Bilingualism*. Clevedon, Avon: Multilingual Matters.

Baker, E.T., Wang, M.C., and Walberg, H.J. (1994–5). The effects of inclusion on learning. *Educational Leadership*, 52, 33–35.

Baranek, G.T. (2002). Efficacy of sensory and motor interventions for children with Autism. *Journal of Autism and Developmental Disorders*, 32, 397–421.

Barker, C., Pistrang, N., and Elliott, R. (2002). 'Research methods'. In: *Clinical Psychology: An Introduction for Students and Practitioners*, (2nd Ed.). London: Wiley.

Barlow, D., Nock, M., and Hersen, M. (2008). *Single Case Experimental Designs*, (3rd revised edn). Needham Heights, MA: Allyn and Bacon.

Baron-Cohen, S. (2002). The extreme male brain theory of autism. *Trends in Cognitive Science*, 6, 248–254.

Baron-Cohen, S., Leslie, A.M., and Frith, U. (1985). Does the autistic child have a 'theory of mind'? *Cognition*, 4, 37–46.

Baron-Cohen, S., Ring, H., Wheelwright, S., Bullmore, E., Brammer, M., Simmons, A., and Williams, S. (1999). Social intelligence in the normal and autistic brain: An fMRI study. *European Journal of Neuroscience*, 11, 1891–1898.

Baroody, A.J. (2003). 'The development of adaptive expertise and flexibility: the integration of conceptual and procedural knowledge'. In: A.J. Baroody and A. Dowker (Eds), *The Development of Arithmetic Concepts and Skills: Constructing Adaptive Expertise*. London: Lawrence Erlbaum Associates, 1–32.

Baroody, A.J., and Dowker, A. (Eds) (2003). *The Development of Arithmetic Concepts and Skills: Constructing Adaptive Expertise*. London: Lawrence Erlbaum Associates.

Barth, R. (1979) Home-based reinforcement of school behaviour: A review and analysis. *Review of Educational Research*, 49, 436–458.

Basic Skills Agency (2003). *Survey into Young Children's Skills on Entry into Education*. London: Basic Skills Agency.

Beaton, A.E., Martin, M.O., Mulla, I.V.S., Gonzalez, E.J., Smith, T.A., and Kelly, D.L. (1996). Science Achievement in the Middle School Years. IEA's Third International Mathematics and Science Survey. Chestnut Hill, MA: TIMSS-Boston College.

Beck, A.T. (1976). *Cognitive Therapy and Emotional Disorders*. New York: Methuen.

Bereiter, C. (1986). Does Direct Instruction cause delinquency? *Early Childhood Research Quarterly*, 1, 289–292.

Bereiter, C., and Englemann, S. (1966). *Teaching Disadvantaged Children in the Preschool*. Englewood Cliffs, NJ: Prentice-Hall.

Berg, I. (1996). 'School avoidance, school phobia and truancy'. In: M. Lewis (Ed.), *Child and Adolescent Psychiatry: A Comprehensive Textbook*, (2nd Ed.). Baltimore: Williams and Wilkins.

Berg, I., Nichols, K., and Pritchard, C. (1969) School phobia – its classification and relationship to dependency. *Journal of Child Psychology and Psychiatry*, 10, 123–141.

Bergin, A., and Strup, H. (1972). *Changing Frontiers in the Science of Psychotherapy*. Chicago, IL: Aldine.

Berry, G., Injejikian, M.A., and Tidwell, R. (1993). The school phobic child and the counsellor: identifying, understanding and helping. *Education*, 114, 37–45.

Bettle, S., Frederickson, N., and Sharp, S. (2001). Supporting a School in Special Measures: implications for the potential contribution of educational psychology. *Educational Psychology in Practice*, 17, 53–68.

Bibby, T. (2002). Shame: an emotional response to doing mathematics as an adult and a teacher. *British Educational Research Journal*, 28, 705–721.

Bickford-Smith, A., Wijayatilake, L., and Woods, G. (2005). Evaluating the effectiveness of an early years language intervention. *Educational Psychology in Practice*, 21, 161–173.

Black, D., and Cottrell, D. (1993). *Seminars in Child and Adolescent Psychiatry. Gaskell*. London: Royal College of Psychiatrists.

Blagg, N. (1987). *School Phobia and its Treatment*. London: Croom Helm.

Blagg, N., and Yule, W. (1984). The behavioural treatment of school refusal – a comparative study. *Behaviour Research and Therapy*, 22, 119–127.

Blair, R.J.R., Peschardt, K.S., Budhani, S., Mitchell, D.G.V, and Pine, D.S. (2006). The development of psychopathy. *Journal of Child Psychology and Psychiatry*, 47, 262–275.

Blakemore, S.J., and Frith, U. (2005). *The Learning Brain: Lessons for Education*. Malden, M.A.: Blackwell Publishing.

Blatchford, P., Burke, J., Farquhar, C., Plewis, I., and Tizard, B. (1987). Associations between pre-school reading-related skills and later reading achievement. *British Education Research Journal*, 13, 15–23.

Boaler, J. (1998). Open and closed mathematics: student experiences and understandings. *Journal for Research in Mathematics Education* 29, 41–62.

Bools, C., Foster, J., Brown, I., and Berg, I. (1990). The identification of psychiatric disorders in children who fail to attend school: a cluster analysis of a non-clinical population. *Psychological Medicine*, 20, 171–181.

Booth, S.R., and Jay, M. (1981). The use of precision teaching technology in the work of the educational psychologist. *Journal of the Association of Educational Psychologists* 5, 21–26.

Bouchey, H.A., and Harter, S. (2005). Reflected appraisals, academic self-perceptions, and math/science performance during early adolescence. *Journal of Educational Psychology*, 97, 673–686.

Bowers, L., Smith, P.K., and Binney, V. (1994). Perceived family relationships of bullies, victims and bully/victims in middle childhood. *Journal of Social and Personal Relationships*, 11, 215–232.

Bowlby, J. (1969). *Attachment and Loss* (Volume 1). New York: Basic Books.

Bozic, N., and Morris, S. (2005). Traumatic brain injury in childhood and adolescence: the role of educational psychology services in promoting effective recovery. *Educational and Child Psychology*, 22, 108–120.

Brand, C. (1996). *The g Factor: General Intelligence and its Implications*. New York: John Wiley.

Brewer, M., and Miller, N. (1984). 'Beyond the contact hypothesis: Theoretical perspectives on desegregation.' In: N. Miller and M. Brewer (Eds), *Groups in Conflict*. New York: Academic Press, 281–302.

Briggs, S., MacKay, T., and Miller, S. (1995). The Edinburgh Playground Project: Changing aggressive behaviour through structured intervention. *Educational Psychology in Practice*, 11, 37–44.

Briskman, J., Happé, F., and Frith, U. (2001). Exploring the cognitive phenotype of Autism: weak "central coherence" of parents and siblings of children with autism II. Real life skills and preferences. *Journal of Child Psychology and Psychiatry*, 42, 309–316.

British Psychological Society (1999). *Dyslexia, Literacy and Psychological Assessment*. Report of a Working Party of the Division of Educational and Child Psychology. Leicester: British Psychological Society.

British Psychological Society, Division of Education and Child Psychology (2002). *Professional Practice Guidelines*. Leicester: British Psychological Society.

British Psychological Society (2006). *Code of Ethics and Conduct*. Leicester: British Psychological Society.

Broadwin, I.T. (1932). A contribution to the study of truancy. *Orthopsychiatry*, 2, 253–259.

Bronfenbrenner, U. (1974). Developmental research, public policy and the ecology of childhood. *Child Development*, 45, 1–5.

Bronfenbrenner, U. (1979). *The Ecology of Human Development: Experiments by Nature and Design*. Cambridge, MA: Harvard University Press.

Bronfenbrenner, U., and Morris, P.A. (2006). 'The bio-ecological model of human development.' In: R.M. Learner and W. Damon (Eds), *Handbook of Child Psychology* (6th Ed.). Volume 1, Theoretical Models of Human Development. Hoboken, N.J.: John Wiley, 793–828.

Brooks, G., Pugh, A.K., and Shagen, I. (1996). *Reading Performance at 9*. Slough: National Foundation for Educational Research.

Brophy, J. (2006). 'History of research on classroom management.' In: C.M. Evertson and C.S. Weinstein (Eds), *Handbook of Classroom Management*. London: Lawrence Erlbaum Associates.

Bruner, J.K. (1966). *Toward a Theory of Instruction*. Cambridge, MA: Harvard University Press.

Burden, R. (2005). *Dyslexia and Self-Concept: Seeking a Dyslexic Identity*. London: Whurr.

Burgess, T. (1980). 'What makes an effective school?' In: B. Tizard, et al. (Eds), *Fifteen Thousand Hours – A Discussion*. London: University of London Institute of Education, 1–14.

Burland, R. (1979). *Social Skills as the Basis for Coping Strategies in School*. Proceedings of the 1979 DECP Annual Course. British Psychological Society.

Caffyn, R. (1989). Attitudes of British secondary school teachers and pupils to rewards and punishments. *Educational Research*, 31, 210–220.

Calfee, R. (1997). Language and literacy, home and school. *Early Child Development and Care*, 127/8, 75–90.

Cameron, L., and Rutland, A. (2006). Extending contact through story reading in school: reducing children's prejudice towards the disabled. *Journal of Social Issues*, 62, 469–488.

Cameron, R.J. (2006). Educational Psychology: The distinctive contribution. *Educational Psychology in Practice*, 22, 289–304.

Cameron, R.J., and Stratford, R.J. (1987). Educational Psychology: a problem-centred approach to service delivery. *Educational Psychology in Practice*, 2, 10–20.

Canter, L., and Canter, M. (1992). *Lee Canter's Assertive Discipline: Positive Behavior Management for Today's Classroom*. Santa Monica, CA: Canter and Associates.

Caravolas, M. (2005). 'The nature and causes of dyslexia in different languages.' In: M.J. Snowling and C. Hulme (Eds), *The Science of Reading: A Handbook*. Oxford: Blackwell.

Carnine, D. (1979). Direct instruction: a successful system for educationally high risk children. *Journal of Curriculum Studies*, 11, 29–46.

Carr, A. (2000) (Ed.). *What Works with Children and Adolescents? A Critical Review of Psychological Interventions with Children, Adolescents and their Families*. London: Routledge.

Carroll, J.B. (1993). *Human Cognitive Abilities: A Survey of Factor Analytic Studies*. New York: Cambridge University Press.

Carroll, J.B. (1996). 'Mathematical abilities: some results from factor analysis.' In: R.J. Sternberg and T. Ben-Zeev (Eds), *The Nature of Mathematical Thinking*. Mahwah, NJ: Lawrence Erlbaum Associates, 3–26.

Carroll, J.B. (2005). 'The three-stratum theory of cognitive abilities.' In: D.P. Flanagan and P.L. Harrison (Eds), *Contemporary Intellectual Assessment: Theories, Tests and Issues* (2nd Ed.). New York: Guilford Press, 69–76.

Chafouleas, S.M., Riley-Tillman, T.C., and McDougal, J.L. (2002). Good, bad, or in-between: how does the daily behaviour report card rate? *Psychology in the Schools*, 39, 157–169.

Chall, J.S. (1983). *Learning to Read. The Great Debate.* (2nd Ed.). Fort Worth: Harcourt Brace College Publishers.

Chapman, S.C., Exing, C.B., and Mozzoni, M.P. (2005). Precision teaching and fluency training across cognitive, physical, and academic tasks in children with traumatic brain injury: a multiple baseline study. *Behavioural Interventions*, 20, 37–49.

Chen, J-Q., and Gardner, H. (2005). 'Assessment based on multiple-intelligences theory.' In: D.P. Flanagan and P.L. Harrison (Eds), *Contemporary Intellectual Assessment: Theories, Tests and Issues* (2nd Ed.). New York: Guilford Press, 77–102.

Cheng, Z.J., and Chan, L.K.S. (2005). Chinese number-naming advantages? Analyses of Chinese pre-schoolers' computational strategies and errors. *International Journal of Early Years Education*, 13, 179–192.

Chisholm, B., Kearney, D., Knight, G., Little, H., Morris, S., and Tweddle, D. (1986). *Preventative Approaches to Disruption*. Basingstoke: Macmillan Education.

Chitiyo, M., and Wheeler, J.J. (2006). School phobia: Understanding a complex behavioural response. *Journal of Research in Special Educational Needs*, 6, 87–91.

Cianciolo, A.T., and Sternberg, R.J. (2004). *Intelligence: A Brief History*. Oxford: Blackwell.

Clark, M.S., and Mills, J. (1979). Interpersonal attraction in exchange and communal relationships. *Journal of Personality and Social Psychology*, 37, 12–24.

Clark, M.S., and Mills, J. (1993). The difference between communal and exchange relationships. *Personality and Social Psychology Bulletin*, 19, 684–691.

Clarke, D.D. (2004). ' "Structured judgement methods" – the best of both worlds?' In: Z. Todd, B. Nerlich, S. McKeown and D.D. Clarke (Eds), *Mixing Methods in Psychology. The Integration Of Qualitative and Quantitative Methods in Theory and Practice*. London: Routledge.

Clay, M. (1987). Learning to be learning disabled. *New Zealand Journal of Educational Studies*, 22, 155–173.

Coie, J.D., and Pennington, B.E. (1976). Children's perceptions of deviance and disorder. *Child Development*, 47, 407–413.

Coie, J.D., Dodge, K.A., and Coppotelli, H. (1982). Dimensions and types of social status; A cross-age perspective. *Developmental Psychology*, 18, 557–570.

Colom, R., Jung, R.E., and Haier, R.J. (2006). Distributed brain sites for the g-factor of intelligence. *NeuroImage*, 31, 1359–1365.

Conti-Ramsden, G., and Botting, N. (2004). Social difficulties and victimization in children with SLI at 11 years of age. *Journal of Speech, Language, and Hearing Research*, 47, 145–161.

Cornah, D. (2000). Explaining children's behaviour. *Special Children*, October 2000, 38–39.

Cornell, D.T., Sheras, P.L., and Cole, J.C.M. (2006). 'Assessment of bullying.' In: S.R. Jimerson and M. Thurlong (Eds), *Handbook of School Violence and School Safety from Research to Practice*. Mahwah, N.J.: Lawrence Erlbaum.

Creese, A., Bhatt, A., Bhojani, N., and Martin, P. (2006). Multicultural, heritage and learner identities in complementary schools. *Language and Education*, 20, 23–43.

Crick, M.R., and Dodge, K.A. (1994). A review and reformulation of social information-processing mechanisms in children's social adjustment. *Psychological Bulletin*, 115, 74–101.

Crick, M.R., and Dodge, K.A. (1996). Social information processing mechanisms on reactive and proactive aggression. *Child Development*, 67, 993–1002.

Crick, M.R., and Dodge, K.A. (1999). 'Superiority' is in the eye of the beholder: A comment on Sutton, Smith and Swettenham. *Social Development*, 8, 128–131.

Critchley, M., and Critchley, E.A. (1978). *Dyslexia Defined*. London: Heinemann Medical.

Croll, P., and Moses, D. (1985). *One in Five. The Assessment and Incidence of Special Educational Needs*. London: Routledge and Kegan Paul.

Croll, P., and Moses, D. (1999). *Special Needs in the Primary School: One in Five?* London: Continuum.

Crozier, R.W., and Alden, L.E. (2005). 'Introduction: The development of social anxiety.' In: R.W. Crozier and L.E. Alden (Eds), *The Essential Handbook of Social Anxiety for Clinicians*. New York: Wiley, 27–32.

Crystal, D. (1988). *Introduction to Language Pathology*, (2nd Ed.). London: Cole and Whurr.

D'Amico, A., and Guarnera, M. (2005). Exploring working memory in children with low arithmetic achievement. *Learning and Individual Differences*, 15, 189–202.

de Castro, B.O., Veerman, J.W., Koops, W., Bosch, J.D., and Monshouwer H.J. (2002). Hostile attribution of intent and aggressive behaviour: a meta-analysis. *Child Development*, 73, 916–934.

Deary, I.J., and Caryl, P.G. (1997). Neuroscience and human intelligence differences. *Trends in Neuroscience*, 20, 365–371.

Deary, I.J., and Stough, C. (1996). Intelligence and inspection time: achievements, prospects, and problems. *American Psychologist*, 51, 599–608.

Department for Education (1993). *Schools Requiring Special Measures*. Circular No. 17/93. London: DfE.

Department for Education (2001). *Code of Practice on the Identification and Assessment of Special Educational Needs*. London: HMSO.

Department For Education and Employment (DfEE) (1998). *Circular 1/98: LEA Behaviour Support Plans*. London. DfEE.

Department for Education and Employment DfEE (1999a). *The National Numeracy Strategy: Framework for teaching mathematics from Reception to Year 6*. London: DfEE.

Department for Education and Employment (DfEE) (1999b). *Social Inclusion: Pupil Support* (Circular 10/99). London: DfEE.

Department for Education and Employment (DfEE) (2000a). *Educational Psychology Services (England): Current Role, Good Practice and Future Directions*. The Report of the Working Group. London: HMSO.

Department for Education and Employment (DfEE) (2000b). *Educational Psychology Services (England): Current Role, Good Practice and Future Directions*. The research report. London: DfEE.

Department For Education and Employment (DfEE) (2000c). *Home–school agreements. Guidance for Schools*. London. DfEE.

Department for Education and Employment (DfEE) (2001). *Special Educational Needs and Disability Act*. London: HMSO.

Department for Education and Science (DfES) (2000). *Bullying – Don't Suffer in Silence. An Anti-bullying Pack for Schools*. London: DfES. http://publications.teachernet.gov.uk

Department for Education and Science (DfES) (2001). *Code of Practice on the Identification and Assessment of Children with Special Educational Needs*. London: DfES.

Department for Education and Science DfES (2003). *Speaking, Listening, Learning: Working with Children in Key Stages 1 and 2. Primary National Strategy Handbook*. DfES Ref. 0626-2003 G. London: DfES.

Department for Education and Science (DfES) (2004). *Every Child Matters: Change for Children*. London: HMSO.

Department for Education and Science (DfES) (2007). *School Discipline and Pupil-Behaviour Policies: Guidance for Schools*. www.teachernet.gov.uk/wholeschool/behaviour/schooldisciplinepupilbehaviourpolicies/

Department of Education and Science (1968). *Psychologists in Education Services* (The Summerfield Report). London: HMSO.

Department of Education and Science (1989). *Discipline in Schools* (The Elton Report). London: HMSO.

Dessent, T. (1988). 'Educational psychologists and the resource issue.' In: N. Jones and J. Sayer (Eds), *Management and the Psychology of Schooling*. Lewis: Falmer Press, 73–88.

Dessent, T. (1992). 'Educational psychologists and the "case for individual case work".' In: S. Wolfendale, T. Bryans, M. Fox, A. Labram and A. Sigston (Eds), *The Profession and Practice of Educational Psychology: Future Directions*. London: Cassell, 34–48.

Dickson, M.D.L. (1938). *Child Guidance*. London: Sands.

Dix, T., Ruble, D.N., and Zambarabno, R.J. (1989) Mothers' implicit theories of discipline: child effects, parent effects and the attribution process. Child Development, 60, 1373–1391.

Doherty-Sneddon, G. (2003). *Children's Unspoken Language*. London: Jessica Kingsley.

Doll, B., Song, S., and Siemers, E. (2004). 'Classroom ecologies that support or discourage bullying.' In: D.L. Espelage and S.M. Swearer (Eds), *Bullying in American Schools: A Social-Ecological Perspective on Prevention and Intervention*. Mahwah, N.J.: Lawrence Erlbaum, 1–12.

Dowling E., and Osborne E. (1994). *The Family and the School. A Joint Systems Approach to Problems with Children*, (2nd Ed.). London: Routledge.

Dowling, E., and Taylor, D. (1989). The clinic goes to school: lessons learned. *Maladjustment and Therapeutic Education*, 7, 24–28.

Du Paul, G.J., Jitendra, A.K., Volpe, R.J., Tresco, K.E., Lutz, J.G., Junod, R.E.V., Cleary, K.S., Flammer, L.M., and Mannella, M.C. (2006). Consultation-based academic interventions for children with ADHD: effects on reading and mathematics achievement. *Journal of Abnormal Child Psychology*, 34, 635–648.

Dunn, L.M. (1968). Special education for the mildly retarded – Is much of it justifiable? *Exceptional Children*, 35, 5–22.

Dunsmuir, S., and Frederickson, N. (Eds) (2005). *Autistic Spectrum Disorders* [CD]. London: Educational Psychology Publishing, University College London.

Duveen, G. (2001). 'Representations, identities, resistance.' In: K. Deaux and G. Philogène (Eds), *Representations of the Social: Bridging Theoretical Traditions*. Oxford: Blackwell, 257–270.

Dyches, T.T., Wilder, L.K., and Obiakor, F.E. (2001). 'Autism: Multicultiural perspectives.' In: T. Walberg, F. Obiakor, S. Burkhardt, et al. (Eds), *Educational and Clinical Interventions*. Oxford: Elsevier Science, 151–177.

Ehri, L.C. (1992). 'Reconceptualizing the development of sight word reading and its relationship to recoding.' In: R. Treiman, P.B. Gough and L.C. Ehri, Linnea (Eds), *Reading Acquisition*. Hillsdale, NJ: Lawrence Erlbaum Associates, 107–143.

Ehri, L.C. (2002). Faces of acquisition in learning to read words and implications for teaching. *British Journal of Educational Psychology: Monograph Series*, 1, 7–28.

Ehri, L.C. (2005). 'Development of sight word reading: phases and findings.' In: M.J. Snowling and C. Hulme (Eds), *The Science of Reading: A Handbook*. Oxford: Blackwell.

Elliott, J. (1996). Locus of control in behaviourally disordered children. *British Journal of Educational Psychology*, 66, 1, 47–57.

Elliott, J. (2000). Editorial. Psychological influences upon educational interventions. *Educational and Child Psychology*, 17, 4–5.

Elliott, J. (2003). Dynamic assessment in educational settings: realising potential. *Educational Review*, 55, 15–32.

Elliot, J.G. (1999). Practitioner review: School refusal: issues of conceptualisation, assessment and treatment. *Journal of Child Psychology and Psychiatry*, 40, 1001–1012.

Elliot, J.G., and Place, M. (2004). *Children in Difficulty: A Guide to Understanding and Helping*, (2nd Ed.). London: Routledge.

Ericsson, K.A., and Charness, N. (1994). Expert performance: its stricture and acquisition. *American Psychologist*, 49, 725–747.

Estes, H.R., Haylett, C.H., and Johnson, A.L. (1956). Separation anxiety. *American Journal of Psychotherapy*, 10, 682–695.

Evans, I.M., Goldberg-Arnold, J.S., and Dickson, J.K. (1998). 'Children's perceptions of equity in peer interactions.' In: L.H. Meyer, H-S Park, M. Grenot-Scheyer, I.S. Schwartz and B. Harry (Eds), *Making Friends: The Influences of Culture and Development*. Baltimore, MD: Paul H. Brooks, 133–147.

Eysenck, H.J. (1949). Training in clinical psychology: an English point of view. *American Psychologist*, 4, 173–176.

Eysenck, M.W., and Calvo, M.G. (1992). Anxiety and performance: The processing efficiency theory. *Cognition and Emotion*, 6, 409–434.

Farrell, P. (2000). The impact of research on developments in inclusive education. *International Journal of Inclusive Education*, 4, 153–162.

Farrell, P., and Smith, N. (1982). A survey of methods educational psychologists use to assess children with learning difficulties. *Occasional Papers of the Division of Educational and Child Psychology*, 6, 31–41.

Farrell, P., Dunning, T., and Foley, J. (1989). Methods used by educational psychologists to assess children with learning difficulties. *School Psychology International*, 10, 47–55.

Farrell, P., Woods, K., Lewis, S., Rooney, S., Squires, G., and O'Connor, M. (2006). *A Review of the Functions and Contribution of Educational Psychologists in England and Wales in light of* "Every child matters: Change for Children". Nottingham: DfES Publications.

Ferguson, E., and Cox, T. (1993). Exploratory factor analysis: a users guide. *International Journal of Selection and Assessment*, 1, 84–94.

Fiske, S.I., and Taylor, S.E. (1984). *Social Cognition*. New York: Random House.

Flanagan, D.P., and Harrison, P.L. (Eds) (2005). *Contemporary Intellectual Assessment: Theories, Tests and Issues*, (2nd Ed.). New York: Guilford Press.

Flewitt, R. (2005). Is every child's voice heard? Researching the different ways 3-year-old children communicate and make meaning at home and in a pre-school playgroup. *Early Years*, 25, 207–222.

Flugel, J. (1947). An inquiry as to popular views on intelligence and related topics. *British Journal of Educational Psychology*, 27, 140–152.

Flynn, J.R. (1999). Searching for justice: The discovery of IQ gains over time. *American Psychologist*, 54, 5–20.

Fombonne, E., and Chakrabarti, S. (2001). No evidence for a new variant of measles–mumps–rubella-induced autism. *Pediatrics*, 108: E58.

Foorman, B.R., Francis, D.J., Fletcher, J.M., Schatschneider, C., and Mehta, P. (1998). The role of instruction in learning to read: Preventing reading failure in at-risk children. *Journal of Educational Psychology*, 90, 37–55.

Forsterling, F. (2001). Attribution: An Introduction to Theories, Research and Applications. Hove: Psychology Press.

Frederickson, N. (1990). 'Systems approaches in educational psychology practice.' In: N. Jones and N. Frederickson (Eds), *Refocusing Educational Psychology*. London: Falmer Press, 130–164.

Frederickson, N. (1993). 'Using Soft Systems Methodology to rethink special educational needs.' In: A. Dyson and C. Gains (Eds), *Rethinking Special Needs in Mainstream Schools: Towards the Year 2000*. London: David Fulton, 1–21.

Frederickson, N., and Cline, T. (2008). *Special Educational Needs, Inclusion and Diversity. A Textbook* (2nd Ed.). Buckingham: Open University Press.

Frederickson, N., and Frith, U. (1998). Identifying dyslexia in bilingual children: a phonological approach within inner London Sylheti speakers. *Dyslexia*, 4, 119–131.

Frederickson, N.L., and Furnham, A.F. (1998). Sociometric status group classification of mainstreamed children who have moderate learning difficulties: An investigation of personal and environmental factors. *Journal of Educational Psychology*, 90, 772–783.

Frederickson, N., and Furnham, A. (2004). The relationship between sociometric status and peer assessed behavioural characteristics of included pupils who have moderate learning difficulties and their classroom peers. *British Journal of Educational Psychology*, 74, 391–410.

Frederickson, N., and Reason, R. (1995). Discrepancy definitions of specific learning difficulties. *Educational Psychology in Practice*, 10, 195–205.

Frederickson, N., and Simmonds, E. (in press). Special needs, relationship type and distributive justice norms in early and later years of middle childhood. *Social Development*.

Frederickson, N., Simmonds, E., Evans, L., and Soulsby, C. (2007). Assessing social and affective outcomes of inclusion. *British Journal of Special Education*, 34, 105–115.

Freeman, J. (1998). *Educating the Very Able: Current International Research*. London: The Stationery Office.

Frith, U. (1985). 'Beneath the surface of developmental dyslexia'. In: K.E. Patterson, J.C. Marshall and M. Coltheart (Eds), *Surface Dyslexia: Neuro-psychological and Cognitive Studies of Phonological Reading*. London: Erlbaum, 301–330.

Frith, U. (1989). Autism: Explaining the Enigma. Oxford: Blackwell.

Frith, U. (1999). Paradoxes in the definition of dyslexia. *Dyslexia*, 5, 192–214.

Frith, U. (2003). *Autism: Explaining the Enigma*, (2nd Ed.) Oxford: Blackwell.

Fry, S. (1997). *Moab is my Washpot: An Autobiography*. London: Random House.

Gallagher, A.M., and Kaufman J.C. (Eds) (2005). *Gender Differences in Mathematics: an Integrative Psychological Approach*. Cambridge, Cambridge University Press.

Gallagher, D.J. (2001). Neutrality as a moral standpoint, conceptual confusion and the full inclusion debate. *Disability in Society*, 16, 637–654.

Gallagher, E. (2006). Improving a mathematical key skill using precision teaching. *Irish Educational Studies*, 25, 303–319.

Galloway, D., and Miller, A. (1978). The use of graded in vivo flooding in the extinction of children's phobias. *Behavioural Psychotherapy*, 6, 7–10.

Galvin, P., Mercer, S., and Costa, P. (1990). *Building a Better Behaved School*. Harlow: Longman.

Gardner, H. (1983). *Frames of Mind: The Theory of Multiple Intelligences*. London, Basic Books.

Gardner, H. (1999). *Intelligence Reframed: Multiple Intelligences for the 21st Century*. New York: Basic Books.

Gay, J., and Cole, M. (1967). *The New Mathematics and an Old Culture*. New York: Holt, Rinehart and Winston.

Gierl, M.J., and Bisanz, J. (1995). Anxieties and attitudes related to mathematics in grades 3 and 6. *Journal of Experimental Education* 63, 139–158.

Gilborn, D., and Mirza, H.S. (2000). *Educational Inequality. Mapping Race, Class and Gender*. London: Ofsted.

Gillham, B. (1978). 'Directions of change.' In: B. Gillham (Ed.), *Reconstructing Educational Psychology*. London: Croom Helm, 11–23.

Gillham, W.E.C. (1978). *Reconstructing Educational Psychology*. London: Croom Helm.

Gipps, C., and Murphy, P. (1994). *A Fair Test? Assessment, Achievement and Equity*. Buckingham: Open University Press.

Goldstein, H. (1980). Critical notice of "Fifteen Thousand Hours". *Journal of Child Psychology and Psychiatry*, 21, 364–366.

Goodman, K.S. (1967). Reading: a psycho-linguistic guessing game. *Journal of the Reading Specialist*, 6,126–135.

Goodman, R., and Scott, S. (2002). *Child Psychiatry*. Oxford. Blackwell.

Goodwin, D.W., and Coates, T.J. (1976). *Helping Students Help Themselves. How You Can Put Behaviour Analysis into Action in Your Classroom*. Englewood Cliffs, NJ: Prentice-Hall.

Gorsuch, R. (1983). *Factor Analysis*. London: Lawrence Erlbaum Associates.

Goswami, U. (2005). Synthetic phonics and learning to read: A cross-language perspective. *Educational Psychology in Practice*, 21, 273–282.

Goswami, U. (2006). Neuroscience and education: from research to practice. *Nature Reviews Neuroscience*, 7, 2–7.

Gough, P.B., and Tunmer, W.E. (1986). Decoding, reading and reading disability. *Remedial and Special Education*, 7, 6–10.

Gough, P.B., Alford, J.A., and Holley-Wilcox, P. (1983). 'Words and contexts.' In: O.J.L. Tzeng and H. Singer (Eds), *Perceptions of Print: Reading Research in Experimental Psychology*. Hillsdale, NJ: Erlbaum, 85–102.

Graham, S., and Folkes, V.S. (1990). *Attribution Theory. Applications to Achievement, Mental Health and Interpersonal Conflict*. Mahwah, NJ: Lawrence Erlbaum Associates.

Gray, C.A. (1998). 'Social stories and comic strip conversations with students with Asperger's Syndrome and high functioning autism.' In: E. Schloper and G.B. Mesibov (Eds), *Asperger's Syndrome or High Functioning Autism? Current Issues in Autism*. New York: Plenum Press, 167–198.

Green, J., and Goldwin, R. (2002). Annotation: attachment disorganization and psychopathology: new findings and attachment research and the potential implications for developmental psychopathology in childhood. *Journal of Child Psychology and Psychiatry*, 43, 835–846.

Gregory, E. (2005). Playful talk: The interspace between home and school discourse. *Early Years*, 25, 223–236.

Greig, A. (2007). A framework for the delivery of cognitive behaviour therapy in the educational psychology context. *Educational and Child Psychology*, 24, 19–35.

Gresham, F.M. (1982). Misguided mainstreaming: The case for social skills training with handicapped children. *Exceptional Children*, 48, 422–433.

Gresham, F.M. (2002). 'Responsiveness to intervention: an alternative approach to the identification of learning disabilities.' In: R. Bradley, L. Danielson and D.P. Hallahan (Eds), *Identification of Learning Disabilities: Researched Practice*. Mahwah, NJ: Erlbaum.

Gresham, F.M., and Macmillan, D.L. (1997a). Autistic recovery? An analysis and critique of the empirical evidence on the early intervention project. *Behavioral Disorders*, 22, 185–201.

Gresham, F.M., and Macmillan, D.L. (1997b). Denial and defensiveness in the place of fact and reason: rejoinder to Smith and Lovaas. *Behavioral Disorders*, 22, 219–230.

Gresham, F.M., and Macmillan, D.L. (1997c). Social competence and affective characteristics of students with mild disabilities. *Review of Educational Research*, 67, 377–415.

Gresham, F.M., Watson, T.S., and Skinner, C.H. (2001). Functional behavioural assessment: Principles, procedures, and future directions. *School Psychology Review*, 30, 156–172.

Guimond, S., Begin, G., and Palmer, D.L. (1989). Education and causal attributions: the development of "person-blame" and "system-blame" ideology. *Social Psychology Quarterly*, 52, 126–140.

Gurney, P. (1987). The use of operant techniques to raise self-esteem in maladjusted children. *British Journal of Educational Psychology*, 57, 87–94.

Gutkin, T.B. (1993). Moving from behavioral to ecobehavioral consultation: What's in a name. *Journal of Educational and Psychological Consultation*, 4, 95–99.

Gutkin, T.B., and Curtis, M.J. (1999). 'School-based consultation: theory and practice.' In: C.R. Reynolds and T.B. Gutkin (Eds), *The Handbook of School Psychology*, (3rd Ed.). New York: Wiley.

Hadwin, J., Baron-Cohen, S., Howlin, P., and Hill, K. (1996). Can children with autism be taught concepts of emotion, belief and pretence? *Development and Psychopathology*, 8, 345–265.

Hadwin, J., Baron-Cohen, S., Howlin, P., and Hill, K. (1997). Does teaching theory of mind have an affect on the ability to develop conversation in children with autism? *Journal of Autism and Developmental Disorders*, 27, 519–537.

Haier, R.J. (1993). 'Cerebral glucose metabolism and intelligence.' In: P.A. Vernon (Ed.), *Biological Approaches to the Study of Human Intelligence*. Norwood, NJ: Ablex, 317–332.

Hallam, S., Ireson, J., and Davies, J. (2004). Primary pupils' experiences of different types of grouping in school. *British Educational Research Journal*, 30, 515–533.

Hamilton, L. (2002). Constructing pupil identity: personhood and ability. *British Educational Research Journal*, 28, 591–602.

Happé, F. (1995). The role of age and verbal ability in the theory of mind task performance of subjects with autism. *Child Development*, 66, 843–855.

Happé, F., Briskman, J., and Frith, U. (2001). Exploring the cognitive phenotype of Autism: weak "central coherence" in parents and siblings of children with autism. One experimental test. *Journal of Child Psychology and Psychiatry*, 42, 299–307.

Harden, R.M. (2003). Learning outcomes and instructional objectives. Is there a difference? *Medical Teacher*, 24, 151–155.

Haring, N.G., and Eaton, M.D. (1978). 'Systematic instructional procedures: An instructional hierarchy.' In: N.G. Haring et al. (Eds), *The Fourth R – Research in the Classroom*. Ohio: Charles E. Merrill.

Harrop, L.A., and McNamara, E. (1979). The behavioural workshop for classroom problems. A re-appraisal. *British Journal of In-Service Education*, 1, 47–50.

Harrop, L.A., and Williams, T. (1992). Rewards and punishments in the primary school: pupils' perceptions and teachers' usage. *Educational Psychology in Practice* 7, 211–215.

Hart, B., and Risley, T.R. (1992). American parenting of language-learning children: persisting differences in family-child interactions observed in natural home environments. *Developmental Psychology*, 28, 1096–1105.

Hastings, N., and Wood, K.C. (2002). *Reorganizing Primary Classroom Learning*. Maidenhead: Open University Press.

Hatcher, P.J., Hulme, C., and Snowling, M.J. (2004). Explicit phoneme training combined with phonic reading instruction helps young children at risk of reading failure. *Journal of Child Psychology and Psychiatry*, 45, 338–358.

Hawker, D.S., and Boulton, M.J. (2001). 'Sub-types of peer harassment and their correlates: a social dominance perspective.' In: J. Juvonen and S. Graham (Eds), *Peer Harassment in School*. New York: Guildford Press.

Hegarty, M., and Kozhevnikov, M. (1999). Types of visual-spatial representations and mathematical problem solving. *Journal of Educational Psychology*, 91, 684–689.

Hegarty, S. (1993). Reviewing the literature on integration. *European Journal of Special Needs Education*, 8, 194–200.

Henderling, J., and Lepper, M.R. (2002). The effects of praise on children's intrinsic motivation: a review and synthesis. *Psychological Bulletin*, 128, 774–795.

Hermelin, B. (2001). *Bright Splinters of the Mind. A Personal Story of Research with Autistic Savants*. London: Jessica Kingsley.

Hersov, L. (1977). 'School refusal.' In: M. Rutter and L. Hersov (Eds), *Child Psychiatry. Modern Approaches*. Oxford: Blackwell.

Hewstone, M., and Brown, R.J. (1986). 'Contact is not enough: An intergroup perspective on the contact hypothesis.' In: M. Hewstone and R. Brown (Eds), *Contact and conflict in intergroup encounters*. Oxford: Blackwell, 1–44.

Heyne, D., and Rollings, S. (2002). *School Refusal*. Oxford: BPS Blackwell.

Heyne, D., King, N., and Olendeck, T.H. (2005). 'School refusal.' In: Graham, P. (Ed.), *Cognitive Behaviour Therapy for Children and Families,* (2nd Ed.). Cambridge: Cambridge University Press.

Hinshelwood, J. (1900). Congenital word blindness. *Lancet*, 1, 1506–1508.

Hmelo-Silver, C.E. (2004). Problem-based learning: What and how do students learn? *Educational Psychology Review*, 16, 235–266.

Ho, I.T. (2004). A comparison of Australian and Chinese teachers' attributions for student problem behaviours. *Educational Psychology*, 24, 375–391.

Holmes, J., and Adams, J.W. (2006). Working memory and children's mathematical skills: implications for mathematical development and mathematics curricula. *Educational Psychology*, 26, 339–366.

Horn, J.L., and Blankson, N. (2005). 'Foundations for better understanding of cognitive abilities.' In: D.P. Flanagan and P.L. Harrison (Eds), *Contemporary Intellectual Assessment: Theories, Tests and Issues,* (2nd Ed.). New York: Guilford Press, 41–68.

House of Commons Education and Skills Committee (2007). *Bullying*. London: The Stationery Office.

Howley, M., and Arnold, E. (2005). *Revealing the Hidden Social Code*. London: Jessica Kingsley.

Howlin, P. (1998). Practitioner review: Psychological and educational treatments for autism. *Journal of Child Psychology and Psychiatry*, 39, 307–322.

Howlin, P., Baron-Cohen, S., and Hadwin, J. (1999). Teaching Children with Autism To Mind-Read: A Practical Guide for Teachers and Parents. London: Wiley.

Hudley, C., Britsch, B., Wakefield, W.D., Smith, T., Demorat, M., and Cho, S.-J. (1998). An attribution retraining program to reduce aggression in elementary school students. *Psychology in the Schools*, 35, 271–282.

Imich, A. (1999). Educational psychologists and the allocation of time. *Educational Psychology in Practice*, 15, 89–97.

Imich, A., and Roberts, A. (1990). Promoting positive behaviour: An evaluation of a behaviour support project. *Educational Psychology in Practice*, 5: 201–209.

Individuals with Disabilities Education Act (IDEA) (1997). 20 US Congress. Chapter 33, Sections 1400–1491.

Infantino, J., and Little, E. (2005). Students' perceptions of classroom behaviour problems and the effectiveness of different disciplinary methods. *Educational Psychology*, 25, 491–508.

Jacobs, J.E., Davis-Kean, P., Bleeker, M., Eccles, J.S., and Malachuk, O. (2005). ' "I can, but I don't want to": the impact of parents, interests, and activities on gender differences in math.' In: A.M. Gallagher and J.C. Kaufmann (Eds), *Gender Differences in Mathematics: an Integrative Psychological Approach*. Cambridge, Cambridge University Press.

James, W. (1899). *Talks to Teachers*. New York: Norton. (Republished 1958).

Jaswal, V.K., and Fernald, A. (2002). 'Learning to communicate.' In: A. Slater and M. Lewis (Eds), *Introduction to Infant Development*. Oxford: Oxford University Press, 244–265.

Jensen, A.R. (1998). *The g Factor: The Science of Mental Ability*. Westport, Connecticut: Praeger.

Jimerson, S.R., Oakland, T.D., and Farrell, P.T. (Eds) (2007). *The Handbook of International School Psychology*. London: Sage.

Johnson, A.M., Falstein E.I., Szurek, S.A., and Svendsen, M. (1941). School phobia. *American Journal of Orthopsychiatry*, 11, 702–711.

Johnson, R.C., McClearn, G.E., Yuen, S., Nagoshi, C.T., Ahern, F.M., and Cole, R.E. (1985). Galton's data a century later. *American Psychologist*, 40, 875–892.

Johnston, C., Patenaude, R.L., and Inman, C.A. (1992). Attributions for hyperactive and aggressive child behaviours. *Social Cognition*, 10, 255–270.

Jones, G. (2002). *Educational Provision for Children with Autism and Asperger Syndrome: Meeting their Needs.* London: David Fulton Publishers.

Jordan, R. (1999). *Autistic Spectrum Disorders: An Introductory Handbook for Practitioners.* London: David Fulton Publishers.

Jordan, R., Jones, G., and Murray, D. (1998). *Educational Interventions for Children with Autism: A Literature Review of Recent and Current Research.* DfEE Research Report 77. London: Department for Education and Employment.

Juvonen, J. (1991). Deviance, perceived responsibility, and negative peer reactions. *Developmental Psychology*, 27, 672–681.

Juvonen, J., and Graham, S. (2004). 'Research-based interventions on bullying.' In: C.E. Sanders and G.D. Phye (Eds), *Bullying: Implications for the Classroom.* San Diego, CA: Elsevier Academic Press, 229–255.

Juvonen, J., Nishina, A., and Graham, S. (2001). 'Self-views versus peer perceptions of victim status among early adolescents.' In: J. Juvonen and S. Graham (Eds), *Peer Harassment in School.* New York: Guilford Press.

Kanner, L. (1943). Autistic disturbances of affective contact. *Nervous Child*, 2, 217–250.

Kazdin, A.E. (1982). *Single-Case Research Designs. Methods for Clinical and Applied Settings.* Oxford: Oxford University Press.

Kearney, C.A. (2003). Bridging the gap among professionals who address youths with school absenteeism: overview and suggestions for consensus. *Professional Psychology: Research and Practice*, 34, 57–65.

Kearney, C.A. (2007). Forms and functions of school refusal behaviour in youth. *Journal of Child Psychology and Psychiatry*, 48, 53–61.

Kearney, C.A., and Silverman, W.K. (1990). A preliminary analysis of a functional model of assessment and intervention of school refusal behaviour. *Behaviour Modification*, 149, 340–66.

Kearney, C.A., Eisen, A.R., and Silverman, W.K. (1995). The legend and myth of school phobia. *School Psychology Quarterly*, 10, 65–85.

Kelley, H.H., and Thibaut, J.W. (1978). *Interpersonal Relations: A Theory of Interdependence.* New York: Wiley.

Kelsey, D.M., Kearney, P., Plax, T.G., Allen, T.H. and Ritter, K.J. (2004). College students' attributions of teacher misbehaviours. *Communication Education*, 53, 1–17.

Kerr, K., Smyth, P., and McDowell, C. (2003). Precision teaching children with autism: helping design effective programmes. *Early Child Development and Care*, 17, 399–410.

Kessissoglou, S., and Farrell, P. (1995). Whatever happened to precision teaching? *British Journal of Special Education*, 22, 60–63.

King, N., and Bernstein, G.A. (2001). School refusal in children and adolescents: A review of the past ten years. *Journal of the American Academy of Child and Adolescent Psychiatry*, 40, 197–205.

King, N., Hamilton, D. and Ollendick, T.H. (1994). Children's Phobias: A behavioural perspective. New York: Wiley.

King, N., Tonge, B.J., Heyne, D., and Ollendick, T.H. (2000). Research on the cognitive-behavioral treatment of school refusal. A review and recommendations. *Clinical Psychology Review*, 20, 495–507.

Kiresuk, T.J., and Sherman, R.E. (1968). Goal attainment scaling: A general method for evaluating community mental health programmes. *Community Mental Health Journal*, 4, 443–453.

Kiresuk, T.J., Smith, A., and Cardillo, J.E. (Eds) (1994). *Goal Attainment Scaling: Applications, Theory and Measurement.* Hillsdale, NJ: Erlbaum.

Klahr, D., and Nigram, M. (2004). The equivalence of learning paths in early science instruction: effects of direct instruction and discovery learning. *Psychological Science*, 15, 661–667.

Klein, P. (1997). Multiplying the problems of intelligence by eight: a critique of Gardner's theory. *Canadian Journal of Education*, 22, 377–394.

Knapman, M., Huxtable, M., and Tempest, A. (1987). Redecorating educational psychology: an alternative approach to service delivery. *Educational Psychology in Practice*, 3, 29–33.

Kohn, A. (1993). *Punished by Rewards. The Trouble with Gold Stars, Incentive Plans, A's, Praise and Other Bribes.* Boston: Houghton Mifflin Company.

Kolvin, I., Garside, R.C., Nicol, A.R., Macmillan, A., Wolstenholme, F., and Leitch, I.M. (1981). *Help Starts Here. The Maladjusted Child in the Ordinary School.* London: Tavistock Publications.

Kounin, J.S. (1970). *Discipline and Group Management in Classrooms.* New York: Holt, Rinehart and Winston.

Kratochwill, T.R., and Stoiber, K.C. (2000). Empirically supported interventions and school psychology: Conceptual and Practice issues – Part II. *School Psychology Quarterly*, 15: 233–253.

Landrum, T.L., and Kauffman, J.M. (2006). 'Behavioural approaches to classroom management'. In: C.M. Evertson and C.S. Weinstein (Eds), *Handbook of Classroom Management*. London: Lawrence Erlbaum Associates.

Lane, D., and Corrie, S. (2006) (Eds) *The Modern Scientist-Practitioner: Practical Approaches to Guide how Professional Psychologists Think*. London: Routledge.

Lauchlan, F. (2003). Responding to chronic non-attendance: a review of intervention approaches. *Educational Psychology in Practice*, 19, 132–146.

LaVigna, G. (2000). *Alternatives to Punishment* (2000). New York: Irvington Publishers.

Law, G.U., Sinclair, S., and Fraser, N. (2007). Children's attitudes and behavioural intentions towards a peer with symptoms of ADHD: does the addition of a diagnostic label make a difference? *Journal of Child Health Care*, 11, 98–111.

Leadbetter, J. (2000). Patterns of service delivery in educational psychology services: some implications for practice. *Educational Psychology in Practice*, 16, 449–460.

Leslie, A., and Frith, U. (1988) Autistic children's understanding of seeing, knowing and believing. *British Journal of Developmental Psychology*, 6, 316–324.

Leslie, A.M., and Thaiss, L. (1992). Domain specificity in conceptual development: Evidence from autism. *Cognition*, 43, 467–479.

Levy, A., and Kahan, B. (1991). *The Pindown Experience and the Protection of Children*. Staffordshire County Council.

Lewis, M. (2002). 'Early emotional development.' In: A. Slater and M. Lewis (Eds), *Introduction to Infant Development*. Oxford: Oxford University Press, 192–209.

Lincoln, A.J., Allen, M.H., and Kilman, A. (1995). 'The assessment and interpretation of intellectual abilities in people with autism.' In: E. Schopler and G.B. Mesibov (Eds), *Learning and Cognition in Autism*. New York: Plenum Press, 89–117.

Lindsay, G. (2003). Inclusive education: A critical perspective. *British Journal of Special Education*, 30, 3–12.

Lindsay, G. (2007). Educational psychology and the effectiveness of inclusive education/mainstreaming. *British Journal of Educational Psychology*, 77, 1–24.

Lindsley, O.R. (1971). Precision teaching in perspective: an interview. *Teaching Exceptional Children*, 3, 114–119.

Lipsky, D.K., and Gartner, A. (1996). Inclusion, school restructuring, and the remaking of American society. *Harvard Educational Review*, 66, 762–795.

Lipsky, M. (1971). Street-level bureaucracy and the analysis of urban reform. *Urban Affairs Review*, 6, 391–409.

Lloyd, B., and Duveen, G. (1992). *Gender Identities and Education: The Impact of Starting School*. Hemel Hempstead, Hertfordshire: Harvester Wheatsheaf.

Locke, A., and Ginsborg, J. (2003). Spoken language in the early years: the development of three- to five-year-old children from socio-economically disadvantaged backgrounds. *Educational and Child Psychology*, 20, 68–79.

Lokke, C., Gersch, I., M'Gadzah, H., and Frederickson, N. (1997). The resurrection of psychometrics: fact or fiction? *Educational Psychology in Practice*, 12, 222–233.

Lovaas, O.I. (1987). Behavioural treatment and normal intellectual and educational functioning in autistic children. *Journal of Consulting and Clinical Psychology*, 55, 3–9.

Lovaas, O.I., Scheffer, B., and Simmons, J.Q. (1965). Building social behaviour in autistic children by use of electric shock. *Journal of Experimental Research and Personality* 1, 99–109.

Lyon, G.R. (1995). Towards a definition of dyslexia. *Annals of Dyslexia*, 45, 3–27.

Ma, X. (2001). Bullying and being bullied: To what extent are bullies also victims? *American Educational Research Journal*, 38, 351–370.

Maas, E., Marecek, J., and Travers, J.R. (1978). Children's conceptions of disordered behavior. *Child Development*, 49, 146–154.

MacBeath, J., and Mortimore, P. (Eds) (2001). *Improving School Effectiveness*. Buckingham: Open University Press.

MacGeorge, E.L. (2004). Gender differences in attributions and emotions in helping contexts. *Behavioural Science*, 48, 175–182.

Macintosh, N.J. (1995) (Ed.). *Cyril Burt: Fraud or Framed?* Oxford: Oxford University Press.

Madden, N.A., and Slavin, R.E. (1983). Mainstreaming students with mild handicaps: Academic and social outcomes. *Review of Educational Research*, 53, 519–569.

Madsen, C.H., Becker, W.C., and Thomas, D.R. (1968). Rules, praise and ignoring: Elements of elementary classroom control. *Journal of Applied Behavioural Analysis*, 1, 139–150.

Maliphant, R. (1998). Educational psychology training: history and lessons from history. *Educational and Child Psychology, Special Edition: 50 years of professional training in educational psychology*, 17–26.

Maras, P., and Brown, R.J. (1996). Effect of contact on children's attitudes to disability: A longitudinal study. *Journal of Applied Social Psychology*, 26, 2113–2134.

Maras, P., and Brown, R.J. (2000). Effects of different forms of school contact on children's attitudes toward disabled and non-disabled peers. *British Journal of Educational Psychology*, 70, 337–351.

Marks, J. (2000). *The Betrayed Generations*. London: Centre for Policy Studies.

Marom, M., Cohen, D., and Naon, D. (2007). Changing disability-related attitudes and self-efficacy of Israeli children via the Partners to Inclusion Programme. *International Journal of Disability, Development and Education*, 54, 113–127.

Martin, J. (1992). *Cultures in Organizations: Three Perspectives*. New York: Oxford University Press.

Mastergeorge, A.M., Rogers, S.J., Corbett, B.A., and Solomon, M. (2003). 'Non medical interventions for autistic spectrum disorders.' In: S. Ozonoff, S.J. Rogers and R.L. Hendren (Eds), *Autism Spectrum Disorders: A Research Review for Practitioners*. Washington, DC: American Psychiatric Publishing, 133–160.

McDougall, J., De Witt, D.J., King, G., Miller L.T., and Killip, S. (2004). High-school aged youths' attitudes towards their peers with disabilities: the role of school and student interpersonal factors. *International Journal of Disability, Development and Education*, 51, 287–313.

McEachin, J., Smith, T., and Lovaas, O.I. (1993). Long-term outcome for children with autism who received early intensive behavioral treatment. *American Journal of Mental Retardation*, 97, 359–372.

McGuinness, D. (1997). *Why Children Can't Read and What We Can Do About It*. London: Penguin.

McNamara, E., and Harrop, L.A. (1979). Behaviour modification in secondary schools – a cautionary tale. *Occasional Papers of the DECP* 3, 38–40.

McNamara, E., and Harrop, L.A. (1981). Behaviour modification in the secondary school: a rejoinder to Wheldall and Austin. *Occasional Papers of the DECP*, 3, 38–40.

McShane, G., Walter, G., and Rey, J.M. (2004). Functional outcome of adolescents with 'school refusal'. *Clinical Child Psychology and Psychiatry*, 9, 53–60.

Medical Research Council (MRC) (2001). *MRC Review of Autism Research Epidemiology and Causes*. London: Medical Research Council. www.mrc.ac.uk

Menyuk, P., and Brisk, M.E. (2005). *Language Development and Education: Children with Varying Language Experience*. New York: Palgrave Macmillan.

Mercer, N. (2005). Thinking together. *NALDIC Quarterly*, 2, 18–22.

Mercer, N., and Littleton, K. (2007). *Dialogue and the Development of Children's Thinking*. London: Routledge.

Mercer, N., Dawes, L., Wegerif, R., and Sams, C. (2004). Reasoning as a scientist: ways of helping children to use language to learn science. *British Educational Research Journal*, 30, 359–377.

Merrett, F., and Blundell, D. (1982). Self-recording as a means of improving behaviour in a secondary school. *Educational Psychology* 2, 147–157.

Merrett, F., and Tang, W.M. (1994). The attitudes of British primary school pupils to praise, rewards, punishments and reprimands. *British Journal of Educational Psychology*, 64, 91–103.

Merrett, F., and Wheldall, K. (1978). Playing the game: a behavioural approach to classroom management in the junior school. *Educational Review*, 30, 1, 41–50.

Miller, A. (1995). Teachers' attributions of causality, control and responsibility in respect of difficult pupil behaviour and its successful management. *Educational Psychology*, 15, 457–471.

Miller, A. (2003). *Teachers, Parents and Classroom Behaviour. A Psychosocial Approach*. Maidenhead: Open University Press.

Miller, A., and Black, L. (2001). Does support for home-school behaviour plans exist within teacher and pupil cultures? *Educational Psychology in Practice* 17, 245–261.

Miller, A., and Frederickson, N. (2006). 'Generalisable findings and idiographic problems: Struggles and successes for educational psychologists as scientist-practitioners.' In: D. Lane and S. Corrie (Eds), *The Modern Scientist-Practitioner: Practical Approaches to Guide How Professional Psychologists Think*. London: Routledge.

Miller, A., Jewell, T., Booth, S., and Robson, D. (1985). Delivering educational programmes to slow learners. *Educational Psychology in Practice*, 1, 99–104.

Miller A., Ferguson, E., and Simpson, R. (1998). The perceived effectiveness of rewards and sanctions in primary schools – adding in the parental perspective. *Educational Psychology*, 18, 55–64.

Miller, A., Ferguson, E., and Byrne, I. (2000). Pupils' causal attributions for difficult classroom behaviour. *British Journal of Educational Psychology*, 70, 85–96.

Miller, A., Ferguson, E., and Moore, E. (2002). Parents' and pupils' causal attributions for difficult classroom behaviour. *British Journal of Educational Psychology*, 72, 27–40.

Miller, G. (1969). On turning psychology over to the unwashed. *Psychology Today*, 3, 53–54, 66–68, 70, 72, 74.

Miura, I.T. (1987). Mathematics achievement as a function of language. *Journal of Educational Psychology*, 79, 79–82.

Monsen, J.J., and Frederickson, N. (in press). 'The problem analysis framework: A guide to decision making, problem solving and action within applied psychological practice.' In: B. Kelly, L. Wolfson and J. Boyle (Eds), *Frameworks for Practice in Educational Psychology: A Textbook for Trainees and Practitioners*. London: Jessica Kingsley.

Morton, J. (2004). *Understanding Developmental Disorders: a Causal Modelling Approach*. Oxford: Blackwell.

Morton, J., and Frith, U. (1995). 'Causal modelling: A structural approach to developmental psychopathology.' In: D. Cilchette, and D.J. Cohen (Eds), *Manual of Developmental Psychopathology*. New York: Wiley, 357–390.

Mroz, M., and Hall, E. (2003). Not yet identified: the knowledge, skills, and training needs of early years professionals in relation to children's speech and language development. *Early Years*, 23, 117–130.

Mundy, P., Sigman, M., and Kasari, C. (1990). A longitudinal study of joint attention and language development in autistic children. *Journal of Autism and Developmental Disorders*, 20, 115–128.

Nabuzoka, D., and Smith, P.K. (1993). Sociometric status and social behaviour of children with and without learning difficulties. *Journal of Child Psychology and Psychiatry*, 34, 1435–1448.

Naglieri, J.A., and Das, J.P. (1997). *Cognitive Assessment System*. Itasca, IL: Riverside Publishing.

Naito, M., and Miura, H. (2001). Japanese children's numerical competencies: age- and schooling-related influences on the development of number concepts and addition skills. *Developmental Psychology*, 37, 217–230.

Nansel, T.R., Overpeck, M., Pilla, R.S., Ruan, W.J., Simons-Morton, B., and Scheidt, P. (2001). Bullying behaviors among US youth. Prevalence and association with psychological adjustment. *Journal of the American Medical Association*, 285, 2095–2100.

National Reading Council (1998). 'Preventing reading difficulties in young children.' In: C.E. Snow, M.S. Burns and P. Griffin (Eds). Washington DC: National Academy.

National Reading Panel (2000). *Teaching Children To Read: An Evidence Based Assessment of the Scientific Research Literature On Reading and its Implications for Reading Instruction*. Washington, DC. National Institute for Child Health and Human Development.

National Research Council (2001). *Educating Children with Autism*. Washington, DC: National Academy Press.

Neisser, U. (1967). *Cognitive Psychology*. New York. Appleton-Century-Crofts.

Newberry, M.K., and Parish, T.S. (1987). Enhancement of attitudes toward handicapped children through social interactions. *Journal of Social Psychology*, 127, 59–62.

Newcomb, A.F., Bukowski, W.M., and Pattee, L. (1993). Children's peer relations: A meta-analytic review of popular, rejected, neglected, controversial and average sociometric status. *Psychological Bulletin*, 113, 99–128.

Newstead, K. (1998). Aspects of children's mathematics anxiety. *Educational Studies in Mathematics*, 36, 53–71.

NHS (2005). *Depression in Children and Young People. Identification and Management in Primary, Community and Secondary Care*. London: National Institute for Health and Clinical Excellence.

Nichols, S.L., Hupp, S.D., Jewell, J.D., and Zeigler, C.S. (2005). Review of social story interventions for children diagnosed with autistic spectrum disorders. *Journal of Evidence Based Practices for School*, 6, 90–120.

Nicolson, R., and Fawcett, A. (1990). *Automaticity: A New Framework for Dyslexia Research?* Cognition, 35, 159–182.

Nippold, M.A. (1998). *Later Language Development: The School-Age and Adolescent Years*, (2nd Ed.). Austin, TX: Pro-Ed.

Nishina, A. (2004). 'A theoretical review of bullying: can it be eliminated?' In: C.E. Sanders and G.D. Phye (Eds), *Bullying: Implications for the Classroom*. San Diego, CA: Elsevier Academic Press.

Noell, G.H., Witt, J.C., Slider, N.J., et al. (2005). Treatment implementation following behavioural consultation in schools: a comparison of three follow-up strategies. *School Psychology Review*, 34, 87–106.

Nowicki, E.A., and Sandieson, R. (2002). A meta-analysis of children's attitudes toward individuals with intellectual and physical disabilities. *International Journal of Disability, Development and Education*, 49, 243–266.

Nunes, T. (2004). *Teaching Mathematics to Deaf Children*. London, Whurr Publishers.

Nunes, T., Schliemann, A.D., and Carraher, D.W. (1993). *Street Mathematics and School Mathematics*. New York: Cambridge University Press.

O'Connor, T.G., Rutter, M., Beckett, C., Keaveney, L., Kreppner, J., and the English and Romanian Adoptees Study Team. (2000). The effects of global severe privation on cognitive competence: Extension and longitudinal follow-up. *Child Development*, 71, 376–390.

Odom, S.L., Vitztum, J., Wolery, R., et al. (2004). Preschool inclusion in the United States: a review of research from an ecological systems perspective. *Journal of Research in Special Educational Needs*, 4, 17–49.

OECD (2003). Learning for Tomorrow's World: First Results from PISA 2003. Paris: Organization for Economic Co-operation and Development (OECD). Retrieved 15 November 2006 from: www.pisa.oecd.org/dataoecd/1/60/34002216.pdf

Ofsted (2005). *The Annual Report of HM's Chief Inspector of Schools 2003/4*. London: DfES.

Olweus, D. (1978). *Aggression in the Schools: Bullies and Whipping Boys*. Washington, DC: Hemisphere (Wiley).

Olweus, D. (1991). 'Bully/victim problems among school children: Basic facts and effects of a school-based intervention programme.' In: D.J. Pepler and K.H. Reuben (Eds), *The Development and Treatment of Childhood Aggression*. Hillsdale, NJ: Erlbaum, 411–448.

Olweus, D. (1993). *Bullying at School*. Oxford: Blackwell Publishing.

Olweus, D. (1994). Annotation: bullying at school: basic facts and effects of a school-based intervention programme. *Journal of Child Psychology and Psychiatry*, 35, 1171–1190.

Orpinas, P., and Horne, A.M. (2006). *Bullying Prevention: Creating a Positive School Climate and Developing Social Competence*. Washington, DC: American Psychological Association.

Orton, S.T. (1925). 'Word-blindness' in school children. *Archives of Neurology and Psychiatry*, 14, 581–615.

Osborne, J.W. (2001). Testing stereotype threat: Does anxiety explain race and sex differences in achievement? *Contemporary Educational Psychology*, 26, 291–310.

Ozonoff, S. (1997). 'Components of executive function deficits in autism and other disorders.' In: J. Russel (Ed.), *Autism as an Executive Disorder*. Oxford: Oxford University Press, 179–211.

Ozonoff, S., and Griffith, E.M. (2000). 'Neuropsychological functioning and the external validity of Asperger syndrome.' In: A. Klin, F. Volkmar and S.S. Sparrow (Eds), *Asperger Syndrome*. New York: Guilford Press, 72–96.

Ozonoff, S., and Miller, J.M. (1995). Teaching theory of mind: a new approach to social skills training for individuals with autism. *Journal of Autism and Development Disorders*, 25, 415–433.

Ozonoff, S., and Rogers, S.J. (2003). 'From Kanner to the Millennium: Scientific advances that have shaped clinical practice.' In: S. Ozonoff, S.J. Rogers and R.L. Hendren (Eds), *Autistic Spectrum Disorders: A Research Review for Practitioners*. Washington, DC: American Psychiatric Publishing, 3–33.

Ozonoff, S., South, M., and Miller, J.N. (2000). DSM-IV-defined Asperger syndrome: cognitive, behavioral and early history differentiation from high functioning autism. *Autism*, 4, 29–46.

Pajares, F., and Kranzler, J. (1995). Self-efficacy beliefs and general mental ability in mathematical problem-solving. *Contemporary Educational Psychology*, 20, 426–443.

Pateman, T. (1980). Can schools educate? *Journal of Philosophy of Education*, 14, 139–148. (A 'lightly revised' version was accessed on 8 August 2007 at www.selectedworks.co.uk/schooleducation.html).

Payne, A.A., and Gottfredson, D.C. (2004). 'Schools and bullying: School factors related to bullying and school-based bullying interventions.' In: C.E. Sanders and G.D. Phye (Eds), *Bullying: Implications for the Classroom*. San Diego, CA: Elsevier Academic Press, 159–176.

Pearson, L., and Howarth, I.C. (1982). Training professional psychologists. *Bulletin of the British Psychological Society*, 35, 375–376.

Pellegrini, A.D. (2001). 'Sampling instances of victimization in middle school: A methodological comparison.' In: J. Juvonen and S. Graham (Eds), *Peer Harassment in School. The Plight of the Vulnerable and Victimized*. New York: Guildford Press, 125–144.

Pellegrini, A.D., and Bartini, M. (2000). An empirical comparison of methods of sampling aggression and victimization in school settings. *Journal of Educational Psychology*, 92, 360–366.

Pellegrini, D. (2007). School non-attendance: definitions, meanings, responses, interventions. *Educational Psychology in Practice*, 23, 63–77.

Pennington, B.F., and Olson, R.K. (2005). 'Genetics of dyslexia.' In: M.J. Snowling and C. Hulme (Eds), *The Science of Reading: A Handbook*. Oxford: Blackwell.

Pepler, D.J., and Craig, W.M. (1995). A peek behind the fence: naturalistic observations of aggressive children with remote audio visual recording. *Developmental Psychology*, 31, 548–553.

Perera, K. (1981). *Children's Writing and Reading: Analysing Classroom Language*. Oxford: Blackwell.

Perry, D.G., Hodges, E.B.E., and Egan, S.K. (2001). 'Determinants of chronic victimization by peers: a review and new model of family influence.' In: J. Juvonen and S. Graham (Eds), *Peer Harassment in School: The Plight of the Vulnerable and Victimized*. New York: Guildford Press, 73–104.

Phares, V., Ehrbar, L.A., and Lum, J.J. (1996). Parental perceptions of the development and treatment of children's' and adolescents' emotional/behavioural problems. *Child and Family Behaviour Therapy*, 18, 19–36.

Pikas, A. (2002). New developments of the shared concern method. *School Psychology International*, 23, 307–326.

Pinker, S. (1997). Foreword. In: D. McGuinness, *Why Our Children Can't Read and What We Can Do About It: A Scientific Revolution in Reading*. London: Penguin Education.

Pitchford, M. (2006). *Responding to Really Challenging Behaviour*. Lecture delivered to the University of Nottingham (23 February 2006).

Place, M., Hulsmeier, J., Davis, S., and Taylor, E. (2002). The coping mechanisms of children with school refusal. *Journal of Research in Special Educational Needs*, 2, 1–10.

Plowden Committee (1967). *Children and their Primary Schools*. (The Plowden Report.) London: HMSO.

Porter J. (2005). 'Severe learning difficulties.' In: A. Lewis and B. Norwich (Eds), *Special Teaching for Special Children: A Pedagogy for Inclusion?*. Milton Keynes: Open University, 53–66.

Porter, L. (2007). *Behaviour in Schools. Theory and Practice for Teachers*. Maidenhead. Open University Press.

Poulou, M., and Norwich, B. (2000). Teachers' causal attributions, cognitive, emotional and behavioural responses to students with emotional and behavioural difficulties. *British Journal of Educational Psychology*, 70, 559–581.

Presland, J. (1981). Modifying behaviour long-term and sideways. *Association of Educational Psychologists Journal*, 5, 27–30.

Pressley, M., Wharton-McDonald, R., Allington, R., Block, C., Morrow, L., Tracey, D., et al. (2001). A study of effective first-grade literacy instruction. *Scientific Studies of Reading*, 5, 35–58.

QAA (2002). *Psychology Subject Benchmark Statements*. Gloucester: Quality Assurance Agency for Higher Education.

Quicke, J. (1982). *The Cautious Expert*. Milton Keynes: Open University Press.

Ramus, F. (2004). Neurobiology of dyslexia: a reinterpretation of the data. *Trends in Neurosciences*, 27, 720–726.

Ramus, F., White, S., and Frith, U. (2006). Weighing the evidence between competing theories of dyslexia. *Developmental Science*, 9, 265–269.

Raybould, E.C., and Solity, J. (1982). Teaching with precision. *Special Education Forward Trends*, 8, 9–13.

Raybould, T. (2004). How teaching with precision helped Roop and Kerry. *Action for Inclusion* (Birmingham City Council), 6, 29–32.

Reisman, J.M. (1991). *A History of Clinical Psychology*, (2nd Ed.). New York: Hemisphere Publishing.

Rennie, E.N.F. (1980). Good behaviour games with a whole class. *Remedial Education*, 15, 187–190.

Resing, W.C.M. (1997). Learning potential assessment: the alternative for measuring intelligence. *Educational and Child Psychology*, 14, 68–82.

Reyna, C., and Weiner, B. (2001). Justice and utility in the classroom: An attributional analysis of the goals of teachers' punishment and intervention strategies. *Journal of Educational Psychology*, 93, 309–319.

Reynhout, G., and Carter, M. (2006). Social stories™ for children with disabilities. *Journal of Autism and Developmental Disorders*, 36, 445–469.

Rigby, K. (2004). Addressing bullying in schools. Theoretical perspectives and their implications. *School Psychology International*, 25, 287–300.

Rigby, K. (2005). Why do some children bully at school? The contribution of negative attitudes towards victims and the perceived expectations of friends, parents and teachers. *School Psychology International*, 26, 147–161.

Rigby, K., and Slee, P.T. (1998). *The Peer Relations Questionnaire (PRQ)*. Point Lonsdale, Vic: The Professional Reading Guide.

Rivers, I., and Soutter, A. (1996). Bullying and the Steiner School ethos: a case study analysis of a group-centred educational philosophy. *School Psychology International*, 17, 359–377.

Robbins, C., and Ehri, L. (1994). Reading storybooks to kindergartners helps them learn new vocabulary words. *Journal of Educational Psychology*, 86, 54–64.

Roberts, C., and Zubrick, S. (1992). Factors influencing the social status of children with mild academic disabilities in regular classrooms. *Exceptional Children*, 59, 192–202.

Roberts, C.M., and Lindsell, J.S. (1997). Children's attitudes and behavioural intentions toward peers with disabilities. *International Journal of Disability, Development and Education*, 44, 133–145.

Roberts, C.M., and Smith, P.R. (1999). Attitudes and behaviour of children towards peers with disabilities. *International Journal of Disability, Development and Education*, 46, 35–50.

Robson, C. (2002). *Real World Research*, (2nd Ed.). Oxford. Blackwell.

Rogers, S.J., and Pennington, B.F. (1991). A theoretical approach to the deficits in infantile autism. *Development and Psychopathology*, 3, 137–162.

Roid, G. (2003). *Stanford-Binet Intelligence Scales*, (5th Ed.). Itasca, IL: Riverside.

Rose, J. (2006). *Independent Review of the Teaching of Early Reading*. London: DfES Publications.

Rosnow, R.L., and Rosenthal, R. (2005). *Beginning Behavioral Research: A Conceptual Primer*, (5th Ed.). New York: Pearson/Prentice Hall.

Rowling, J.K. (1997). *Harry Potter and the Philosopher's Stone*. London: Bloomsbury.

Rushton, J.P. (2002). New evidence on Sir Cyril Burt: His 1964 speech to the Association of Educational Psychologists. *Intelligence*, 30, 555–567.

Rust, J., and Smith, A. (2006). How should the effectiveness of social stories to modify the behaviour of children on the autistic spectrum be tested? Lessons from the literature. *Autism*, 10, 125–138.

Rutter, M. (1996). Autism research: prospects and priorities. *Journal of Autism and Developmental Disorders*, 26, 257–275.

Rutter, M. (1999). Autism: two-way interplay between research and clinical work. *Journal of Child Psychology and Psychiatry*, 40, 169–188.

Rutter, M., Tizard, J., and Whitmore, K. (1970). *Education, Health and Behaviour*. London: Longman.

Rutter, M., Maughan, B., Mortimore, P., Ouston, J., and Smith, A. (1979). *Fifteen Thousand Hours: Secondary Schools and Their Effects on Children*. Somerset: Open Books.

Salmivalli, C. (1999). Participant role approach to school bullying: Implications for interventions. *Journal of Adolescence*, 22, 453–459.

Sampson, O. (1980). *Child Guidance: Its History, Provenance and Future*. British Psychological Society Division of Educational and Child Psychology Occasional Papers, Volume 3, No. 3. London: British Psychological Society.

Scarr, S. (1984). *Race, Social Class and Individual Differences in IQ*. London: Lawrence Erlbaum Associates.

Schon, D. (1987). *Educating the Reflective Practitioner*. San Francisco: Jossey Bass.

Schopler, E., and Mesibov, G. (1995). *Learning and Cognition in Autism*. New York: Plenum Press.

Schopler, E., Short, B., and Mesibov, G. (1989). Relation of behavioral treatment to normal functioning: Comment on Lovaas. *Journal of Consulting and Clinical Psychology*, 57, 162–164.

Schwartz, D., Dodge, K.A., Pettit, G.S., and Bates, J.E. (1997). The early socialization of aggressive victims of bullying. *Child Development*, 68, 665–675.

Schweinhart, L.L., Weikart, D.P., and Larner, M.B. (1986). Consequences of three preschool curriculum models through age 15. *Early Childhood Research Quarterly*, 1, 15–45.

Scottish Executive (2002). *Review of Provision of Educational Psychology Services in Scotland*. Edinburgh: Scottish Executive Education Department.

Scottish Parliament Information Centre (SPICe) (2004). *Abuse of Children and Young People in Residential Care*. 04/85. Edinburgh: Scottish Parliament Information Centre.

Sdorow, L.N., and Rickabaugh, C.A. (2002). *Psychology*, (5th Ed.). New York: McGraw Hill.

Sebba, J. (2004). 'Developing evidence-informed policy and practice in education.' In: G. Thomas and R. Pring (Eds), *Evidence-Based Practice in Education*. Maidenhead: Open University Press/McGraw-Hill Education, 34–43.

Sebba, J., and Sachdev, D. (1997). *What Works in Inclusive Education?* Barkingside: Barnardo's.

Sepie, A.C., and Keeling, B. (1978). The relationship between types of anxiety and under-achievement in mathematics. *Journal of Educational Research*, 72, 15–19.

Seymour, P.H.K., and Duncan, L.G. (2001). Learning to read in English. *Psychology: The Journal of the Hellenic Psychological Society*, 8, 281–299.

Seymour, P.H.K., Aro, M., and Erskine, J.M. (2003). Foundation literacy acquisition in European orthographies. *British Journal of Psychology*, 94, 143–174.

Shah, A., and Frith, U. (1993). Why do autistic individuals show superior performance on the block design task? *Journal of Child Psychology and Psychiatry*, 34, 1351–1364.

Shallice, T., and Warrington, E.K. (1975). Word recognition in a phonemic dyslexic patient. *Quarterly Journal of Experimental Psychology*, 27, 187–199.

Shallice, T. (1988). *From Neuropsychology to Mental Structure*. Cambridge: Cambridge University Press.

Sharp, S. (1999). 'Bullying behaviour in schools.' In: N. Frederickson and R.J. Cameron (Eds), *Psychology in Education Portfolio*. Maidenhead: NFER-Nelson.

Sheridan, S.M., Welch, M., and Orme, S.F. (1996). Is consultation effective: A review of outcome research. *Remedial and Special Education*, 17, 341–354.

Shipstone, K., and Burt, S. (1973). Twenty-five years on: A replication of Flugel's (1947) work on lay popular views of intelligence and related topics. *British Journal of Educational Psychology*, 56, 183–187.

Siegel, B. (1996). Is the emperor wearing clothes? Social policy and the empirical support for full inclusion of children with disabilities in the preschool and early elementary grades. *Social Policy Report, Society for Research in Child Development*, X (2 and 3), 2–17. Available to download at: www.srcd.org/documents/publications/spr/spr10-2_3.pdf

Siegel, L.S. (1992). An evaluation of the discrepancy definition of dyslexia. *Journal of Learning Disabilities*, 25, 616–629.

Sigelman, C.K., and Begley, N.L. (1987). The early development of reactions to peers with controllable and uncontrollable problems. *Journal of Paediatric Psychology*, 12, 99–115.

Simonoff, E., Pickles, A., Chadwick, O., et al. (2006). The Croydon Assessment of Learning Study: Prevalence and educational identification of mild mental retardation. *Journal of Child Psychology and Psychiatry*, 47, 828–839.

Simos, P.G., Breier, J.I., Fletcher, J.M., Bergman, E., and Papanicolau, A.C. (2000). Cerebral mechanisms involved in word reading in dyslexic children. *Cerebral Cortex*, 10, 809–816.

Simos, P.G., Fletcher, J.M., Bergman, E., et al. (2002). Dyslexia-specific brain activation profile becomes normal following successful remedial training. *Neurology*, 58, 1203–1213.

Simos, P.G., Fletcher, J.M., Sarkari, S., Billingsley, R.L., Denton, C., and Papanicolaou, A.C. (2007). Altering the brain circuits for reading through intervention: A magnetic source imaging study. *Neuropsychology*, 21, 485–496.

Siraj-Blatchford, I., Sylva, K., Muttock, K., Gilden, R., and Bell, D. (2002). *Researching Effective Pedagogy in the Early Years*. DfES Ref. RR356. London: DfES.

Skemp, R.R. (1976). Relational understanding and instrumental understanding. *Mathematics Teaching*, 77, 20–26.

Sladeczek, I.E., Elliott, S.N., Kratochwill, T.R., Robertson-Mjaanes, S., and Stoiber, K.C. (2001). Application of goal attainment scaling to a conjoint behavioral consultation case. *Journal of Educational and Psychological Consultation*, 12, 45–58.

Slee, P.T., and Rigby, K. (1993). The relationship of Eysenck's personality factors and self esteem to bully-victim behaviour in Australian schoolboys. *Personality and Individual Differences*, 14, 371–373.

Smith, C. (2003). *Writing and Developing Social Stories*. Bicester, Oxon: Speechmark.

Smith, F. (1978). *Understanding Reading: A Psycho-linguistic Analysis of Reading and Learning to Read*, (2nd Ed.). New York: Holt, Rinehart and Winston.

Smith, P.K. (2001). Should we blame the bullies? *The Psychologist*, 14, 61.

Smith, P.K. (2004). Bullying: Recent Developments. *Child and Adolescent Mental Health*, 9, 98–103.

Smith, T., Eikeseth, S., Klevstrand, M., and Lovaas, O.I. (1997). Intensive behavioural treatment for pre-schoolers with severe mental retardation and pervasive developmental disorder. *American Journal of Mental Retardation*, 102, 238–249.

Smith, T., Groen, A.D., and Wynn, J.W. (2000). Randomised trial of intensive early intervention for children with Pervasive Developmental Disorder. *American Journal of Mental Retardation*, 105, 269–285.

Snow, C.E. (2002). 'Second language learners and understanding the brain.' In: A.M. Galaburda, S.M. Kosslyn and C. Yves (Eds), *The Languages of the Brain*. Cambridge, MA: Harvard University Press, 151–165.

Snow, C.E., and Juel, C. (2005). 'Teaching children to read: What we know about how to do it'. In: M.J. Snowling and C. Hulme (Eds), *The Science of Reading: a Handbook*. Oxford: Blackwell.

Snowling, M., and Hulme, C. (1989). A longitudinal case study of developmental phonological dyslexia. *Cognitive Neuropsychology*, 6, 379–401.

Snowling, M.J. (2000). *Dyslexia*, (2nd Ed.). Oxford: Blackwell.

Snowling, M.J., Muter, B., and Carroll, J. (2007). Children at family risk of dylexia: a follow up in early adolescence. *Journal of Child Psychology and Psychiatry*, 48, 609–618.

Snyder, J., Cramer, A., Afrank, J., and Patterson, G.R. (2005). The contributions of ineffective discipline and parental hostile attributions of child misbehaviour to the development of conduct problems at home and school. *Developmental Psychology*, 41, 30–41.

Solberg, M.E., Olweus, D. and Endresen, I.M. (2007). Bullies and victims at school: Are they the same pupils? *British Journal of Educational Psychology*, 77, 441–464.

Solity, J. (1996). Discrepancy definitions of dyslexia: an assessment through teaching approach. *Educational Psychology in Practice*, 12, 141–151.

Solity, J., Deavers, R., Kerfoot, S., Crane, G., and Cannon, K. (2000). The Early Reading Research: the impact of instructional psychology. *Educational Psychology in Practice*, 16, 109–129.

Solvason, C. (2005). Investigating specialist school ethos . . . or do you mean culture? *Educational Studies*, 31, 85–94.

Spence, S.H. (2003). Social skills training with children and young people: theory, evidence and practice. *Child and Adolescent Mental Health*, 8, 84–96.

Squires, G., and Farrell, P.T. (2007). 'Educational psychology in England and Wales'. In: S.R. Jimerson, T.D. Oakland and P.T. Farrell (Eds), *The Handbook of International School Psychology*. London: Sage, 81–90.

Stage, S.A., Abbott, R.D., Jenkins, J.R., and Berninger, V.W. (2003). Predicting response to early reading intervention from verbal IQ, reading-related language abilities, attention ratings and verbal IQ – word reading discrepancy: Failure to validate discrepancy method. *Journal of Learning Disabilities*, 36, 24–33.

Stanovich, K. (1991). Discrepancy definitions of reading disability: has intelligence led us astray? *Reading Research Quarterly*, 26, 7–29.

Stanovich, K.E. (1986). Matthew effects in reading: some consequences of individual differences in the acquisition of literacy. *Reading Research Quarterly*, 21, 360–407.

Stassen Berger, K. (2007). Update on bullying at school: Science forgotten? *Developmental Review*, 27, 90–126.

Steele, C. (1997). A threat in the air: how stereotypes shape intellectual identity and performance. *American Psychologist*, 52, 613–629.

Stein, J., and Talcott, J. (1999). Impaired neuronal timing in developmental dyslexia – the magnocellular hypothesis. *Dyslexia* 5, 59–77.

Sternberg, R.J. (1981). Intelligence and nonentrenchment. *Journal of Educational Psychology*, 73, 1–16.

Sternberg, R.J. (1999). Successful intelligence: finding a balance. *Trends in Cognitive Sciences*, 3, 436–442.

Sternberg, R.J., and Grigorenko, E.L. (2002). The theory of successful intelligence as a basis for gifted education. *Gifted Child Quarterly*, 46, 265–277.

Stobart, G. (1986) Is integrating the handicapped psychologically defensible? *Bulletin of the British Psychological Society*, 39, 1–3.

Stratford, R.J. (1990). Creating a positive school ethos. *Educational Psychology in Practice*, 5, 183–191.

Stuart, M., and Coltheart, M. (1988). Does reading develop in a sequence of stages? *Cognition*, 30, 139–181.

Stuebing, K.K., Fletcher, J.M., Le Doux, J.M., Lyon, G.R., Shaywitz, S.E., and Sheywitz, B.A. (2002). Validity of IQ-discrepancy classifications of reading disabilities: A meta-analysis. *American Educational Research Journal*, 39, 469–518.

Summerfield Committee (1968). *Psychologists in Education Services*. London: HMSO.

Sutherland, A.E. (1990). Selection in Northern Ireland: from 1947 Act to 1989 Order. *Research Papers in Education*, 5, 29–48.

Sutton, J. (2001). Bullies: thugs or thinkers? *The Psychologist*, 14, 430–434.

Sutton, J., Smith, P.K., and Swettenham, J. (1999a). Bullying and 'theory of mind': a critique of the 'social skills deficit' view of anti-social behaviour. *Social Development*, 8, 117–127.

Sutton, J., Smith, P.K., and Swettenham, J. (1999b). Social cognition and bullying: Social inadequacy or skilled manipulation? *British Journal of Developmental Psychology*, 17, 435–450.

Sutton, J., Smith, P.K., and Swettenham, J. (2001). 'It's easy, it works, and it makes me feel good' – A response to Arsenio and Lemerise. *Social Development*, 10, 74–78.

Swanson, H.L. (2000). 'What instruction works for students with learning disabilities? Summarizing the results from a meta-analysis of intervention studies.' In: R. Gersten and E.P. Schiller (Eds), *Contemporary Special Education Research: Synthesis of the Knowledge Base on Critical Instructional Issues*. Mahwah, NJ: Lawrence Erlbaum Associates.

Swearer, S.M., and Espelage, D.L. (2004). 'Introduction: A social-ecological framework of bullying among youth.' In: D.L. Espelage and S.M. Swearer (Eds), *Bullying in American Schools: A Social-Ecological Perspective on Prevention and Intervention*. Mahwah, NJ: Lawrence Erlbaum, 1–12.

Swearer, S.M., Song, S.Y., Cary, P.T., Eagle, J.W., and Mickleson, W.T. (2001). Psychosocial correlates in bullying and victimization: The relationship between depression, anxiety and bully/victim status. *Journal of Emotional Abuse*, 2, 95–121.

Tajfel, H. (1978). 'Social categorization, social identity and social comparison.' In: H. Tajfel (Ed.), *Differentiation Between Social Groups: Studies in the Social Psychology of Intergroup Relations*. London: Academic Press, 61–76.

Tallal, P. (1980). Auditory temporal perception, phonics, and reading disabilities in children. *Brain and Language*, 9, 182–198.

Tallal, P. (2004). Improving language and literacy is a matter of time. *Nature Reviews Neuroscience*, 5, 721–728.

Taylor, A.R., Asher, S.R., and Williams, G.A. (1987). The social adaptation of mainstreamed mildly retarded children. *Child Development*, 58, 1321–1334.

Taylor, B., Miller, E., Lingam, R., Andrews, N., Simmons, A., and Stowe, J. (2002). Measles, mumps and rubella vaccination and bowel problems or developmental regression in children with autism. *British Medical Journal*, 324, 393–396.

Taylor, B.M., Pearson, P.D., Clark, K., and Walpole, S. (2000). Effective schools and accomplished teachers: lessons about primary-grade reading instruction in low income schools. *Elementary School Journal*, 101, 121–165.

Teddlie, C., and Reynolds, D. (Eds) (2000). *International Handbook of School Effectiveness Research*. London: RoutledgeFalmer.

Thibaut, J.W., and Kelley, H.H. (1959). *The Social Psychology of Groups*. New York: Wiley.

Thomas, G., Walker, D., and Webb, J. (1998). *The Making of the Inclusive School*. London: Routledge.

Tizard, B. (1990). Research and policy: is there a link? *The Psychologist*, 3, 435–440.

Tizard, B., and Hughes, M. (1984). *Young Children Learning: Talking and Thinking at Home and School*. London, Fontana.

Tomlinson, S. (1982). *A Sociology of Special Education*. London: Routledge and Kegan Paul.

Tonnessen, F.E. (1997). How can we best define dyslexia? *Dyslexia*, 3, 78–92.

Tony, T.S.K. (2003). Locus of control, attributional style and discipline problems in secondary schools. *Early Child Development and Care*, 173, 455–466.

Topping, K.J., Smith, E., Barrow, W., Hannah, E., and Kerr, C. (2007). 'Professional educational psychology in Scotland.' In: S.R. Jimerson, T.D. Oakland and P.T. Farrell (Eds), *The Handbook of International School Psychology*. London: Sage, 339–350.

Torgersen, C.J., Brooks, G., and Hall, J. (2006). *A Systematic Review of the Research Literature on the Use of Phonics in the Teaching of Reading and Spelling*. Nottingham: Department for Education and Skills (DfES).

Torgesen, J.K. (2002). The prevention of reading difficulties. *Journal of School Psychology*, 40, 7–26.

Torgesen, J.K. (2005). 'Recent discoveries on remedial interventions for children with dyslexia.' In: M.J. Snowling and C. Hulme (Eds), *The Science of Reading: A Handbook*. Oxford: Blackwell.

Torgesen, J.K., Alexander, A.W., Wagner, R.K., et al. (2001). Intensive remedial instruction for children with severe reading disabilities: immediate and long term outcomes from two instructional approaches. *Journal of Learning Disabilities*, 34, 33–58.

Tripp, A., French, R., and Sherrill, C. (1995). Contact theory and attitudes of children in physical education programs toward peers with disabilities. *Applied Physical Activity Quarterly*, 12, 323–332.

Trujillo, K.M., and Hadfield, O.D. (1999). Tracing the roots of mathematics anxiety through in-depth interviews with pre-service elementary teachers. *College Student Journal*, 33, 219–232.

Tsoi, M.M., and Yule, W. (1976). The effects of group reinforcement in classroom behaviour modification. *Educational Studies*, 2, 129–140.

Tutt, R., Powell, S., and Thornton, M. (2006). Educational approaches in autism: What we know about what we do. *Educational Psychology in Practice*, 22, 69–81.

US Department of Education, Office of Special Education Programmes (2002). *Specific Learning Disabilities: Finding Common Ground*. Washington DC: US Department of Education.

UNESCO (1994). *The Salamanca Statement and Framework for Action on Special Needs Education*. Paris: UNESCO.

Unnever, J.D., and Cornell, D.G. (2004). Middle school victims of bullying: who reports being bullied? *Aggressive Behaviour*, 30, 373–388.

Uusimaki, L., and Nason, R. (2004). *Causes Underlying Pre-service Teachers' Negative Beliefs and Anxieties about Mathematics*. Proceedings of 28th Conference of the International Group for the Psychology of Mathematics Education, 4, 369–376. Retrieved 5.10.06 from Conference web site: www.emis.de/proceedings/PME28

Valsiner, J. (2000). *Culture and Human Development: An Introduction*. London: Sage Publications.

Van Bourgondien, M.E. (1987). Children's responses to retarded peers as a function of social behaviour, labeling and age. *Exceptional Children*, 53, 432–439.

Van der Klift, E., and Kunc, N. (2002). 'Beyond benevolence.' In: J.S. Thousand, R.A. Villa and A.I. Nevin (Eds), *Creativity and Collaborative Learning: The Practical Guide to Empowering Students, Teachers, and Families*. Baltimore, MA: Paul H. Brookes, 21–28.

van Garderen, D., and M. Montague (2003). Visual-spatial representation, mathematical problem solving and students of varying abilities. *Learning Disabilities Research and Practice*, 18, 246–254.

Vaughn, S., and Fuchs, L.S. (2003). Redefining learning disabilities as inadequate response to instruction: The promise and potential problems. *Learning Disabilities Research and Practice*, 18, 137–146.

Vellutino, F.R. (1987). Dyslexia. *Scientific American*, 256, 34–41.

Vellutino, F.R., and Fletcher, J.M. (2005). 'Developmental dyslexia.' In: M.J. Snowling and C. Hulme (Eds), *The Science of Reading: a Handbook*. Oxford, Blackwell.

Vellutino, F.R., Scanlon, D.M., Sipay, E., Small, S., Pratt, A., Chen, R., et al. (1996). Cognitive profiles of difficult-to-remediate and readily-remediated poor readers: early intervention as a vehicle for distinguishing between cognitive and experiential deficits as basic causes of specific reading disability. *Journal of Educational Psychology*, 88, 601–638.

Vellutino, F.R., Scanlon, D.M., and Tanzman, M.S. (1998). The case for early intervention in diagnosing specific reading disability. *Journal of School Psychology*, 36, 367–397.

Vellutino, F.R., Fletcher, J.M., Snowling, M.J., and Scanlon, D.M. (2004). Specific reading disability (dyslexia): what have we learned in the past four decades. *Journal of Child Psychology and Psychiatry*, 45, 2–40.

Volkmar, F.R., Lord, C., Bailey, A., Schultz, R.T., and Klin, A. (2004). Autism and pervasive developmental disorders. *Journal of Child Psychology and Psychiatry*, 45, 135–170.

Vossekuil, B., Fein, R.A., Reddy, M., Borum, R., and Modzeleski, W. (2004). *The Final Report and Findings of the Safe School Initiative: Implications for the Prevention of School Attacks in the United States*. Washington, DC: US Secret Service and US Department of Education.

Vouloumanos, A., and Werker, J.F. (2007). Listening to language at birth: evidence for a bias for speech in neonates. *Developmental Science*, 10, 159–164.

Vygotsky, L.S. (1978). Mind in Society: The Development of Higher Psychological Processes. Cambridge, MA: Harvard University Press.

Ward, J. (1971). Modification of deviant classroom behaviour. *British Journal of Educational Psychology*, 41, 304–313.

Warwickshire County Council (2005). *An ASD Tool Kit for Teachers*. Warwickshire County Council.

Wasserman, J.D., and Tulsky, D.S. (2005). 'A history of intelligence assessment.' In: D.P. Flanagan and P.L. Harrison (Eds), *Contemporary Intellectual Assessment: Theories, Tests and Issues*, (2nd Ed.). New York: Guilford Press, 3–22.

Webster-Stratton, C., and Reid, J.M. (2003). Treating conduct problems and strengthening social and emotional competence in young children: the dinosaur treatment programme. *Journal of Emotional and Behavioural Disorders*, 11, 130–143.

Weiner, B. (1985). An attributional theory of achievement motivation and emotion. *Psychological Review*, 92, 548–573.

Weiner, B. (1986). *An Attributional Theory of Motivation and Emotion*. New York. Springer.

Weiner, B. (2000). Intrapersonal and interpersonal theories of motivation from an attributional perspective. *Educational Psychology Review*, 12, 1–14.

West, P., Sweeting, H., and Leyland, A. (2004). School effects on pupils' health behaviours: evidence in support of the health promoting school. *Research Papers in Education*, 19, 261–291.

Wheldall, K. (1981). '"A" before "C" or the use of behavioural ecology in the classrooms.' In: P. Gurney (Ed.), *Behaviour Modification in Education*. Perspectives 5. Exeter: University of Exeter.

Wheldall, K., Morris, M., Vaughn, P., and Ng, Y.Y. (1981). Rows versus tables: an example of the use of behavioural ecology in two classes of 11-year old children. *Educational Psychology*, 1, 171–184.

White, J. (2004). *Howard Gardner: the myth of Multiple Intelligences*. Lecture at the Institute of Education, University of London (17 November 2004). Downloaded on 19 September 2007 from – www.ioe.ac.uk/schools/mst/LTU/phil/HowardGardner_171104.pdf

White, S., Milne, E., Rosen, S., Hansen, P., Swettenham, J., Frith, U., and Ramus, F. (2006). The role of sensory motor impairments in dyslexia: a multiple case study of dyslexic children. *Developmental Science*, 9, 237–255.

Whitney, I., and Smith, P.K. (1993). A survey of the nature and extent of bullying in junior/middle and secondary schools. *Educational Research*, 35, 3–25.

Williams, H., and Muncey, J. (1982). Precision teaching before behavioural objectives. *Journal of the Association of Educational Psychologists*, 5, 40–42.

Willis, P. (1977). *Learning to Labour. How Working-Class Kids Get Working Class Jobs*. New York: Columbia University Press.

Wimmer, H., and Perner, J. (1983). Beliefs about beliefs: Representations and constraining function of wrong beliefs in young childrens' understanding of deception. *Cognition*, 13, 103–128.

Wing, L., and Gould, J. (1979). Severe impairments of social interaction and associated abnormalities in children: epidemiology and classification. *Journal of Autism and Developmental Disorders*, 9, 11–29.

Wing, L., and Potter, D. (2002). The epidemiology of autism: Is the prevalence rising? *Mental Retardation and Developmental Disabilities Research Reviews*, 8, 151–161.

Winnet, R.A., and Winkler, R.C. (1972). Current behaviour modification in the classroom: Be still, be quiet, be docile. *Journal of Applied Behaviour Analysis*, 8, 259–262.

Witkins, H., Oltman, P., Raskin, E., and Karp, S. (1971). *A Manual for Embedded Figures Test, Children's Embedded Figures Test and Group Embedded Figures Test*. Mountain View, CA: Consulting Psychologists Press.

Wolpe, J. (1954). Reciprocal inhibition as the main basis of psychotherapeutic effects. *Archives of Neurological Psychiatry*, 72, 205–226.

Wood, A. (1998). OK then: What do EPs do? *Special Children*, May 1998, 11–13.

Woods, K., and Farrell, P. (2006). Approaches to psychological assessment in England and Wales. *School Psychology International*, 27, 387–404.

Woolfolk Hoy, A.M., and Weinstein, C.S. (2006). 'Student and teacher perspectives on classroom management.' In: C.M. Evertson and C.S. Weinstein (Eds), *Handbook of Classroom Management: Research, Practice and Contemporary Issues*. London: Lawrence Erlbaum Associates.

Woolfson, L., Whaling, R., Stewart, A., and Monsen, J.J. (2003). An integrated framework to guide educational psychologist practice. *Educational Psychology in Practice*, 19, 283–302.

World Health Organization (1995). *International Classification of Disability – Version 10 (ICD-10)*. Geneva: WHO.

Wrigley, T. (2004). 'School effectiveness': the problem of reductionism. *British Educational Research Journal*, 30, 227–244.

Wydell, T.N., and Butterworth, B. (1999). A case study of an English–Japanese bilingual with monolingual dyslexia. *Cognition*, 70, 273–305.

Wyse, D., and Styles, M. (2007). Synthetic phonics and the teaching of reading: the debate surrounding England's 'Rose Report'. *Literacy*, 41, 35–42.

Yang, S., and Sternberg, R.J. (1997). Taiwanese Chinese people's conceptions of intelligence. *Intelligence*, 25, 21–36.

Young, S. (1998). Support group approach to bullying in schools. *Educational Psychology in Practice*, 14, 32–39.

Zelli, A., Dodge, K.A., Lochman, J.E., Laird, R.D. Conduct Problems Prevention Research Group (1999). The distinction between beliefs legitimizing aggression and deviant processing of social queues: testing measurement validity and the hypothesis that bias processing mediates the effects of beliefs on aggression. *Journal of Personality and Social Psychology*, 77, 150–166.

Zhou, Z., Peverly, S.T., and Lin, J. (2005). Understanding early mathematical competencies in American and Chinese children. *School Psychology International*, 26, 413–427.

Zigler, E. (1999). 'The individual with mental retardation as a whole person.' In: E. Zigler and D. Bennett-Gates (Eds), *Personality Development in Individuals with Mental Retardation*. Cambridge: Cambridge University Press, 1–16.

Index